CU01510886

THE MENACE UNDER THE ICE

Cryptoterrestrials in the Frost, UAP and Secret Facilities

Gaylord Knowles

Echoes of Ink Editions

COPYRIGHT

Title: **The Menace Under the Ice: Cryptoterrestrials in the Frost, UAP and Secret Facilities**

Subtitle: **The truth about what lies at the poles: evidence of unknown civilizations, unexplained anomalies, UFOs and alien activity**

Author: **Gaylord Knowles**

Edition: **First Edition**

Copyright © 2025 Gaylord Knowles

All rights reserved. Without the written permission of the publisher or author, no part of this book may be copied, stored, or transmitted in any manner or by any means, electronic, mechanical, photocopying, or recording, except in the case of brief quotations incorporated in critical reviews and other noncommercial uses permitted by copyright law. Applicable laws punish copyright infringement.

DISCLAIMER

This book was written for informational and educational purposes. The author has made every effort to ensure the accuracy of the information presented. However, he assumes no responsibility for any errors, omissions, or misinterpretations of the information in the book. Readers should consult appropriate sources and professionals to confirm information and obtain specific advice.

This book is a translation of the original text written by the author in his language of origin, this translation is done with automated and manual tools. Although efforts have been made to ensure the accuracy of the translation, errors or inaccuracies may occur. The author assumes no responsibility for any misunderstandings or misinterpretations resulting from such errors.

TRADEMARKS AND INTELLECTUAL PROPERTY

All product names, logos and trademarks mentioned in this book, if any, are the property of their respective owners. Their inclusion does not imply any endorsement of or affiliation with the author.

IMAGES

This book contains no pictures to ensure a reading entirely focused on descriptive content, designed to stimulate the reader's imagination and allow for in-depth exploration of curiosities through words alone. The absence of pictures also avoids any visual interruptions and makes the format more accessible, suitable for those who want immersive reading without visual distractions.

TERMS, WORDS AND ACRONYMS IN OTHER LANGUAGES

This book may contain many terms in languages different from those in the book and/or words and/or acronyms specific to the subject matter. To make the terms understandable in practice, it will be necessary to know the terms in the original language of the term and not in the language of the book, so the author has preferred to leave them in their original language without translating them so as to ensure maximum consistency and correspondence on the subject matter and to enable you to learn them right away.

REPETITIONS

Some concepts and terms may be repeated in multiple chapters to ensure a complete understanding and because they are inherent to different topics covered in the book. This repetition is intentional and is intended to emphasize the importance of certain principles and practices related to the subject matter.

Each repetition aims to reinforce key concepts, offering the reader greater clarity and consolidation of knowledge.

However, it is important to note that repetition of content is not synonymous with a lack of variety or originality. Each repetition is uniquely contextualized and can offer new perspectives or insights into topics already covered.

Readers are advised to consider these repetitions as opportunities to reinforce understanding and practical application of the principles set forth, rather than as mere redundancy.

CONTACT INFORMATION

For permit requests or other, please contact:

Gaylord Knowles to this e-mail address: **echoesofinkeditions@gmail. com**

If you'd like to share thoughts or suggestions, feel free to get in touch. Your feedback matters. If you found this book helpful, we'd be delighted to read your review on Amazon.

INDEX

Theories on the connection between the tunnels and the Hollow Earth

Advanced technologies to explore the frozen underground

Testimonies and documents on secret pole entrances

What might these tunnels conceal and why is no one talking about them?

What do the Cryptoterrestrials want?

Who are the cryptoterrestrials and what are the theories about their origin?

Interactions with humanity: contacts, secrets and manipulations?

Are they a threat or a civilization that wants to maintain anonymity?

Occult influence in political and scientific decisions?

Assumptions about their ultimate purpose: adaptation, domination, or study?

If they exist, what should we do?

Who will control this secret?

A new race to conquer the poles

Hidden resources in the ice: a disputed treasure

The interests of multinational corporations: exploitation or conservation?

How climate change will redefine the control of the poles

The military use of the poles: secret bases and global surveillance

Archaeology, Myth, and Alternative Theories
Official Reports and Declassified Documents
Independent Research and Testimonies

PREFACE

For centuries, the Earth's poles have represented the last frontier of the unknown, inaccessible places, extreme and charged with mystery. Shrouded in frost for millions of years, these territories have held secrets that could rewrite human history, challenging the beliefs of science and the certainties of modern civilization. Yet despite technological advances and the advancement of scientific research, many of the fundamental questions about the polar regions remain unanswered.

Why are some parts of Antarctica inaccessible even to scientists? What lies beneath miles of ice, detected only by radar instruments but never explored directly? Why do some ancient maps seem to know the morphology of Antarctica even before its official discovery? And, most importantly, what information is being withheld from the public, and why?

This book is not a collection of mere speculation, nor an attempt to feed baseless theories. It is a thorough and documented investigation of all that we know, and all that we are still denied, about the mysteries of the poles. Each chapter is the result of rigorous analysis, based on scientific data, historical documents, explorers testimonies and declassified reports, to reconstruct a picture that challenges the official narrative and opens up unexpected scenarios.

From Operation Highjump, which saw the United States engaged in a massive military expedition to Antarctica without convincing justification, to unexplained magnetic and light phenomena, to geometric structures detected under the ice, anomalies abound. Sightings of unidentified flying objects in the polar skies, speculation about hidden underground bases, and the strategic interest of powers such as Russia, China, and the United

States in controlling these wastelands clearly indicate that the poles are not just an expanse of ice and wind, but a strategic territory where a much bigger game is being played than is generally believed.

But the issue is not just about the past. Global warming is accelerating the melting of ice, and with it the release of millennia-old secrets. Fossils, prehistoric viruses, lost cities, geological anomalies-what comes to light in the coming years could change our understanding of history and our place in the universe. If traces of a forgotten civilization or life forms that defy our biological understanding are found in the poles, will humanity be prepared for them?

And again, who will decide what we can know and what must remain hidden? If world powers already have access to this information, how will they use it? Will it be shared with humanity or exploited for military and geopolitical purposes?

This book is an invitation to look beyond the veil of officialdom, to explore anomalies, to ask questions that no one seems to want to address openly. It does not offer definitive answers, but it lays the groundwork for a debate that can no longer be ignored.

Because the mysteries of the poles are not just stories of explorers and remote glaciers. They are a reflection of a larger truth, a secret just waiting to be revealed.

And when the ice melts, it will be too late to ignore it.

THE SECRET OF THE POLES

A FORBIDDEN ZONE?

The mysterious restrictions of Antarctica

Antarctica is the most remote and inhospitable region on the planet, but what makes it even more enigmatic is not just its extreme climate or icy vastness, but the severe restrictions imposed on access and travel within the continent. Travel to Antarctica is extremely difficult not only for logistical and environmental reasons, but mainly because of the extremely strict regulations that limit human presence and, in particular, independent exploration. Although it is officially stated that these restrictions are due to the need to protect the fragile ecosystem and to preserve the scientific integrity of ongoing research, questions arise about some areas that remain completely off limits to even the most qualified scientists. What lies behind these inaccessible areas and why can't they be accessed even with special permissions?

Scientists who obtain permission to conduct studies in Antarctica must abide by strict regulations. Expeditions are monitored by government agencies and, in many cases, restricted to specific predetermined areas. Some researchers have reported receiving peremptory orders not to venture beyond certain coordinates, without plausible explanations. Added to this is the surprising presence of military installations, secret facilities and air exclusion zones, which seem to contradict the official narrative of a territory dedicated exclusively to scientific research and international cooperation. Why does an uninhabited region with no immediate strategic resources need such levels of surveillance and interdiction?

Another element fueling the mystery is the small number of civilian flights flying over Antarctica. Commercial air routes routinely avoid the continent, officially due to adverse weather conditions and lack of emergency infrastructure. However, some former pilots and aviation officials have revealed that the overflight ban covers specific geographic coordinates, suggesting the possible presence of installations or anomalies that should not be observed or documented. Testimonies from independent explorers speak of unexplained communication blockages, magnetic interference, and even veiled threats received from unknown authorities in the case of attempts to penetrate beyond the boundaries of permitted zones.

There are also accounts of military missions conducted in great secrecy, the purposes of which remain unknown. Some declassified documents reveal operations conducted by powerful nations, with means and facilities that far exceed simple scientific research. Whether they are secret experiments, undisclosed archaeological discoveries or underground bases hidden under the ice, the level of secrecy employed suggests the presence of something far beyond simple environmental conservation. It is no accident that even private expeditions, organized by wealthy explorers, are systematically discouraged, blocked or diverted from their route, as if there were a deliberate attempt to prevent access to certain areas.

If Antarctica were really just an icy wilderness devoid of strategic interest, why would the world's most powerful governments impose such strict restrictions and maintain such rigid control over activities conducted on the continent? More importantly, what is in the areas banned to the public and even to officially recognized scientists? The answer to these questions could rewrite not only the history of polar exploration, but also our understanding of the planet itself.

The Antarctic Treaty: protection or cover-up?

The Antarctic Treaty, signed in 1959 and entered into force in 1961, is an international agreement establishing the principle of non-militarization and scientific cooperation on the Antarctic continent. Ostensibly, the treaty serves to ensure that Antarctica remains a natural reserve, intended solely for peaceful research, without economic exploitation or territorial claims. However, a closer look at its provisions reveals a number of clauses and limitations that raise more than one suspicion. Is it really just a matter of environmental protection, or does the treaty conceal a secret agenda aimed at covering up inconvenient discoveries?

One of the most disturbing aspects of the Antarctic Treaty is the level of control exercised by the signatory powers. Any attempt at independent exploration is subject to extremely restrictive regulations, with severe fines and penalties for anyone attempting to trespass into designated areas without authorization. This means that, in effect, only government agencies and approved scientific institutions can conduct research, while any other initiative is immediately stopped. This rigidity has led some to speculate that the treaty is actually a tool to prevent sensitive information from emerging outside the control of global elites.

The presence of military bases disguised as scientific research stations is another suspect element. Officially, the treaty prohibits any military activity, but there is documented evidence of covert operations being conducted in various parts of Antarctica, often under the cover of research missions. The discovery of underground structures, man-made tunnels and even anomalous objects buried under the ice has led some researchers to speculate that there are relics of unknown civilizations or advanced technology hidden from the eyes of the world. The fact that this information is strictly classified suggests that the Antarctic Treaty is actually a sophisticated system for maintaining control over something much larger than just environmental protection.

Another critical point is how the treaty prevents the exploitation of the continent's natural resources. Although this may seem like a measure to prevent ecological damage, some analysts argue that it actually serves to protect geopolitical or scientific secrets. Some unofficial expeditions have reported the existence of geological anomalies and non-natural structures detected under the ice using advanced remote sensing technologies. If this information is confirmed, it would mean that the treaty was not signed to preserve Antarctica, but to hide what is found there.

The surprising cohesion between often-conflicting nations is another aspect worthy of attention. The Antarctic Treaty is one of the few international agreements respected by all world powers, without exception. How is it that countries with conflicting political visions, from the United States and Russia to China, cooperate in an unusual way when it comes to Antarctica? Is it possible that there is a secret understanding between governments to conceal something that, if revealed, could upset the entire historical and scientific narrative accepted to date?

If the Antarctic Treaty was really established only for environmental protection, there would be no reason to maintain such a level of secrecy. Yet everything about the continent is shrouded in an aura of mystery, from unexplained restrictions to off-limits areas to the disturbing accounts of those who have attempted to explore it without permission. The real question is: What are they hiding at the poles and why should humanity not know?

Military missions and covert operations

Antarctica and the Arctic, while officially areas dedicated to scientific research and international cooperation, have always attracted the interest of major military powers. Their strategic location, inaccessible vastness and prohibitive environmental conditions make them ideal places for covert operations, technological testing and difficult-to-detect underground installations. Declassified documents and testimony from former military personnel and researchers suggest that, far from being unused wastelands, the poles are actually the scene of some of the most mysterious operations in modern history, conducted by the United States, Russia, China and other superpowers.

During the Cold War, both the United States and the Soviet Union had a strong interest in controlling the poles, using them as strategic observation points and bases for secret military tests. The presence of underground installations has been speculated since the 1950s, with projects such as the Camp Century Base in Greenland, a network of underground tunnels developed by the United States to house nuclear missiles in a theoretically "neutral" area. Although the base was officially dismantled due to environmental difficulties, many argue that it actually served as an experiment for more advanced and secret facilities. In parallel, the Soviet Union conducted a number of undisclosed operations, including experimental weapons testing and underground engineering projects in the Arctic regions of Siberia.

In Antarctica, the mystery deepens further. The 1959 Antarctic Treaty explicitly prohibits any military activity on the continent, but numerous reports indicate the presence of secret installations disguised as scientific research stations. One of the most controversial cases involves Vostok Station, a Russian base located above a subglacial lake more than 4,000 meters deep. Some theories suggest that an ancient structure, perhaps of nonhuman origin, may lie beneath the ice, and that Russian scientists have discovered something so extraordinary as to justify the base's isolation and complete secrecy about its operations.

The United States, for its part, has built several bases in West Antarctica, including the Amundsen-Scott base, located exactly at the South Pole. Officially a research station, this facility features an unusual amount of atmospheric and magnetic monitoring equipment, raising suspicions about its real purpose. Some claim that it is involved in advanced surveillance projects or even in testing unknown technologies. In addition, there are reports of geological anomalies detected with ground-penetrating radar, which would have revealed immense underground cavities under the ice. These spaces could be natural, but their perfect symmetry and strategic placement near military bases suggest possible artificial use.

Military presence in the poles is not limited to the construction of secret bases. In recent decades, strange events have occurred that indicate undisclosed operations, such as sightings of unidentified aircraft, satellite communication blackouts, and even the disappearance of entire expeditions. One of the most disturbing stories involves the mysterious disappearance of a U.S. science team in 2001, the recovery of which was handled abnormally by the U.S. government, with total censure on the cause of the incident. Some theorists claim that these events are related to experiments on advanced technologies, perhaps based on principles still unknown to official science.

Covert operations at the poles could also include tests on new forms of propulsion or climate control devices. The boldest theories speak of technologies capable of influencing the Earth's magnetic field, a hypothesis reinforced by the use of facilities such as HAARP (High-Frequency Active Auroral Research Program) in Alaska. Although officially this is an ionosphere research program, some believe it is involved in climate modification or underground anomaly detection.

In light of this evidence, a fundamental question emerges: if the poles were really just frozen deserts with no strategic value or mystery to hide, why do the great powers continue to invest enormous resources in them and maintain such a high level of secrecy? Perhaps the answer is hidden under miles of ice, far from the eyes of the public.

Banned flights: why are some airspaces banned?

One of the most enigmatic aspects related to the poles is the strict ban on certain air routes over Antarctica and the Arctic. Although there are official reasons why most airlines avoid flying over these regions-including extreme weather conditions, lack of emergency infrastructure, and communication difficulties-there are specific areas completely banned from air traffic, raising questions about the real motivations behind these bans.

The Arctic, with its proximity to Russia, Canada and the United States, is already subject to strict military restrictions. The presence of secret installations and missile tests has led to the creation of extensive no-fly zones over some sensitive areas, such as the archipelago of Novaja Zemlja, known for Soviet nuclear tests. However, some restrictions cannot simply be explained by military security. For example, the area around the North Pole itself is considered a dangerous flight zone because of alleged magnetic anomalies that would interfere with navigation systems, but some pilots have reported unexplained phenomena, such as sudden radio interruptions or malfunctions of onboard instruments.

Antarctica presents an even greater mystery. Most airlines deliberately avoid flying over it, and the few flights that cross the continent's borders follow rigidly prescribed routes. There are specific areas that are totally prohibited, including areas above some glaciers and subglacial lakes, such as the aforementioned Lake Vostok, access to which is strictly restricted.

Some say the reason is the presence of gravitational anomalies or hidden structures under the ice, which the authorities want to keep secret.

One particular case concerns the so-called Magnetic South Pole, which gradually shifts every year. This point is one of the most difficult to fly over, and some pilots who have ventured into its vicinity have reported strange phenomena, such as unexplained variations in compasses and temporary blackouts of electronic systems. Is it possible that there are metallic masses or energy fields under the ice sheet that are not yet understood by official science?

Another theory suggests that commercial flights avoid Antarctica not only for practical reasons, but because the continent harbors secrets that should not be documented. Government surveillance satellites can monitor the area, but a commercial flight might accidentally capture images or phenomena that should not be revealed. These could be secret installations, advanced technologies being tested, or even ancient structures that great powers want to keep hidden.

The anomalous interdiction of air traffic over the poles continues to raise questions without definitive answers. If the explanation were really only logistical in nature, there would be no need for such secrecy. But then, what lies beneath the ice or behind the silence of the authorities?

Strange reports and censored testimonies

Over the decades, numerous explorers, pilots and scientists who have had the opportunity to operate at the poles have reported puzzling experiences, often characterized by unexplained phenomena. However, many of these tales have never reached the public eye, having been censored, downplayed or completely covered up by the relevant authorities. This raises questions about what is really happening in these remote regions and what information is being deliberately withheld.

One of the best-known cases concerns Admiral Richard E. Byrd, a U.S. explorer who led several expeditions to Antarctica between the 1920s and 1950s. According to some accounts, during his famous 1947 Operation Highjump, Byrd witnessed anomalous aerial phenomena and unknown structures under the ice. Although the official version of the operation speaks of a military exercise to test troops capabilities in extreme environments, some documents suggest that there was an encounter with unidentified aircraft, described as "flying saucers" capable of maneuvers unthinkable for the technology of the time. Byrd would discuss these findings in a personal diary, the contents of which would later be classified as top secret. After the operation, the admiral made enigmatic statements about an "unknown enemy" and the need for enhanced national security, fueling speculation about what he had actually seen.

Other accounts come from commercial and military pilots who have flown over the polar regions. Many have reported instrument anomalies, such as sudden changes in the magnetic field, radio interference, and even the temporary disappearance of visual landmarks. Some claim to have spotted huge openings in the ice, similar to cave entrances or man-made structures, that do not appear on official maps. One particularly disturbing case involves a 1971 U.S. military flight that was allegedly diverted over a forbidden zone in Antarctica, according to leaked documents. The crew reported seeing geometric structures buried under the ice, but were later forced to keep quiet. Crew members were transferred to undisclosed assignments and all traces of the incident were erased from official records.

Similar accounts also come from civilian researchers. In 2002, a group of scientists working near Lake Vostok - one of the largest subglacial lakes in Antarctica - suddenly disappeared for several weeks. When they returned, they refused to make any statements about what had happened, and the Russian agency overseeing the mission imposed total confidentiality on the data they collected. Some claimed they found evidence of unknown life forms or traces of a civilization buried under the ice. Russian authorities dismissed the incident as a simple "loss of radio contact", but the case remains shrouded in mystery.

Some independent explorers have also reported incidents of intimidation and threats after trying to document anomalies in the poles. Several adventurers who attempted to reach unauthorized areas reported being intercepted by military personnel and forced to abort their missions. Some reported finding their photographic materials and recordings mysteriously deleted, as if someone wanted to prevent the release of certain information. This raises an inescapable question: why does the simple act of exploring theoretically uninhabited regions elicit such an aggressive reaction from the authorities?

A constant element in these testimonies is the feeling of being confronted with something that must not be revealed to the world. Whether it is geological anomalies, secret bases, or discoveries that could rewrite human history, the systematic censorship of these reports suggests that there is a hidden agenda behind the control of the poles.

Who guards the secrets of the poles?

Control over the poles is not left to chance. Although Antarctica and the Arctic are theoretically international zones, access to these areas is regulated by a small elite of governments, space agencies and private corporations that impose strict restrictions on who can explore the territory and what information can be released. The official motive is environmental protection and scientific regulation, but there are indications that suggest a much deeper and more strategic control.

The main nations involved in pole management are the United States, Russia, China, the United Kingdom, France and some other European and Asian powers. These countries have established research bases in the polar regions, but many of these facilities seem to have characteristics more akin to military installations than simple scientific stations. For example, the U.S. Amundsen-Scott base at the South Pole is equipped with advanced atmospheric and magnetic sensing systems, instruments that could be used for purposes quite different from environmental research. Russia's Vostok base, located above a subglacial lake, is the subject of much speculation, especially after it was revealed that some of its operations are classified as "restricted access" even for the scientific community.

Space agencies, particularly NASA and Roscosmos, have shown increasing interest in the polar regions, launching satellites dedicated to their constant observation. NASA, for example, has repeatedly monitored gravitational and geological anomalies in Antarctica, but the data collected are not always made public. Some believe the agency may have information on unknown underground structures or unconventional atmospheric phenomena. ESA (European Space Agency) and CNSA (Chinese Space Agency)

11

have also conducted intensive studies of the poles, but without providing clear explanations for certain aspects of their surveys.

In addition to governments and space agencies, another key player in pole control is private corporations, especially in the energy and advanced technology sectors. Companies such as Lockheed Martin, Raytheon and other military industries are involved in research projects in the poles, officially for the development of new infrastructure and communication systems. However, their involvement in an area that should have no strategic value raises questions about the real nature of their activities. Some companies are developing drilling technologies to reach deep beneath the ice, raising suspicions that they may be searching for unknown energy resources or even materials of non-terrestrial origin.

If these entities cooperate in keeping the secret, it means that the poles are hiding something extraordinary. Could they be remnants of an ancient civilization buried under the ice? Evidence of geophysical anomalies that challenge our understanding of the Earth? Or advanced technological installations not revealed to the public? The presence of no-go zones and constant surveillance suggest that the truth is far from the official narrative. The mystery of the poles is not just a geographical issue, but an enigma involving the highest spheres of global power.

THE STRUCTURES BURIED UNDER THE ICE

Satellite images reveal unexplained structures

In recent decades, the use of satellites to monitor Antarctica has led to the discovery of a series of geometric anomalies buried under kilometers of ice. Some of these structures have shapes that can hardly be attributed to natural phenomena, fueling speculation about the possible existence of man-made constructions hidden in the polar subsurface. Images obtained from government and private satellites have revealed symmetrical patterns, right angles and linear formations that do not conform to known geological processes.

One of the most striking examples is the images taken by NASA through the Operation IceBridge program, an airborne mission launched to map the morphology under Antarctic ice. In 2012, a detailed analysis showed the presence of a huge rectangular structure buried under the ice, with dimensions exceeding 2 kilometers in length. This formation, located in the Queen Maud Land area, is characterized by a series of perfectly right angles and a geometric arrangement incompatible with simple glacial erosion or natural fractures in the Earth's crust.

Other satellite images revealed huge circular formations, some of them more than 400 meters in diameter. Some of these structures, detected through infrared imaging techniques, show a thermal difference from their surroundings, suggesting the presence of materials other than ice or common rock. This type of discovery is significant because ice should maintain homogeneous temperatures, while the presence of areas with residual heat could indicate a still active energy source or the presence of underground cavities isolated from the rest of the polar environment.

One of the most mysterious cases involves anomalies detected near Lake Vostok, a subglacial basin located some 4,000 meters below the Antarctic ice sheet. Satellite images showed a series of parallel lines and rectangular structures that appear to correspond to a non-natural conformation. When a Russian team drilled through the ice layer above the lake in 2001 to take water samples, strange phenomena occurred: interference in radio communications, instrument malfunctions and even the temporary isolation of the research team. After their return, the researchers refused to make public statements about their findings, and the Russian government imposed strict secrecy on the entire operation.

Also, in 2017, Google Earth accidentally released images of a strange structure emerging from the ice, located near the Princess Elizabeth Earth mountain range. The image showed a formation that resembled an ancient pyramid, with four sides perfectly aligned. Although some have tried to explain the phenomenon by simple unusual-looking mountain formations, the regular arrangement and symmetry of the structure has sparked debate among scholars and independent researchers. Some speculate that it is the remains of a civilization buried under the ice for thousands, if not millions of years, while others suggest that it could be an artificial structure created by advanced technology.

The fact that many of these anomalies are not officially investigated in depth and that numerous satellite images are obfuscated, censored or removed from publicly accessible databases suggests that there is a deliberate attempt to hide something. But what could justify such a level of secrecy? Could it be ancient ruins belonging to a forgotten civilization? Or perhaps technological installations left behind by another form of intelligence? As long as governments and space agencies continue to maintain secrecy, satellite images remain one of the most important clues to unraveling the truth about structures buried under the ice.

Radar discoveries and buried cavities

Parallel to satellite imagery, another key tool for investigating anomalies under polar ice is ground penetrating radar (GPR). This technology makes it possible to obtain a detailed scan of the subsurface, revealing the presence of cavities, structures and materials other than the surrounding ice. In recent decades, research missions have revealed a number of anomalies buried in the poles, many of which have yet to be officially explained.

One of the most controversial findings was made in 2016, when a team of American and British scientists used deep-wave radar to explore the Queen Maud Land region. The data revealed a huge underground structure, located about 3,000 meters below the ice, with a series of cavities connected by linear passages. Some have speculated that it could be an ancient buried city, while others believe it may be an underground base built in more recent times and kept secret by some military power.

Another remarkable discovery involves the huge cavities under the Thwaites Glacier, located in the western part of Antarctica. In 2019, NASA revealed the presence of a huge cavity about 40 kilometers wide and 300 meters high, located under the ice sheet. The reason for its existence remains unexplained: officially, scientists suggest that it was formed by melting ice, but its perfectly symmetrical shape and the presence of thermal anomalies have led some to speculate that it may be hiding man-made structures or even an unidentified heat source.

In 2018, a team of British Antarctic Survey researchers reported a similar anomaly in the depths of the Antarctic ice sheet, this time in the Wilkes Land region. Radar detected a vast oval depression, with apparently regular walls, located about 800 meters below the surface. Some experts suggested that it may be an underground chamber containing unidentified materials. Scientific authorities quickly downplayed the discovery, stating that the structure was probably the result of an ancient meteoric impact. However, the total lack of further analysis leaves room for alternative hypotheses.

Some theorists believe that these cavities may be underground shelters built by ancient civilizations to protect themselves from global cataclysms, while others suggest that they may house structures of nonterrestrial origin, perhaps dating back thousands or millions of years. There is also the possibility that these enormous caverns may be connected to a global network of underground tunnels, an idea echoed in numerous myths and legends of ancient peoples.

The fact that many of these discoveries are quickly being scaled back or subsequent research blocked leaves room for a disturbing question: what really lies beneath the ice and why should no one know? Radar technologies are slowly revealing a truth that could shock the world, but it seems that someone is trying to prevent this information from becoming public knowledge.

Cyclopean structures under the ice: signs of a lost architecture?

Recent discoveries at the poles suggest that massive structures of unknown origin may lie beneath kilometers of ice. Anomalies detected by satellite imagery and ground-penetrating radar show regular geometric formations whose arrangement and symmetry leave little doubt that they may be man-made works. These constructions, which are characterized by monumental proportions and conformations reminiscent of ancient megalithic structures, have fueled speculation about the presence of lost architecture dating back to remote eras when the poles might have had a completely different climate than today.

One of the most emblematic cases involves the Wilkes Land anomaly, a huge mass buried under the ice in East Antarctica that has been detected through satellite scans and measurements of the Earth's gravitational field. The anomaly features an oval depression about 300 kilometers wide and several kilometers deep, which appears to contain regular structures and geometric lines, completely incompatible with random natural formations. Some scholars have speculated that this region may hide the remains of an ancient buried city, perhaps belonging to a forgotten civilization that existed before the glaciation of Antarctica.

Another extraordinary discovery has emerged near the Gamburtsev subglacial mountain range, a mountain system hidden under more than 4 kilometers of ice. Here, radar scans revealed cyclopean wall-like structures composed of blocks that appear to have an orderly and symmetrical arrangement. The mountains themselves, while natural in origin, appear to host rectilinear formations, which could indicate the presence of ancient settlements now completely buried. The idea that an ancient civilization may have built buildings on this mountain range, before Antarctica became an ice-covered land, finds some confirmation in paleoclimatic studies that suggest that the continent, millions of years ago, was covered with forests and rich in lakes and rivers.

Among the most enigmatic structures ever observed is the alleged Ellsworth Pyramid, a mountain formation that, when viewed from satellite images, appears incredibly symmetrical, with four perfectly sloping sides and an orientation reminiscent of the Great Pyramid of Giza. Some scholars believe that this may be simple pareidolia, or the human tendency to recognize familiar patterns in natural features, but the near-perfect symmetry of the formation continues to raise suspicions. If it were confirmed that this structure was shaped by human hand, it would mean that an advanced civilization existed in Antarctica before the last ice age, upsetting current historical knowledge.

In addition to rectilinear and pyramidal structures, several studies have revealed the presence of underground tunnels, some of which reach several kilometers in length and appear to have been dug intentionally. Ground-penetrating radar has revealed that some of these tunnels have smooth walls and regular angles, incompatible with natural phenomena of erosion or ice melting. Some of these passages lead to immense cavities, so large that they could contain entire underground cities.

The presence of cyclopean structures under the ice cannot be easily ignored. If these formations are not the result of simple geological processes, then the only alternative is that they are the product of an ancient civilization, perhaps existing at a time when Antarctica was a habitable continent. If so, what events led to its disappearance? More importantly, who built these massive structures and for what purposes? The answers to these questions could rewrite the history of humanity and our understanding of lost civilizations.

Technologies used to map the polar subsurface: what do they reveal?

In recent decades, advances in science and technology have made it possible to obtain detailed mapping of the polar subsurface, revealing structures and anomalies that were previously completely unknown. Among the most advanced tools used for ice exploration are ground-penetrating radar (GPR), thermal and gravimetric sensing satellites, autonomous subglacial drones, and next-generation drilling probes.

Ground Penetrating Radar (GPR) is the most widely used tool for exploring the depths beneath the ice. This technology sends electromagnetic waves into the subsurface and measures the time it takes for the waves to bounce back, allowing identification of anomalous stratifications, cavities, and buried solid structures. Using this technique, large empty chambers and underground passages have been detected, some of which have smooth, regular walls, suggesting the presence of man-made structures.

Another effective method is infrared and gravimetric satellite remote sensing. Satellites such as NASA's GRACE and ICESat programs have revealed anomalous variations in the gravitational field over some polar regions, suggesting the presence of large underground masses of higher density than ice or rock. These gravitational anomalies could indicate buried structures or even entire cities submerged under the ice, as suggested by some theories related to the lost civilization of Antarctica.

Drilling probes, such as those used in the Lake Vostok explorations, are another key tool. These probes can dig through miles of ice to take samples and measure subsurface composition. However, much of the data collected remains classified or undisclosed to the public, fueling suspicions that items of extraordinary significance have been discovered.

In recent years, autonomous subglacial drones have also been deployed, such as the Boaty McBoatface, an underwater vehicle designed to explore the oceans beneath the Antarctic ice sheet. These drones have detected immense submerged caverns, some of which extend tens of kilometers beneath the ice. The discovery of these cavities suggests the possibility that there are entire hidden ecosystems, and perhaps even man-made structures submerged beneath the water.

Data collected with these technologies indicate that unexplained anomalies lie beneath the polar ice, which cannot be easily attributed to natural causes. The fact that some of these findings are systematically censored or downplayed suggests that governments and scientific institutions may be privy to secrets they do not want to share with the public. Perhaps because evidence of a technologically advanced ancient civilization or man-made structures under the ice could completely overturn our understanding of history?

The only way to discover the truth is to continue exploring and deciphering the information emerging from the depths of the poles. What has been found so far is only the tip of the iceberg... and the secret that lies beneath may be the greatest in human history.

Why are these findings not disseminated?

Despite the enormous potential of discoveries made at the poles, their disclosure is often hampered by governments, scientific bodies and international organizations. Data collected through ground-penetrating radars, satellites and drill probes show unexplained anomalies that could rewrite the history of humanity and Earth's geology, yet the information is filtered out or only partially made public. But why? What reasons might justify this cover-up?

One of the main factors behind censorship is the geopolitical control of information. Antarctica and the Arctic, although officially neutral areas or protected by international treaties, are the subject of strong strategic interests by the world's superpowers. If theories about the presence of man-made structures under the ice were confirmed, it would open up scenarios in which knowledge of such findings could secure a technological, military or economic advantage for those in control. This would explain why governments such as that of the United States, Russia and China maintain the utmost secrecy about certain discoveries, preventing them from becoming public knowledge.

Another crucial element is the potential historical and cultural impact. If it turns out that advanced civilizations existed on Earth much earlier than official history suggests, a complete reexamination of human chronology would be necessary. This would mean revising theories about the origin of civilizations, technological evolution and even possible interaction with non-Earth intelligences. Such a upheaval could destabilize not only the scientific community, but also religious and political institutions, generating a global culture shock.

Official science also tends to reject anything that does not fit into accepted paradigms. Any discovery that might challenge current knowledge is often ridiculed or ignored. Many scientists and independent researchers who have tried to explore anomalies in the poles have been pressured, threatened, or even had their funding revoked. Some of them have reported being approached by representatives of government agencies who have discouraged them from continuing their investigations.

The role of large space agencies such as NASA, ESA, and Roscosmos is another aspect to consider. Why have agencies that should be in charge of space exploration invested significant resources in the constant monitoring of Antarctica? Some experts believe that the data collected by the satellites revealed non-terrestrial technological objects or structures, the study of which could provide crucial information about the origins of humanity and advanced technologies. If so, governments would have every interest in keeping this information secret.

There is the issue of lack of transparency in scientific research. Many of the data collected at the poles are never published in full. Some of the most important polar research missions, such as those to Lake Vostok or Wilkes Land magnetic anomalies, have produced results that have only been made available in partial form, while the most sensitive information remains classified. This suggests that the most significant findings are reserved for an elite few, while the public is told a purified version of the truth.

The fundamental question remains: what are they afraid to reveal? If science were completely free from political and economic pressures, we could know much more today about the structures buried under the ice. However, as long as power continues to control access to information, the most shocking discoveries will remain hidden.

The role of science in the future of polar exploration

Despite attempts at a cover-up, new technologies are making it increasingly difficult to keep anomalies at the poles a secret. Scientific advances are making it possible to explore previously inaccessible areas, and in the coming years we may see discoveries that can change our understanding of Earth's history and geology.

One of the most powerful tools for investigating the polar subsurface is ground-penetrating radar (GPR), which in recent years has been improved with the integration of higher-resolution systems. This technology makes it possible to obtain three-dimensional images of the subsurface with unprecedented accuracy. If used on a large scale, it could reveal new structures hidden beneath the ice, perhaps even entire submerged cities.

Another revolutionary method is artificial intelligence applied to satellite data analysis. Neural networks and advanced algorithms can recognize geometric patterns and anomalies in satellite images with greater accuracy than humans. This means that even if authorities try to obscure or censor certain data, new automated analysis tools could enable independent scientists to identify artificial structures buried in ice.

New self-contained cryogenic probes are another key innovation. Unlike traditional drills, these probes use heat and pressure to drill through ice without contaminating the samples taken. Some prototypes currently being tested may be able to explore subglacial lakes and hidden caves, such as those beneath Lake Vostok, and detect any traces of artificial structures or unknown life forms.

The use of autonomous subglacial drones is also opening up new frontiers. These vehicles, capable of navigating through the waters beneath the ice, could explore huge submerged caverns and discover man-made tunnels or unknown technological devices. Some experts speculate that such drones could even find ancient artifacts hidden in the polar depths, if indeed in the past the climate was conducive to human presence.

Another promising technology is the use of neutrinos and gravitational waves to probe the polar subsurface. These techniques, which use subatomic particles to penetrate deeply into the Earth's crust, could reveal the presence of hidden structures without the need to drill through the ice, thus eliminating the risk of contamination and the research blockade imposed by governments and organizations.

Space missions could indirectly contribute to understanding polar mysteries. NASA and other agencies are developing technologies to explore icy worlds such as Europa (Jupiter's moon) and Enceladus (Saturn's moon), where it is believed underground oceans may exist. These same technologies could be applied to Antarctic exploration, revealing hidden structures with a level of detail never before achieved.

If science is able to break free from political pressures and use these technologies without restrictions in the coming years, we may be faced with unprecedented discoveries. We may finally answer the questions: who built these structures under the ice? When? And most importantly, why were they hidden? The future of polar exploration could reveal the greatest secret in human history.

THE COVERT OPERATIONS OF THE GREAT POWERS

Operation Highjump: the beginning of the mystery

Operation Highjump, officially named The United States Navy Antarctic Developments Program, was a massive expedition conducted by the United States Navy between 1946 and 1947 under the direction of Admiral Richard E. Byrd. Officially, the operation was intended to test equipment under extreme conditions, train personnel and establish a strategic presence in Antarctica. However, the enormous scale of the mission-which involved 4,700 men, 13 ships and 33 aircraft-has fueled theories for decades about far more ambitious goals and, more importantly, secret discoveries that would be concealed from the public.

From the beginning, Operation Highjump aroused suspicion. The huge deployment of military forces appeared disproportionate to a simple training mission, especially considering that Antarctica was considered a neutral territory with no immediate strategic interest. Some historians believe that the real reason for the mission was related to the Nazi presence in Antarctica. During World War II, Nazi Germany had conducted expeditions to the area and established a supposed secret base known as "Neuschwabenland", where, according to declassified documents, the Germans allegedly built underground installations for the development of advanced technologies.

The most controversial theories state that Operation Highjump was a reconnaissance and neutralization mission of the alleged German base, and that during the expedition American forces encountered unexplained phenomena. According to some documents and testimony from crew members, pilots flying over some regions of Antarctica reported strange structures emerging from the ice, unidentified lights, and flying objects moving with speeds and maneuvers impossible for the technology of the time.

One of the most enigmatic reports is related to Admiral Byrd himself. After the mission, Byrd made disturbing statements to Chilean journalists, claiming that the United States should prepare for a threat from the poles, from aircraft capable of flying from one end of the planet to the other in minutes. These claims were quickly censored, and shortly thereafter Byrd was forced into silence, being confined under close military surveillance. Some claim that he documented his actual findings in a secret diary, the contents of which remain a mystery to this day.

The most puzzling fact about Operation Highjump is that although it was planned to last six months, the expedition was abruptly terminated after just eight weeks, with the immediate return of the fleet to the United States. No official explanation was given, and documents related to the details of the mission remained secret for decades. Some theorists believe that the sudden retreat was due to a confrontation with unknown forces, perhaps advanced technology discovered in the Antarctic depths that far exceeded the U.S. warfare capability of the time.

The truth about what happened during Operation Highjump remains hidden among classified documents and missing testimonies. However, one thing is certain: after this expedition, Antarctica suddenly became one of the most controlled and secretive areas in the world, with close surveillance by global superpowers and strict control of information. The mystery of what Byrd and his team discovered among the ice remains to this day one of the greatest enigmas in modern history.

Secret bases in the polar regions

While officially Antarctica and the Arctic are territories dedicated to scientific research, there are numerous clues that suggest the presence of secret underground bases, built by the world's superpowers for military and technological purposes or to guard discoveries of extraordinary magnitude. Satellite data, testimony from former military personnel and researchers, and some declassified clandestine operations indicate that the United States, Russia, China and other nations have developed installations in the poles, many of them off-limits even to the scientific community.

One of the most suspicious bases is Vostok Station, officially a Russian research base located above the mysterious Lake Vostok, an isolated subglacial basin for more than 15 million years. In the 1990s, radar scans revealed the presence of anomalous structures under the ice, which did not correspond to natural formations. In 2012, when Russian researchers drilled into the ice to take water samples from the lake, the entire mission was suddenly classified as a state secret, and the scientists involved disappeared for weeks before reappearing without making any statements. Some claim that they discovered unknown life forms or traces of a lost civilization, but that the Russian government decided to keep the secret for strategic reasons.

The United States, for its part, has built numerous bases in West Antarctica. The Amundsen-Scott base, located exactly at the South Pole, is one of the most heavily guarded in the world. Although officially an atmospheric research center, its underground structure and the level of security around some sections suggest that it may be hiding classified activities. Some former staff members have reported areas to which access is strictly forbidden, even to authorized scientists, raising doubts about the true nature of operations conducted inside.

China has also recently intensified its presence at the poles. Its Antarctic bases, such as Kunlun Station, are located in strategic areas and are equipped with sophisticated communication and surveillance systems. Beijing has invested billions of dollars in polar infrastructure development, raising suspicions that it may be seeking hidden resources or advanced technologies buried under the ice.

But polar bases are not limited to Antarctica. The Arctic, due to its strategic location and the presence of huge reserves of resources, is home to numerous secret installations. Russia, in particular, has developed a network of underground bases in Siberia and Arctic islands, many of them inherited from Soviet times. Declassified documents indicate that secret experiments, nuclear tests and research into unexplained phenomena, often shrouded in the utmost secrecy, have been conducted at these facilities.

The increasing militarization of the polar regions suggests that world powers are not just exploring these territories for scientific purposes, but are protecting something. Could it be unknown energy resources, advanced technologies, or even remnants of an ancient civilization? The secrecy surrounding the bases in the poles indicates that the answer may be more extraordinary than we imagine. As long as governments continue to classify these sites as "top secret", the world will remain in the dark about their true purposes.

Scientific experiments and testing of new technologies

The polar regions, due to their remote location and extreme climate, have always been used as secret laboratories for scientific experiments and testing of advanced technologies. From the Cold War era to the present day, the world's superpowers have invested enormous resources in researching climate weapons, new energy sources, and experimental technologies, many of which are classified as top secret.

One of the most controversial projects is related to climate control. Evidence exists to suggest that the United States and Russia have conducted experiments to alter the climate in the polar regions, with the goal of developing meteorological weapons capable of influencing large-scale weather events. The U.S.-developed High-Frequency Active Auroral Research Program (HAARP) has often been associated with ionospheric alteration tests, and some believe that more advanced variants of these experiments have been conducted in Antarctica, taking advantage of the continent's conformation and its isolation to avoid prying eyes. Theories about these experiments are based on detections of anomalous electromagnetic pulses, strange variations in the magnetosphere, and mysterious radio blackouts recorded near secret bases.

Another area of research concerns the exploitation of unknown energy resources. Geological formations beneath polar ice could conceal rare materials or even energy sources not yet understood by modern science. Some reports indicate that geothermal anomalies and unexplained heat sources have been found in the Antarctic subsurface. If these were natural energy deposits, their exploitation could revolutionize the world's energy sector, but if they were technologies left behind by an ancient civilization or of non-terrestrial origin, interest in their study would be even greater. According to some theories, projects classified as the "IceCube Project", officially dedicated to the study of cosmic neutrinos, could conceal far more ambitious goals, such as the detection of gravitational anomalies or unknown sources of energy beneath the ice.

Experiments conducted at the poles are not limited only to energy and climate. Some declassified documents suggest that the possibility of exploiting the polar regions to test new forms of propulsion, including technologies based on advanced electromagnetism and gravitational levitation systems, has also been explored. The fact that some areas are completely off limits even to accredited scientists reinforces the hypothesis that superpowers are conducting very high-level experiments, the implications of which could alter the planet's geopolitical balance.

Another crucial aspect is the possible use of the polar regions for advanced biological and genetic experiments. The extreme environment of Antarctica is considered ideal for studying the adaptation of organisms to extreme conditions, which could have implications for biotechnology, space medicine, and even human genetic manipulation. Some secret laboratories in the polar regions could be used for genetic engineering experiments, testing of extremophilic organisms and the development of new forms of biological resistance.

Taken together, these projects suggest that Antarctica and the Arctic are not simply uninhabited territories, but true centers of highly advanced research, where world powers are testing technologies that could change the future of humanity. The question remains: how much of this will ever be made public?

Nazi interest in Antarctica and the myth of Base 211

During World War II, the German Third Reich developed a strong interest in Antarctica, conducting a series of expeditions to the continent and establishing an alleged secret base, known as Base 211 or Neuschwabenland. The idea that the Nazis built an underground outpost in Antarctica is one of the greatest mysteries in modern history and continues to generate debate among independent researchers and historians.

German interest in Antarctica officially began in 1938, when the Reich sent an expedition led by Captain Alfred Ritscher for the purpose of exploring and claiming territories in the frozen continent. During the mission, German planes mapped a vast region and dropped flags with the swastika symbol, officially marking the territory as part of Nazi Germany. This territory was christened Neuschwabenland (New Swabia), and, according to some documents, the expedition identified underground caverns and subglacial passages, which would have made it possible to build a secret base.

According to some theories, the Nazis not only established a settlement in Antarctica, but moved scientists, engineers and advanced technologies there, with the aim of creating a secret refuge inaccessible to the Allies. Some claim that during the last days of the war, German ships and submarines transported materials, documents and even high-ranking officers to this base, hoping to continue their research away from the eyes of the world.

One of the elements that reinforces this theory is the disappearance of several Kriegsmarine U-boats (submarines) at the end of the war. Some of these mysteriously reappeared in Argentina, while others were never found. The submarine U-977, for example, turned itself in to the Allies in Argentina in 1945, months after Germany's surrender, fueling speculation that it had made a secret voyage to Antarctica before resurfacing in South America.

The most controversial theories suggest that Base 211 was dedicated to the development of advanced technologies, including prototype flying saucers based on electromagnetic propulsion principles. Some documents and accounts indicate that Nazi scientists, such as Viktor Schauberger, worked on anti-gravity systems and experimental aircraft. If Base 211 had really existed, it could have housed such experiments, away from the war and Allied interference.

Another key element is the link between the Nazis and esotericism. Antarctica was considered by some German secret societies, such as the Thule Gesellschaft, to be a place of great importance, potentially linked to lost civilizations or technologies of non-terrestrial origin. Some believe that the Nazis were searching Antarctica for traces of an ancient advanced civilization whose knowledge could have given them a decisive technological advantage.

After the war, many of these theories were considered fanciful, but Operation Highjump, conducted by the United States in 1946-47, fueled new doubts. If there was nothing in Antarctica, why did the United States send such a large military expedition immediately after the war ended? Some suggest that the goal was precisely to hunt for the last Nazis hiding in the polar depths.

Today, Base 211 remains an enigma. There is no definitive evidence of its existence, but the continued interest in Antarctica by superpowers and the secrecy surrounding its operations suggest that something extremely important may still lie beneath the ice.

The race for polar resources: a new geopolitical battleground

The polar regions, long considered remote and inhospitable territories, are now at the center of a silent but fierce geopolitical battle. As global warming steadily shrinks the ice caps, new opportunities for strategic resource extraction are opening up, drawing governments and multinational corporations into unprecedented competition for control of the vast riches buried beneath the ice. Oil, natural gas, rare minerals and even fresh water are among the most coveted resources, turning the Arctic and Antarctica into new economic and strategic battlegrounds.

The Arctic, in particular, is one of the most contested areas. According to geological studies, an estimated 13 percent of the world's untapped oil reserves and 30 percent of its natural gas reserves lie beneath its seabed. This immense wealth has prompted nations such as Russia, the United

States, Canada, Norway and Denmark to claim ever larger portions of Arctic territory, often with justifications based on geological and historical data. Russia, in particular, has made the region a strategic priority, establishing new military bases, strengthening its icebreaker fleet and sending submarines to map the ocean floor. In 2007, a Russian expedition symbolically planted a flag at the bottom of the North Pole, declaring that the Lomonosov submarine ridge was part of the Russian continental shelf, an act that sparked international tensions.

The United States has also intensified its presence in the Arctic, especially in Alaska and Greenland, where oil companies such as ExxonMobil and Shell are seeking concessions for hydrocarbon extraction. In parallel, China-though not an Arctic country-has invested billions of dollars in infrastructure development in the region, declaring itself a "quasi-Arctic nation" and advancing plans for a New Polar Silk Road, which would give it easier access to the resources of the North.

Antarctica, unlike the Arctic, is protected by the 1959 Antarctic Treaty, which prohibits all commercial exploitation of natural resources until 2048. However, several nations are already preparing the ground for future expansion of their activities. China has built new scientific bases in strategic locations, while Russia has begun exploring mineral reserves under the polar ice cap. Some reports suggest that both countries are conducting secret studies of Antarctic resources, intending to get ahead of other global players when the treaty is renegotiated.

The consequences of this resource race are potentially devastating. Oil and gas extraction in the Arctic could accelerate global warming and damage delicate ecosystems, while militarization of the region increases the risk of geopolitical conflict. In Antarctica, the opening of mines and extraction facilities could lead to environmental catastrophe, as well as pose a threat to any archaeological or technological discoveries hidden beneath the ice.

The real danger is that this competition is not only economic, but also strategic and military. Control of polar resources could become a new point of contention between the superpowers, with unpredictable consequences for global stability. If the Arctic and Antarctica harbor deeper secrets than we have been told, the race for resources could be just a facade to cover up even darker and more secretive interests.

What is the real purpose of military operations in the poles?

Although Antarctica is officially a demilitarized zone, and the Arctic is presented as a region of international cooperation, the military presence in polar areas has never been stronger. Major powers are enhancing their presence in the poles, establishing advanced bases, testing new technologies, and keeping the real goals of their operations secret. But what lies behind this increasing militarization?

One of the most immediate explanations concerns strategic control. The Arctic has become a key national security area for many nations, especially for Russia and the United States. Climate change is opening up new sea routes, making the Arctic a crucial passage for international trade and resource transport. Controlling these routes means dominating global trade and gaining military advantage. For this reason, Russia has built more than 50 military installations in the region, including an elite base on the Franz Josef Islands equipped with sophisticated radar systems and missile defenses. The United States has responded by strengthening its icebreaker fleet and expanding operations in Alaska and Greenland.

However, there are more disturbing theories. Some believe that the real purpose of military operations at the poles is not just to control resources or sea routes, but to protect extraordinary discoveries. According to rumors, underground structures of unknown origin have been identified in Antarctica, and some leaked documents suggest that the armies of major powers are involved in their exploration and study. This may explain why areas of Antarctica are inaccessible even to accredited scientists and why operations such as Operation Highjump have been conducted with massive military resources.

Another hypothesis involves secret experiments and testing of new technologies. Some researchers claim that the polar regions are used as testing grounds for climate weapons, new propulsion systems and advanced devices, away from prying eyes. The isolated nature of the poles allows highly classified technologies to be tested without the risk of being observed or filmed. Operations could include tests of experimental air vehicles, electromagnetic thrusters, or even experiments related to manipulating the Earth's magnetic field.

Another possibility is that world powers are trying to recover and study technology of unknown origin. Some declassified documents mention anomalous electromagnetic emissions detected in Antarctica, and the discovery of immense underground cavities that seem to house structures that cannot be traced to natural processes. If these structures were of artificial origin, they could be bases built by ancient civilizations or non-human entities, which would justify the level of secrecy imposed by governments and military agencies.

The real reason for the increasing militarization of the polar regions may go far beyond simple competition for natural resources. If bold speculation were true, governments are protecting discoveries of such extraordinary importance that they could rewrite human history. Control of information and operations at the poles may not just be an economic or geopolitical issue, but a battle for dominance over knowledge and technologies that the world is not yet ready to learn about.

THE MAP OF PIRI REIS

CLUES TO A FORGOTTEN PAST

Who was Piri Reis and what does his map represent?

Piri Reis, whose real name was Hadji Muhiddin Piri Ibn Hadji Mehmed, was an admiral, cartographer and navigator of the Ottoman Empire who lived between the 15th and 16th centuries. Born around 1465, Piri Reis spent his life plying the seas of the Mediterranean, acquiring enormous knowledge of sea routes, landmasses and navigation techniques. He was known for his strategic skills in battle and his talent for cartography, which led him to compile one of the greatest atlases of the time, the "Kitab-ı Bahriye", a compendium of nautical information and detailed maps.

However, his most enigmatic work is undoubtedly the 1513 map, discovered in 1929 in the Topkapi Palace in Istanbul. This ancient document depicts with surprising accuracy the western coasts of Europe and Africa, South America and, according to some interpretations, even ice-free Antarctica, a fact that defies official history.

What makes this map extraordinary is not only its accuracy, but the context in which it was made. According to conventional historians, Antarctica was not discovered until 1820, more than 300 years after Piri Reis map was made. Moreover, 16th-century cartography lacked the knowledge to chart with such accuracy the coasts of South America, much less those of a continent that officially no one had yet explored. Still, the map shows geographical details that would have required advanced surveying technologies, such as measuring longitude, which would not be perfected until the 18th century.

According to notes written by Piri Reis himself, his map was compiled on the basis of ancient sources, including older maps from earlier civilizations. The Ottoman cartographer explicitly mentioned that he had used "20 maps and globes", including documents from the time of Alexander the Great and the Arabs, but mostly much older maps of unknown origin. This detail has fueled speculation that the Piri Reis map may be a copy of an even older map made by a lost civilization at a time when Antarctica was not yet covered by ice.

The main enigma of the map concerns precisely the portion that, according to some scholars, would depict the coast of Antarctica without the ice sheet. This would suggest that, in the remote past, the region was ice-free and known to an ancient civilization with advanced navigational skills. But how could such a detailed map exist if humanity, according to the official story, did not possess the technology to explore those latitudes at that time?

The Piri Reis map remains one of the greatest mysteries in cartography, a document that may hold clues to a forgotten past and the true history of Earth exploration. But the most disturbing question is: by whom and when were the original maps on which Piri Reis based made?

How could Piri Reis have known about Antarctica before its official discovery?

The hypothesis that the Piri Reis map depicts Antarctica without ice raises profound questions about the geographical knowledge of ancient civilizations. If indeed the Ottoman document is based on older maps, it means that, in a remote era, someone possessed accurate information about a continent that would not be officially discovered until three centuries later. But who could have explored Antarctica before the modern era?

One of the most fascinating theories suggests that Antarctica was a habitable continent at a much earlier time, before it was covered by ice. This hypothesis finds possible support in geological and paleoclimatic research, which indicates that millions of years ago Antarctica was covered by forests, lakes and even complex life forms. However, according to conventional history, humans could not have explored the continent in such remote eras. Unless there was a prehistoric advanced civilization that was able to navigate and map the globe long before the birth of known civilizations.

Another striking aspect is the map's accuracy in depicting the Antarctic coastline, which matches surveys obtained in 1958 by the Seismic Survey of the British Royal Navy. This study, conducted with advanced radar technology, revealed the morphology of the Antarctic coast hidden under the ice, showing a surprising correspondence with the details on the Piri Reis map. In other words, the Ottoman map appears to show Antarctica as it appeared thousands of years ago, before it was covered by ice.

But how could Piri Reis-or anyone before him-have access to information that only modern science has been able to confirm? Some researchers speculate that the sources used by Piri Reis were derived from a pre-diluvian civilization capable of mapping the world with an accuracy we now associate only with satellite technologies. This theory ties in with the myths of Atlantis and other vanished cultures, which according to some traditions were destroyed by global cataclysms, leaving only fragments of their knowledge in ancient maps.

Another possible explanation is that advanced geographical knowledge was secretly preserved and passed down by groups of navigators, astronomers and priests throughout history. It is known that many ancient civilizations, such as the Egyptians, Phoenicians and Carthaginians, possessed highly developed nautical knowledge. Some scholars suggest that these peoples may have inherited maps from even older civilizations, dating back to forgotten ages, and that these documents were progressively copied and updated over the centuries until they reached the hands of Piri Reis.

There are also those who speculate that the map is evidence of contact with non-terrestrial knowledge. Some bolder theories suggest that if our planet had been visited by higher intelligences in the past, they might have left traces of their knowledge, including detailed maps of the world. Although this hypothesis remains highly speculative, the fact that a 16th-century map could contain information that science only confirmed in the 20th century continues to be an unexplained enigma.

In light of these considerations, it seems clear that the history of exploration and geographic knowledge is much more complex than the traditional narrative suggests. If Antarctica was already known in ancient times, who possessed this knowledge? How was it transmitted through the millennia? And most importantly, what other secrets might it still be hiding beneath its ice?

The Piri Reis map is not just a cartographic document, but a clue to an alternate past, when human civilization-or perhaps someone else-knows much more about Earth than we are willing to admit today.

Unknown sources and lost maps

Piri Reis's map is not only a masterpiece of Renaissance cartography, but may be the last vestige of a much older knowledge, passed down through the centuries by vanished or unknown civilizations. While Piri Reis himself claimed to have based his work on older maps, the real question is: where did these maps come from and who drew them?

One of the most intriguing clues concerns the possibility that Piri Reis had access to cartographic documents of Greco-Egyptian origin, inherited from the famous Library of Alexandria. This ancient center of knowledge, founded in the third century B.C., housed countless documents from all over the known world, including, according to some ancient texts, extremely detailed maps of unknown lands. Some historians suggest that the original maps on which Piri Reis relied may have been copied from documents kept by the Egyptians, who in turn may have inherited their knowledge from an earlier civilization.

Another fascinating hypothesis links this knowledge to the Phoenician and Carthaginian navigators, who allegedly explored vast areas of the Atlantic Ocean and may have mapped lands beyond the borders of the known world. It is believed that the Carthaginians, with their advanced naval technology, possessed secret routes and maps, which were destroyed or concealed by the Romans after the fall of Carthage. If some of this knowledge had been passed down through the Middle Ages to Piri Reis, it might explain the presence of such precise geographical details in his map.

Some researchers suggest instead that the original maps used by Piri Reis may date back to a much earlier time, perhaps even to a pre-diluvian civilization such as Atlantis. This theory, although controversial, is based on a number of historical and mythological clues that indicate that, in the distant past, a highly advanced people would have possessed extraordinary knowledge, including the ability to map the entire globe. Had Atlantis existed and been in contact with other ancient cultures, it is possible that some of its knowledge may have survived through copies of maps preserved over the centuries.

Another extreme but fascinating hypothesis is that the cartographic information that led to the creation of the Piri Reis map was not of human origin, but was provided by a technologically superior civilization. Some independent scholars point out how the accuracy of the map-especially in the depiction of Antarctica's coastline under the ice-exceeded the technological capabilities of the time and suggest that the only way to obtain such information would have been through aerial or satellite surveys, a technology that humanity did not possess in 1513. If an advanced ancient civilization had access to more sophisticated exploration technologies, such as aircraft or satellites, the Piri Reis map might be one of the few remaining evidences of such knowledge.

The mystery of the sources of the Piri Reis map remains unsolved, but the implications are enormous. If Antarctica is shown to have been known and mapped long before the modern era, it would be definitive proof that human history is far more complex and ancient than currently accepted.

Geological evidence and the possibility of an ice-free Antarctica

The idea that Antarctica may have been ice-free in the relatively recent past is not only a fascinating theory, but is supported by geological and paleoclimatic evidence gathered over the past decades. Scientific studies show that, in a remote era, the Antarctic continent was not an ice desert, but a land rich in vegetation, rivers and even animal life.

Evidence for this theory emerges from drilling into Antarctic ice, which has uncovered fossilized plant and tree sediments, indicating that the continent millions of years ago was home to flora similar to that of today's temperate forests. According to studies published in the journal Nature, traces of fossilized pollen and remnants of rainforests have been found under Wilkes Land Ice, suggesting that Antarctica had a much milder climate, similar to that of present-day New Zealand.

Research on the ocean floor off the Antarctic coast has revealed the presence of sediments typical of freshwater rivers and lakes, confirming that, in a remote era, the continent was not always covered by ice. Some climate models suggest that this period may have occurred between 12,000 and 40,000 years ago, a time frame that coincides with theories about a possible major global cataclysm that may have altered Earth's climate.

One of the most surprising clues comes from radar scans of the Antarctic ice sheet, which have revealed the presence of canyons, mountains and subglacial lakes, some of which are still active and have liquid water, such as Lake Vostok. This indicates that, in the not too distant past, Antarctica might have been habitable and, consequently, explorable by advanced civilizations.

But the most puzzling evidence concerns the discovery of ancient rock carvings and maps in various parts of the world that seem to depict Antarctica without ice. Some hieroglyphs found in South America and Egypt show representations of the ancient world with a mysterious continent to the south, which could correspond to Antarctica. If these representations were thousands of years old, it would mean that someone had explored the continent before it was covered by ice.

Another interesting theory is related to the phenomenon of crustal dislocation, a theory put forward by Charles Hapgood, which suggests that the Earth's crust may have undergone sudden shifts, shifting entire continents to new locations. If Antarctica was once located further north, in an area with a more temperate climate, it could explain why ancient civilizations may have explored and mapped it.

If it were confirmed that Antarctica was habitable in relatively recent times, it would open up incredible questions: who lived there? Were there advanced cultures living there before the Ice Age? Are there remains of ancient cities still buried under the ice?

Modern science is slowly unraveling Antarctica's hidden past, but much of the most important information seems to be controlled or kept secret. The fact that some areas of the continent are rigidly inaccessible and that many exploration missions are surrounded by an aura of secrecy suggests that what has been discovered so far may only be the tip of the iceberg.

If one day the mystery of Antarctica is completely unraveled, we could be faced with a rewriting of human history, with implications that would go far beyond simple geology. It could be definitive proof that long before known civilizations, Earth was inhabited by highly advanced cultures of which we have now lost all trace.

More anomalous maps that could rewrite history

The Piri Reis map is not an isolated case. Other maps from eras before the official discovery of Antarctica show similarly puzzling details, suggesting that the world was known far better than official history admits. Among them, Oronteus Finaeus's map, Philippe Buache's map, and other ancient geographic representations bear striking similarities to modern maps of the Antarctic continent, but with one key difference: they depict it ice-free, as if it had been explored at a time when the climate was very different.

Oronteus Finaeus, a 16th-century French cartographer, published a map in 1531 showing an Antarctic continent with rivers, mountain ranges and detailed coastlines, devoid of the ice cap that covers it today. When this map was analyzed in the 20th century, experts noticed a surprising correspondence with seismic surveys taken under the ice, which would have revealed the real morphology of the region. What is surprising is that the geographic conformation of the Oronteus Finaeus map predates discoveries made with modern scientific instruments by centuries, raising the question of who could have gathered this information long before technology allowed it.

Another equally enigmatic map is that of Philippe Buache, an 18th-century French geographer, who produced a map of Antarctica based, according to him, on ancient documents. The peculiarity of Buache's map is that it shows the continent divided into two large land masses separated by a vast inland sea, a configuration that only in the 20th century was confirmed by radar scans under the ice. If this information were correct, it would mean that, in a remote era, someone had already studied the structure of Antarctica with advanced surveying techniques.

In addition to these, other mysterious maps depict geographical details that defy official history. Some ancient Chinese maps show the American continent long before its "discovery" by Christopher Columbus, while medieval European maps show features of unknown lands with an accuracy that can hardly be attributed to mere guesswork. Even in Arabic cartography there are examples of maps that seem to depict the Earth with a knowledge of longitude that, according to historians, would not be acquired until several centuries later.

If it were accepted that these maps are based on even older sources, we would have to ask who produced the original maps. The possibility exists that they came from advanced prehistoric civilizations that were able to explore the globe and map its continents long before classical civilizations. If this were true, it would mean that the history of human exploration is much longer and more complex than we are taught, and that ancient knowledge, perhaps kept in secret for millennia, has been lost with time.

What do these discoveries imply for our view of the past?

If the Piri Reis map and other ancient maps are really based on prior knowledge, the implications for human history would be enormous. It would mean that long before the era of great exploration, unknown civilizations were able to navigate the oceans, map the world with extreme precision, and collect advanced geological data. This would challenge the traditional narrative that global geographical knowledge developed only with the age of discovery in the 15th and 16th centuries.

One of the most puzzling possibilities is that the world saw one or more advanced civilizations earlier than known history, perhaps thousands of years before the Sumerians, Egyptians or Mayans. If so, these cultures would have had a sufficient level of technology and organization to conduct global explorations, and their knowledge would then have been passed down through the centuries in the form of maps and documents, all the way to Renaissance scholars. But if such a civilization existed, what happened to it? A global cataclysm, natural event or internal collapse may have wiped out all traces of it, leaving behind only fragments of knowledge that survived in documents such as the Piri Reis map.

If Antarctica was truly ice-free in the not-too-distant past, this would support theories that the planet has undergone extreme climate and geological changes in a much more recent period than previously thought. Some scholars have speculated that a catastrophic event, such as a shift in the Earth's crust or an inversion of the magnetic poles, may have drastically altered the global climate, rendering Antarctica uninhabitable and erasing any traces of civilization that might have existed previously.

These discoveries could also have a significant impact on our understanding of the connections between ancient cultures scattered around the globe. If prehistoric populations had access to detailed maps of the Earth, this could explain the striking similarities between seemingly unrelated civilizations such as the Egyptians, Mayans, Sumerians, and the mysterious megalithic cultures of Europe and Asia. All of these civilizations seem to have possessed advanced knowledge in astronomy, engineering and navigation, suggesting the existence of an ancient global network of communication and information exchange.

But the more disturbing question concerns why this information was forgotten or concealed. Is it possible that, throughout history, some knowledge was deliberately concealed by elites or power groups who wished to maintain control? Some speculate that lost libraries, such as the one at Alexandria, contained evidence of this ancient knowledge, and that their destruction was no accident. Even today, information about certain archaeological and geological findings is often classified or downplayed, fueling suspicions that there is control over discoveries that could rewrite the past.

If we accepted that the Piri Reis map and other anomalous maps are based on real and accurate data, we would have to completely reconsider how we view history. We might be faced with evidence that our planet was explored and studied much earlier than we think, and that ancient civilizations were far more advanced than official history would like to admit. If this knowledge had been passed down to the present day without interruption, we might today have a much broader understanding of our origins and our place in the universe.

Perhaps the real mystery is not only how these maps were made, but why their existence continues to be ignored or downplayed. If evidence of forgotten knowledge exists, who has an interest in keeping it secret? And what more could we discover if research into these anomalies were conducted without bias? The answers might be buried under millennia of ice... or kept in the lost maps of a past the world is not yet ready to accept.

THE MYSTERIOUS LIGHT PHENOMENA OF THE POLES

ONLY AURORA BOREALIS?

Beyond the aurora borealis: mysterious lights in the polar skies

The Northern and Southern Lights are among Earth's most fascinating natural spectacles, light phenomena that dance across the polar sky due to the interaction between solar particles and Earth's magnetic field. However, over the decades, numerous explorers, scientists and residents of the Arctic regions have reported unexplained light phenomena, lights that do not fit known scientific models and seem to obey as yet unknown physical laws.

One of the most well-documented phenomena is the presence of intermittent flashes and sudden flashes of light, observed not only in areas typical of auroras but also in regions where they are not supposed to occur. Arctic explorers have reported bluish or greenish lights that appear to pulsate at regular intervals, resembling huge flashes in the sky, often with no correlation to solar or geomagnetic activity. Some of these events also occur on polar nights, when the lack of sunlight makes their unknown origin even more apparent.

Another anomalous phenomenon involves horizontal streaks of light, observed by pilots and scientists who have flown over the polar regions.

These light beams do not follow the behavior of traditional auroras, but appear motionless or move independently of the solar wind. In some cases, they have been spotted coinciding with magnetic anomalies, leading some researchers to speculate that they could be the result of unknown electrical phenomena or interactions between the Earth's magnetic field and a yet unidentified energy source.

In some expeditions, especially in Antarctica, light phenomena from the ground, similar to glows emerging from the ice sheet, have been reported. Some scientists have theorized that these could be electrostatic discharges or effects of geothermal pressure beneath the ice crust, but the intermittent nature and unnatural coloration of these events continue to raise questions. If energy sources exist beneath the polar ice, they could be linked to even more extraordinary phenomena, perhaps even to buried structures generating unexplained electromagnetic effects.

There are also reports of lights that seem to respond to human presence, blinking or moving in seemingly intelligent ways. Some researchers have speculated that these phenomena may be manifestations of natural plasmas, but the fact that many of these lights have shown anomalous behavior compared to known atmospheric phenomena leaves room for more speculative theories. Is it possible that some of these light manifestations are of artificial origin or related to unknown presences?

Pulsating lights and orbs of energy: unexplained sightings

In addition to atmospheric anomalies, one of the most enigmatic accounts comes from pilots, scientists and inhabitants of the polar regions, who over the years have reported the appearance of floating luminous orbs, often described as pulsating globes of light that move in ways incompatible with traditional physics.

Some of these sightings date back to ancient times. Indigenous peoples of the Arctic, such as the Inuit, have passed down legends for centuries about "dancing lights" that chased people in the dark and seemed to have a consciousness of their own. In some tales, these glowing orbs were considered spiritual entities or signs of impending events, but the similarity to modern descriptions of unidentified energy phenomena suggests that this may be a recurring phenomenon in human history.

In the 20th and 21st centuries, military and civilian pilots have reported spherical luminous objects that moved against the wind, accelerated suddenly and changed direction instantaneously, characteristics typical of what are now called UFOs or unidentified aerial phenomena (UAPs). Some of these sightings occurred near military bases located at the poles, leading some to speculate that they were experimental technologies. However, no known aircraft possess the movement capabilities observed in these phenomena.

One of the most extraordinary sightings occurred in 1985, when a scientific expedition to Antarctica reported seeing three blue-white orbs of light floating above their base camp for about 15 minutes. The lights, according to witnesses, appeared to move in formation and changed color and light intensity in response to sounds from the camp. This event was reported to scientific agencies, but received no official explanation.

In a similar case in 2004, a research mission in the vicinity of the Magnetic South Pole documented on radar and optical instrumentation a sphere of light accelerating from a static position to supersonic speeds, without emitting any sound or signs of propulsion. This event was dismissed as an "atmospheric anomaly", but some members of the mission stated that the phenomenon was so extraordinary that it suggested the intervention of an unknown technology.

The energy spheres observed at the poles could be the result of interactions between the Earth's magnetic field and extreme atmospheric phenomena, or they could be manifestations of a type of energy still unknown to science. Some physicists have speculated that they could be natural plasmoids, similar to globular lightning, but their frequency of appearance and behavior seem to indicate something more complex.

Another hypothesis is that these phenomena could be surveillance probes of unknown origin, perhaps connected to secret installations at the poles or to presences of a nonterrestrial nature. If there were advanced technologies buried beneath the ice or tested by the great powers at the poles, it could be possible that these glowing orbs are the result of classified scientific activities or tests of new forms of propulsion based on electromagnetic energy.

Some theorists have suggested that pulsating lights and energy spheres may represent an even more mysterious phenomenon, perhaps related to unknown dimensions of reality or to interactions with forces that humanity is not yet able to understand. Their presence at the poles, areas of Earth characterized by intense magnetic and gravimetric anomalies, could indicate that these phenomena are a symptom of something much deeper and more complex, an aspect of reality that eludes conventional science.

Questions remain: is this an as-yet unexplained natural phenomenon, secret tests, unknown presences, or something beyond our current understanding of the universe? What is certain is that things are happening in the polar skies that defy scientific explanation, and perhaps one day we will discover that these mysterious lights are the key to understanding a still-hidden aspect of our existence.

Electromagnetic phenomena and unknown atmospheric interactions

The mysterious light phenomena observed in the polar regions could be related to anomalous electromagnetic interactions between the Earth's atmosphere and magnetic field. Polar areas, in particular, are characterized by intense geomagnetic activities and the presence of plasma corridors and charged particle streams interacting with the ionosphere. However, some of the manifestations observed in Arctic and Antarctic skies do not fit into the classical patterns of boreal and austral auroras, suggesting that there may be other physical processes at play.

One of the most advanced hypotheses involves the phenomenon of electromagnetic resonance in the ionosphere, similar to the operation of standing waves in a closed system. Under certain conditions, natural radio waves emitted by the Earth can interact with the magnetic field, creating intermittent light effects and plasma spheres. This might explain some of the light globes that have been observed at the poles, but it would not explain the intelligent motion and sudden accelerations reported by reliable witnesses such as pilots and scientists.

Another hypothesis is that some of these phenomena are the result of as-yet-ununderstood atmospheric electrical discharges, similar to globular lightning but on a much larger scale. In particular, it is hypothesized that the strong polar magnetic field may generate high-energy plasmas, which manifest as bright spheres that can move rapidly and change shape. Some of these plasmas could be linked to Birkeland currents, immense electric currents that flow between the Sun and Earth, powering auroras but also generating side phenomena that have yet to be studied.

One interesting aspect concerns correlations between these luminous phenomena and gravitational anomalies detected in some polar areas, particularly in Antarctica. Some scientists believe that intense variations in the Earth's magnetic field at the poles may generate electromagnetic distortion effects, which could cause luminous manifestations of an as yet unknown nature. In some cases, satellites flying over Antarctica have detected strange magnetic fluctuations coinciding with the appearance of unexplained lights. This has led some researchers to speculate that the polar subsurface may be hiding geological structures or materials with high electrical conductivity, capable of interacting with the Earth's magnetic field and producing unconventional optical phenomena.

Some scientists have suggested that man-made activities may be behind some of these phenomena. Programs such as HAARP (High-Frequency Active Auroral Research Program) have shown that it is possible to manipulate the ionosphere via high-frequency radio waves, creating light effects similar to auroras. If such technologies had been developed in secret by military powers, it is possible that some of the sightings at the poles are the result of advanced testing of the ionosphere and atmospheric electromagnetic interactions. However, the fact that some of the phenomena were recorded long before the era of radar technology and high-frequency transmissions leaves room for the possibility that this is a natural process that is still unknown.

Military reports of unexplained luminous events

The military archives of several nations contain declassified documents reporting sightings of anomalous light phenomena at the poles, often recorded by operating bases and air patrols. Most of these reports have been classified for decades, fueling suspicions that the military has been trying to cover up information about unexplained events occurring in the polar regions.

One of the best-known reports concerns an event that occurred in 1965 at the U.S. McMurdo military station in Antarctica. On that occasion, base personnel reported orbs of blue and orange light floating above the field for more than 20 minutes, moving in a coordinated manner and changing direction suddenly. The phenomenon was recorded both visually and by radar instruments, but the official report at the time attributed the event to an "atmospheric anomaly". However, some witnesses later stated that the lights seemed to respond to the presence of observers, stopping suddenly when flashlights were pointed and resuming movement only after a few seconds.

Another interesting document comes from the archives of the Soviet Air Force, which conducted numerous operations in the Arctic between the 1970s and 1980s to monitor U.S. military activities. On several occasions, Soviet pilots reported sightings of glowing orbs that suddenly accelerated and disappeared into thin air, leaving no trace on conventional radar. In 1978, a Soviet reconnaissance plane intercepted three spherical luminous objects over the Kara Sea that appeared to move with a smart trajectory, avoiding contact with the plane and then disappearing at incredible speed. The event was classified as a UAP (Unidentified Aerial Phenomenon) and dismissed without an official explanation.

The British Ministry of Defense has also released declassified documents referring to unexplained light phenomena over Canada's Arctic bases. In 1981, during a joint U.K.-Canadian operation to monitor Soviet activities in the Arctic, a military patrol observed pulsating red and white lights for over an hour that appeared to form geometric patterns in the sky. Radar detected no aircraft or drones in the area, and witnesses described the phenomenon as "luminous intelligence" that seemed to follow a deliberate path.

In 2010, a leaked document from sources inside the Norwegian military spoke of unknown lights observed in the Svalbard region, a strategic territory in the Arctic. The lights were seen both by pilots and by radar at a monitoring base, and some reports suggested that they appeared to be going in and out of the ice surface, as if plunging underground. This feature, which is completely incompatible with conventional atmospheric phenomena, has led some analysts to speculate that secret underground structures or as yet unknown natural anomalies may exist beneath the ice.

Military interest in these events is not limited to passive observation. Some sources suggest that secret monitoring experiments and intercept attempts have been conducted by various nations to study these phenomena closely. If these glowing objects were drones or unknown technologies developed in secret, then the great powers would be engaged in a strategic game of surveillance at the poles. However, if the lights and energy orbs observed in the polar skies are not of human origin, their true purpose and nature remain a mystery.

Whether they are natural electromagnetic phenomena, advanced technological experiments or manifestations of unknown origin, the fact that militaries around the world have documented unexplained events at the poles is a clear signal that these anomalies deserve thorough research. The poles, with their secrets buried under miles of ice and their skies charged with unknown phenomena, may hold the key to revealing truths that still elude our understanding.

Theories of dimensional inputs and space-time anomalies

Earth's poles are not only the most extreme and inhospitable regions of the planet, but also places where magnetic, gravitational and atmospheric anomalies occur that continue to challenge our understanding of physics. Some researchers have speculated that these phenomena may be related to dimensional gaps or space-time distortions, and that the mysterious lights spotted in Arctic and Antarctic skies could be manifestations of phenomena that transcend our current understanding of reality.

One of the most significant clues concerns Earth's magnetic field, which behaves very differently at the poles than at the rest of the planet. Here, the magnetic field lines curve sharply, generating a particularly intense interaction with charged particles from the Sun. However, in some cases, detection instruments have recorded unexplained fluctuations in the magnetic field, events that do not appear to be attributable to solar activity alone. Some theoretical physicists have speculated that such perturbations may indicate the presence of gravitational interference or time distortions, concepts that, although they seem to belong to science fiction today, find some parallels in Einstein's theory of relativity.

The hypothesis that dimensional gaps may exist at the poles is based on two main elements: gravitational anomalies recorded in the polar regions and unexplained light phenomena that appear to violate the laws of conventional physics. Some scientists have suggested that, under certain conditions, the immense magnetic and gravitational pressures present at the poles could generate effects similar to those predicted by wormholes (Einstein-Rosen bridges), hypothetical structures in theoretical physics that would allow connection between distant points in space-time.

Further confirmation of the existence of possible spatiotemporal distortions comes from the testimony of pilots and explorers, who on several occasions reported anomalous alterations in on-board instruments, such as compasses gone mad, stopwatches marking discordant times, and GPSs recording unexplained changes in position. One famous case involves a military flight that, in the 1990s, crossed an anomalous area of Antarctica and reported a discrepancy of more than 30 minutes in the flight logs, as if the plane had been "moved" to a different point in space-time for a short period.

There are also more extreme accounts of temporary disappearances of entire groups of explorers, reappearing hours or days later with no recollection of what happened. Although these incidents are difficult to verify, their persistence in accounts raises questions about what might really be happening in the less explored areas of the poles.

If space-time distortion phenomena do indeed exist at the poles, these could explain the presence of mysterious lights, fast-moving objects, and even spheres of energy that seem to suddenly appear and disappear. Could these be manifestations of energy from another dimension? Or perhaps signs of an interaction with a parallel reality that, under certain conditions, becomes temporarily visible in our world?

Is something communicating with us? The hypothesis on intelligent signals

If the mysterious lights observed in the polar skies were not simply natural phenomena or space-time anomalies, but rather attempts at communication by unknown entities, then we would be facing one of the most revolutionary discoveries in human history. Some scientists and independent researchers have speculated that some of these light phenomena could be messages, signals or even energy-based life forms.

One particularly fascinating aspect is the fact that some of these lights appear to respond to human stimuli, such as artificial lights, radio waves, or even movements of people at the site. There are numerous accounts of explorers, military personnel and researchers who have reported sudden changes in the intensity or color of lights in response to sounds, gestures or light signals sent from the ground. If these phenomena were purely natural, why do they seem to interact with observers?

One emblematic case occurred in 2003 at Concordia Base, Antarctica, when a group of scientists noticed a pulsating light moving slowly over the base camp. After attempting to signal their presence with light beams directed toward the object, the light suddenly changed color and accelerated upward until it disappeared into the sky. The event was recorded on multiple cameras, but was dismissed without an official explanation.

Military bases in the poles have also reported instances of unexplained radio interference that appear to follow non-random patterns. Some of these signals, picked up by monitoring antennas, showed repetitive and structured modulations, similar to those that would be used to transmit coded information. If this were a natural phenomenon, the question is, why do these signals occur so regularly and with frequency variations reminiscent of intelligent transmissions?

An even bolder hypothesis is that some of the bright orbs observed at the poles may be probes of unknown origin, perhaps autonomous devices designed to gather information or attempt a form of communication. If so, who sent them? Some suggest that they might be manifestations of an intelligence that exists in a nonmaterial form, perhaps beings composed of pure energy inhabiting a parallel reality and manifesting only under special conditions.

There are also theories linking these phenomena to ancient indigenous traditions and legends. Peoples such as the Inuit and Sami have for centuries spoken of "spirits of light" or "guardians of the sky", described in a strikingly similar way to modern sightings of glowing orbs at the poles. Is it possible that these civilizations had contact with an unknown form of intelligence and passed on their experiences in the form of myths and stories?

If the polar light phenomena indeed represent an attempt at communication, this could mean that something or someone is trying to make contact with humanity, using light and energy signals that we are not yet able to decipher. Could it be an advanced life form using the physics of the poles to send messages? Or an interdimensional intelligence that manifests itself only under certain conditions?

The key to unraveling this puzzle may lie in the deeper study of the interactions between these lights and human observers. If we could decode the signals, we might discover not only who is trying to communicate with us, but also what message they are trying to convey. In that case, the poles might not just be remote territories of Earth, but gateways to something much larger, perhaps a dialogue with an intelligence that has long been waiting to be heard.

A CIVILIZATION HIDING UNDER THE ICE?

Hypotheses on underground civilizations: an ancient presence in the poles

The idea that an unknown civilization may exist beneath the ice at the poles is one of the boldest, but also among the most intriguing hypotheses. Anomalies detected over the decades by scientists, explorers and even satellites suggest that Antarctica and the Arctic may not simply be barren expanses of ice, but places that harbor deep secrets, perhaps traces of a civilization that found refuge in the depths of the Earth in ancient times.

Some researchers have hypothesized that, in the distant past, Antarctica was habitable and home to an advanced culture that, for unknown reasons, later retreated beneath the ice. If Antarctica had been a warmer, greener region in past eras-a hypothesis supported by geological and fossil evidence-then it is plausible that a civilization may have lived there before a climatic catastrophe or an unknown event that forced it into hiding in the depths.

One of the most widely discussed theories is that of cryptoterrestrials, intelligent beings who would have found refuge beneath the Earth's surface, developing a society hidden from the eyes of the world. This hypothesis is based on a number of clues, including the huge underground cavities detected under Antarctic ice, some of them so large that they could contain entire cities.

A significant example is the Wilkes Land anomaly, a huge depression under the ice detected through gravitational measurements. This structure, more than 300 kilometers in diameter, has been officially interpreted as a possible meteor impact crater, but some alternative theories suggest that it could be an ancient buried city or an underground base abandoned by unknown beings.

Some documents and secret missions have hinted at the existence of underground tunnels in the polar regions, some of which would be too perfect and symmetrical to be simple natural formations. Could they have been built by a technologically advanced civilization, able to burrow under the ice to protect itself from a catastrophic event or to maintain its isolation from the rest of humanity?

There are also ancient myths and legends about beings coming from the depths of the Earth or knowledge held in the poles. According to some esoteric accounts, particularly those related to the Hollow Earth theory, there would be openings in the poles leading to an underground world inhabited by advanced entities. If this hypothesis were even partially true, the implications would be extraordinary: we may not be the only intelligent species on the planet, only those living on the surface, while other beings have evolved in environments inaccessible to most.

The growing interest of governments and institutions in the polar regions, accompanied by strict secrecy about many of the operations conducted there, has fueled suspicions that something significant has been discovered beneath the ice, something that could change our understanding of history and humanity itself.

Ancient explorers chronicles of strange presences in the ice

The polar regions have been the scene of numerous enigmatic tales by explorers and sailors over the centuries who have reported strange presences, unexplained sounds and mysterious movements in the frozen lands. While officially these stories are dismissed as suggestions or errors of perception, their persistence over time raises questions about what really lies at the poles.

One of the earliest accounts comes from the diaries of Admiral Richard E. Byrd, the famous explorer who led several missions to Antarctica and the Arctic in the 20th century. Although his official documents have been censored or classified, there are accounts that claim Byrd referred to strange shadows moving under the ice, unknown flying objects and even the existence of "a world beyond the Pole". Some theorists believe that Byrd may have discovered underground entrances or lost cities, but that this information was covered up by the U.S. government.

Another interesting case dates back to the 1845 British expedition led by Sir John Franklin, which sought to explore the Northwest Passage in the Canadian Arctic. The mission mysteriously disappeared and was not found until years later, with the bodies of the crew frozen in unexplained conditions and with hints of strange atmospheric phenomena and light apparitions recorded in the few documents recovered. Some Inuit legends suggest that the expedition may have encountered "ice guardians", mysterious beings who would influence the fate of the mission.

Another disturbing tale is that of the missing 1959 Soviet science team operating in a remote area of Antarctica. According to reports leaked only years later, a group of Soviet scientists allegedly disappeared without a trace for weeks, only to reappear with severe symptoms of shock and fuzzy memories about unexplained events. Some team members spoke of metallic sounds coming from under the ice, shadows moving in the dark, and structures that should not have existed in the heart of the Antarctic desert. After their return, the Soviet government classified every document related to the mission, fueling speculation that they had discovered something extraordinary.

The indigenous peoples of the Arctic, such as the Inuit and Sami, have also passed down stories about creatures living under the ice, luminous entities emerging from cavities, and secret passageways leading to underground worlds. According to some Inuit legends, "the Unga" are beings that inhabit the Arctic underground and occasionally interact with humans, but only with those who can find their entrances. Some researchers have related these stories to accounts of the unexplained disappearances of entire Inuit villages, events that remain a mystery to this day.

A recurring element in these accounts is the presence of strange sounds and vibrations from underground, which are often described as metallic hums or deep echoes. Some scientists have tried to explain these phenomena as acoustic effects related to the movement of glaciers, but their repetition in multiple areas of the poles and the fact that they were reported at different times by unrelated witnesses suggests that there may be more to it.

If we consider the possibility that hidden tunnels and cavities exist beneath the poles, then it is plausible that some of the historical evidence may refer to accidental contact with something or someone living below. It could be a technologically advanced civilization, an isolated people who developed their own culture hidden over time, or phenomena still beyond our understanding.

Explorers reports and accounts of strange presences in the ices raise a crucial question: what is really hiding under the poles? Most importantly, if there is a civilization hidden in the depths of the Earth, has it remained there by choice or necessity?

Speculation on submerged cities under the ice: remnants of a lost world?

The idea that the remains of an ancient civilization may lie beneath the ice of Antarctica and the Arctic is not only a fascinating hypothesis, but is supported by geological discoveries, satellite images, and structural anomalies that seem to defy official history. If, in the distant past, the poles were ice-free and harbored environments conducive to life, it is possible that they hosted thriving cities, ports and settlements that later disappeared under a blanket of ice following a global cataclysm.

One of the most significant clues comes from high-resolution satellite images, which have revealed anomalous geometric structures, formations resembling walls, pyramids and even networks of subterranean channels under the ice of Antarctica. Some of these anomalies have been detected in areas such as Queen Maud Land, Wilkes Land, and the region near Lake Vostok. In particular, in Princess Elizabeth Land, scientists have discovered a perfectly symmetrical pyramidal structure, which some experts consider a rare case of natural erosion, but which has features that are difficult to explain without considering an artificial origin.

Theories of submerged cities under the ice find further support in radar surveys by the British Antarctic Survey and NASA, which have revealed the presence of immense cavities and formations that do not appear to be of natural origin. In some cases, kilometer-long underground passages with smooth walls and sharp edges have been identified, suggesting the possibility of man-made constructions.

Another key element is ancient maps, such as those of Piri Reis, Oronteus Finaeus, and Philippe Buache, which show Antarctica free of ice and with detailed coastlines. If these maps were based on older sources, then someone in ancient times not only knew about the continent but described it as a habitable area. This opens up the possibility that Antarctica was home to an ancient, technologically advanced civilization that perhaps flourished before a catastrophic event caused its demise.

Some researchers believe that the Antarctic continent may have been affected by a shift in the Earth's crust, a hypothesis put forward by Charles Hapgood. According to this theory, about 12,000 years ago, Antarctica was in a more temperate position and could have hosted developed civilizations. A sudden shift in the crust would have brought the continent to its current location, instantly freezing all life and burying entire cities under the ice.

Also supporting this hypothesis are the stories handed down by ancient civilizations, such as the tales of the Egyptians, Sumerians and Mayans, which speak of an ancient frozen land inhabited by wise and technologically advanced beings that disappeared due to a great cataclysm. These myths coincide with the legend of Atlantis, which according to Plato disappeared as a result of a drastic climate change or global catastrophic event.

If the structures identified under the Antarctic ice were indeed the remains of a lost civilization, then we would be facing one of the greatest archaeological discoveries in history, capable of rewriting our understanding of the origins of human civilization. The fact that much of this research is classified and scientific missions are often terminated without detailed explanations fuels the suspicion that something extraordinary has been discovered but is being kept secret for reasons not yet known.

Archaeological evidence of settlements under the ice

Although the idea of ancient cities submerged under the ice is still considered speculative by the official scientific community, there are archaeological findings at the poles that suggest an ancient human presence in the polar regions, challenging traditional theories.

One of the most surprising finds was found in 1912 during a British expedition to Antarctica. The explorers discovered remnants of handmade tools, flint arrowheads and pottery fragments, objects that should not have been found in an area considered uninhabited for millions of years. Some of these artifacts were analyzed and dated to thousands of years ago, a fact unexplained by the conventional narrative of human history.

In 1958, a Soviet mission discovered in a remote area of Antarctica a piece of what appeared to be a precisely crafted pillar buried under layers of ice at least 10,000 years old. The find was immediately transferred to Moscow and classified as a state secret. A few years later, leaked reports suggested that the pillar had geometric carvings and markings that appeared to belong to an unknown language.

In recent decades, evidence of ancient human presence in the polar regions has also been found in Greenland. In 2016, an expedition of archaeologists discovered megalithic structures buried under the permafrost, similar to the stone circles found in various parts of the world. Some scholars suggest that these monuments may belong to a forgotten culture that inhabited the region before the last ice age, a hypothesis that contradicts conventional theories that no organized civilization could have existed in such climatic conditions.

Another significant clue comes from radar surveys conducted near Lake Vostok, a huge subglacial basin located 4,000 meters below Antarctic ice. The scans revealed the presence of regular structures and thermal anomalies, suggesting that something man-made may lie beneath the surface. Some researchers have speculated that these may be the remains of a submerged city, frozen in time under the millennia-old ice sheet.

In addition to material objects, there are also unusual petroglyphs and rock carvings found in some polar areas, which appear to depict humanoid figures, abstract symbols and star maps. If these signs were authentic, they could indicate that ancient cultures had advanced knowledge of astronomy and geography, and may have explored the polar regions much earlier than official history recognizes.

If all these clues are confirmed, it would mean that human presence at the poles goes back much farther than expected, and that evidence of a civilization that thrived before a major global disaster may lie beneath the ice. This would explain why research missions to Antarctica are tightly controlled and why much scientific data is secreted.

If there were indeed settlements under the ice, who built them? Were they humans, a technologically advanced culture lost in time, or perhaps a non-human civilization that inhabited the Earth in a remote era? The answers to these questions may lie under miles of ice, waiting to be discovered.

Ancient buried cities: myth or reality?

The idea that buried cities from a remote era may lie beneath polar ice is a hypothesis that fascinates scholars and independent researchers alike. If confirmed, it could completely rewrite human history, forcing us to reconsider the evolution of civilizations and their ability to adapt to extreme conditions. But does this theory have concrete foundations or is it just the result of speculation and legends?

A key element in favor of this hypothesis is the geological anomalies identified beneath the Antarctic and Arctic ice. Radar scans and satellite surveys have revealed the presence of large rectilinear structures, similar to submerged walls or roads, extending for hundreds of kilometers. Some of these formations lie at such depths that, to be explained, we would have to assume that the Antarctic continent was once ice-free and habitable.

Ancient maps, such as that of Oronteus Finaeus and Philippe Buache, seem to support this hypothesis, as they depict Antarctica with a geography compatible with surveys obtained only in the 20th century through radar remote sensing. If these documents were authentic and based on older knowledge, it would mean that an advanced civilization mapped Antarctica before it was covered by ice, implying its existence at a much earlier time than official history acknowledges.

Lake Vostok, a huge expanse of liquid water located under 4 km of ice in Antarctica, has also been the focus of speculation. Some radar data have revealed anomalous geometric structures at the bottom of the lake, suggesting the possibility of settlements or even remains of a submerged city. If confirmed, this would find parallels with megalithic structures discovered under the ocean in different parts of the world, such as the mysterious Yonaguni Monument in Japan, which some believe to be the remains of an ancient civilization sunk into the depths.

The legends of many ancient cultures speak of lands that disappeared due to great catastrophes, such as Atlantis described by Plato or the kingdom of Hyperborea, which according to Greek mythology was located in an icy land inhabited by extraordinary beings. Could these tales be interpreted as allegories or as distorted historical recollections of real events?

Some scientists speculate that a global cataclysmic event, such as a rapid shift in the Earth's crust, a reversal of the magnetic poles or a meteoric impact, may have caused the disappearance of an entire polar civilization, forcing the survivors to take refuge elsewhere or hide underground. If so, libraries, temples and material evidence of a very ancient knowledge left behind by those who inhabited the region before the ice age may lie beneath the ice.

The only way to test this hypothesis is to continue exploring the poles with the latest technology, but much of the data collected so far is either secreted or difficult for the public to access. If world powers really did find evidence of a lost civilization under the ice, what would be their reaction? And why would this information not be released?

The implications of such a discovery: what would it mean for human history?

If it were confirmed that the remains of an ancient advanced civilization lie beneath the polar ice, the impact on all areas of human knowledge would be immense. History as we know it would have to be completely revised, and many of our fundamental assumptions about the evolution of civilization would be challenged.

The first and most obvious consequence would be a redefinition of the chronology of human civilizations. If an ancient city existed under the ice, it would mean that an advanced culture flourished long before what we now consider the cradles of civilization, such as Sumer and Egypt. This would imply that human history is much older and more complex than we think, and that there are whole chapters of our cultural and technological evolution that have been forgotten or removed from official historical accounts.

Another important consequence would concern science and technology. If an Antarctic civilization existed and possessed advanced knowledge, one might ask: How advanced was it? Did it possess technologies superior to ours? If, for example, it had developed an in-depth knowledge of energy, astronomy or the manipulation of natural resources, the recovery of such information could be a revolution for modern science.

In addition, this discovery could strengthen the hypothesis that humanity received outside influences in its evolution. Some theories suggest that ancient civilizations may have had contact with higher intelligences, terrestrial or otherwise, who left signs of their presence under the ice. If the structures buried in Antarctica reveal knowledge that is not compatible with the technological level of known civilizations, we would be facing the possibility that human evolution was guided by external factors or an ancient civilization prior to our own.

Politically and geopolitically, the discovery of an ancient civilization under the ice would have enormous strategic implications. If a nation discovered advanced technologies buried in Antarctica, it could gain an unprecedented advantage. This could explain why Antarctica is tightly regulated by international treaties and why there are continuous scientific expeditions with results that are rarely disclosed in their entirety.

On a philosophical and cultural level, the recognition of a lost civilization would forever change the way we view our place in history. The mythological and religious narratives of many cultures speak of bygone eras, vanished peoples and great catastrophes, and this discovery could give them a basis of historical truth. It could also open questions about how safe our civilization actually is from a similar fate: if an advanced culture disappeared under the ice, might we be destined to suffer the same fate?

This discovery could redefine the whole concept of historical memory and forbidden knowledge. If human history has been altered or forgotten over the millennia, who has benefited? And what more could we discover if research were conducted without restrictions?

The recognition of a civilization under the ice would not only be an archaeological discovery, but a revelation that would change our past, our present, and our future. If the world were ready to accept this reality, we could stand on the brink of a new era of human knowledge, in which the veil of the unknown is finally lifted to reveal the secrets of our planet and the civilizations that have inhabited it before us.

THE ROLE OF ESKIMOS AND NATIVE PEOPLES OF THE ARCTIC

Who are the Inuit and indigenous peoples of the Arctic?

The indigenous peoples of the Arctic, including the Inuit, Yupik, Chukchi and Sami, have inhabited the polar regions for thousands of years, developing an extraordinarily resilient culture in an extreme environment. The Inuit, in particular, are one of the most mysterious and fascinating peoples in human history, bearers of an ancestral knowledge that seems to defy our conventions about adaptation, navigation, and perception of the environment.

The Inuit, formerly known by the term "Eskimo" (meaning "raw meat eaters" in the Algonquian language, a term now considered inappropriate), call themselves "the people" or "the men", in the Inuktitut language, to emphasize their deep connection with nature and their territory. Originating in Siberia, they gradually moved across the Bering Strait, colonizing the North American Arctic and reaching as far as Greenland.

Their survival in such extreme environments has been made possible by skillful use of natural resources and exceptional knowledge of climate, ice, and sea currents. Their culture is based on a combination of hunting, fishing, and spirituality, and their mythology is rich with tales of mysterious beings, spirits inhabiting the ice, and creatures emerging from the depths of sea and sky.

Their oral traditions pass down stories of encounters with nonhuman beings, described as creatures with supernatural powers inhabiting the underground, ice caves and even the sky. Some of these tales surprisingly coincide with modern sightings of unidentified aerial phenomena (UAPs) and strange lights in polar skies, suggesting that the Inuit may harbor forgotten knowledge about energy and interactions between the natural world and other possible forms of intelligence.

Some of their beliefs speak of invisible doors in the ice and travelers suddenly disappearing without a trace, as if they had been swallowed by another dimension or a secret passage underground. There is a legend, for example, of an entire Inuit village that disappeared without explanation, leaving behind intact tents, weapons and supplies, but with no sign of struggle or sudden escape. This event, documented by Western explorers in the 19th century, remains one of the great mysteries of the Arctic.

These accounts suggest that the Inuit may be the keepers of ancient knowledge, perhaps dating back to a time when the Arctic was very different from today. Is it possible that they had contact with cultures now lost, or that they inherited knowledge that dates back to an advanced prehistoric civilization, perhaps one that was submerged by ice millennia ago?

How Inuit navigate and orient themselves with signals invisible to modern explorers

One of the most incredible aspects of Inuit culture is their ability to navigate and orient themselves in an environment seemingly devoid of landmarks, an ability that Western scientists still struggle to fully explain today.

The Inuit can move hundreds of kilometers across the ice desert without modern tools, relying solely on their memory, reading sea waves, cloud formations and even imperceptible variations in wind and light. Their method of orientation seems to be based on a combination of direct observation, orally handed down experience, and an innate ability to perceive patterns and signals that elude most Western explorers.

One of the most mysterious ways the Inuit orient themselves is known as "ice feeling", an ability that allows them to sense the stability and safety of an ice sheet simply by walking on it. While scientists must use sonar and radar instruments to detect the risk of fractures in the ice, the Inuit can do so with their senses, relying on minute vibrations and sounds that are imperceptible to less experienced ears.

Another remarkable aspect of their navigation concerns the way they read ocean waves even at great distances. Even when the sea is covered with ice and invisible to their eyes, the Inuit are able to sense the movements of currents beneath the surface and predict the weather with impressive accuracy. Some scientists have speculated that this ability is a form of "resonance" with the environment, similar to how some animals perceive Earth's magnetic fields.

Another unexplained technique is the Inuit method of predicting storms and atmospheric variations days in advance, without any instruments. Some scholars have found that this ability may be related to reading the lights in the sky and variations in the quality of light reflected from ice, suggesting that the Inuit can sense changes in the Earth's ionosphere and magnetic fields long before they become apparent with scientific instruments.

There are also accounts of a mysterious phenomenon known as "the ice song", a sound the Inuit perceive in certain weather conditions that seems to guide them through the most inaccessible landscapes. Some explorers have reported hearing these sounds during their expeditions, describing them as low, almost ultrasonic vibrations that seem to come directly from the ice and surrounding air.

Another remarkable aspect of Inuit navigation is their ability to find their way home even after being disoriented by blizzards or long journeys through unknown territory. While Western explorers rely on compasses and GPS instruments, the Inuit seem to possess a kind of highly developed "geographic memory" that allows them to reconstruct their location through minute details of the landscape.

Some scholars have speculated that this ability may be the result of a form of ancestral knowledge inherited through generations, perhaps related to a sensory intelligence that modern civilization has forgotten. But there are also those who suggest that the Inuit have developed a special connection with the forces of nature, and that their ability to find their way in such a hostile world may derive from lost knowledge dating back to ages before our own.

If the Inuit really do possess knowledge handed down from time immemorial, is it possible that it contains clues about ancient vanished civilizations, the true history of the poles, and even anomalies that still elude modern science? Could their tales and extraordinary abilities provide evidence of a hidden world beneath the ice or phenomena we do not yet understand?

What is certain is that Inuit knowledge, often ignored by Western science, could reveal even deeper secrets about the mysteries of the Arctic and Antarctica, and perhaps offer us a new key to understanding the anomalies that lurk at the poles of our planet.

Encounters with "Snowmen" and other unexplained creatures

The legends of the Inuit and other Arctic peoples are replete with tales of mysterious beings, creatures that seem to share their habitat with humans but elude scientific classification. Among these, one of the most enigmatic figures is that of the "Snowmen", described as humanoid creatures, tall and robust, covered in fur and endowed with extraordinary strength.

The Inuit call them "Tornit", and their stories portray them as primitive but intelligent beings, capable of building shelters and using rudimentary tools. According to local lore, the Tornit were once more numerous and lived near the Inuit, but they were wary and preferred to remain hidden in caves and ice. Some accounts tell of clashes between the Inuit and the Tornit, who were reportedly taller and stronger than the common men, but less agile and with a more rudimentary culture.

The descriptions of the Tornit bear a striking resemblance to those of other legendary beings scattered around the world, such as the Bigfoot of North America, the Yeti of the Himalayas or the Almasty of Siberia. This has led some scholars to speculate that they may be an archaic human species that survived in remote and inhospitable areas, escaping extinction due to their ability to live in isolation.

Numerous Western explorers have reported sightings of strange figures in the polar ice, describing large beings moving with incredible agility through the Arctic mountains and forests. In 1943, a U.S. military mission to Greenland reported giant footprints in the snow, a sign of the passage of something much larger than a human being. Similar tracks have also been found in Siberia, where some local hunters tell of beings that walk on two legs but move with unnatural swiftness, disappearing into the tundra before they can be observed closely.

Another extraordinary tale comes from the expedition of Danish explorer Knud Rasmussen, who in the early 1900s collected accounts from the Inuit about the presence of semi-human creatures that move through the ice without leaving a visible trace. According to the accounts, these beings have superior knowledge of the land to humans, managing to avoid contact with humans and disappear into the ice as if they were part of the environment itself.

In addition to the Snowmen, other mysterious creatures are part of Inuit lore. Some hunters tell of seeing luminous figures moving under the ice, as if something lived deep in the Arctic ice. These stories connect to the mysterious light phenomena sighted in the polar skies and raise the question of whether there is a connection between these beings and the magnetic and atmospheric anomalies recorded in the polar regions.

Some alternative researchers suggest that the Tornit and other Arctic creatures may be descendants of an ancient civilization that chose to take refuge in the most inaccessible places on Earth, living in isolation for millennia. If this theory is correct, then the Inuit may have had contact with a parallel species of humanoids, perhaps a separate evolutionary line or even the descendants of an advanced prehistoric civilization that preferred to hide rather than disappear.

Although official science does not acknowledge the existence of these beings, the fact that Inuit accounts are so consistent and that similar accounts exist in many other cultures around the world leaves open the possibility that there is something still unknown among the Arctic ice.

The Inuit and their knowledge of the extreme climate: technology or legacy of ancient civilizations?

The Inuit possess advanced knowledge of the Arctic climate and its variations, knowledge that has enabled them to survive in a hostile environment for thousands of years. However, this knowledge seems to go beyond mere practical experience: in many cases, the Inuit can predict storms, ice shifts, and climate change with an accuracy that baffles modern scientists.

One of the Inuit's most amazing abilities is their weather forecasting system based on observation of clouds and light reflected from ice. Without the use of instruments, they can predict the arrival of storms days in advance, an ability that some scholars attribute to ancient knowledge passed down through generations. Some have speculated that this method relies on electromagnetic variations or atmospheric signals imperceptible to most people, a phenomenon that could indicate a hypersensitivity developed through millennia of adaptation.

Another interesting aspect concerns the construction of igloos and Arctic dwellings, which follow a precise pattern of thermal insulation and air distribution. Their structure is so efficient that a relatively warm temperature can be maintained inside even when outside temperatures are below -40°C. This advanced knowledge of thermal dynamics and aerodynamics may be a legacy of ancient knowledge from a time when the Earth's climate was changing and populations had to develop advanced techniques to survive.

Some researchers have speculated that the Inuit may have inherited some of their knowledge from a vanished prehistoric civilization, which would have bequeathed not only the technology to cope with extreme climates, but also advanced maps, symbols and orientation systems. This theory is based on the fact that some of the techniques used by the Inuit, such as orientation through sea waves even when they are invisible, resemble the navigation techniques of ancient Polynesians and Pacific Islanders, suggesting a possible cultural connection between distant peoples.

Another fascinating theory concerns the possibility that the Inuit are descendants of an ancient advanced Arctic civilization, which may have developed superior knowledge before being forced to take refuge in the remotest parts of the planet. If so, their extraordinary ability to adapt could be the result of knowledge much older than official history acknowledges.

There are even accounts of Inuit shamans who claim to have a spiritual connection with ice and wind, a form of knowledge that goes beyond mere physical experience and may be a remnant of an ancient science now forgotten. If these tales had a kernel of truth, it could mean that the indigenous peoples of the Arctic hold an ancestral memory of catastrophic climatic events and perhaps of encounters with cultures or beings of which our history has preserved no record.

If the Inuit and other Arctic peoples have inherited knowledge that eludes modern science, this could mean that there are still secrets hidden among the ice, mysteries that could rewrite human history and our relationship with the past. The question remains: is this knowledge the result of millennia of natural adaptation or the legacy of a much older civilization that left behind fragments of extraordinary knowledge?

Ancient Inuit tools and their incredible survival skills

The Inuit, with their extraordinary ability to survive in one of the most inhospitable environments on the planet, have developed a range of traditional tools that not only reflect their deep knowledge of the natural world, but also suggest a surprisingly advanced understanding of polar conditions and climate dynamics. These tools, ranging from weapons to igloo construction, are tangible evidence of how survival in such an extreme environment can require knowledge and techniques that go far beyond immediate adaptation to nature.

One of the best-known tools of the Inuit is the spear (or harpoon), used for hunting whales, seals, and other marine animals. These weapons were designed to penetrate the thick blubber of marine animals and were often equipped with sharp points and release mechanisms, which allowed hunters to grab and hold their prey at a distance. These sophisticated hunting techniques, combined with the ability to bind the strengths of ice and snow, show that the Inuit possessed an advanced knowledge of the physics of movement and the strength of materials, a skill that would be necessary to survive extreme conditions.

The Inuit also used kayaks, a traditional craft constructed from natural materials such as wood and whalebone, lined with seal skin to ensure buoyancy. These extraordinarily agile and maneuverable kayaks were not only tools of transportation, but also highly specialized hunting vehicles that allowed the Inuit to move silently through icy water and hunt seals without disturbing their surroundings. The kayak is not only an example of adapted engineering, but also of a deep understanding of natural materials and environmental forces. Indeed, the Inuit also exploited biomimicry, studying how animals and plants adapted to polar conditions to create technologies that mimicked those observed in nature.

In addition, the construction of igloos is another example of advanced knowledge. These snow structures not only offered protection from extreme cold, but also utilized the thermal properties of snow itself. Snow, in fact, is an insulating material that, while freezing on the outside, maintains a more stable temperature on the inside. The igloos, with their perfect shape, exploited this characteristic, creating a shelter that, inside, could remain relatively warm, even when the temperature outside dropped as low as -40°C (-104°F).

These techniques and tools are not only the result of millennia of practical experience, but also reflect an intuitive scientific understanding of materials, thermodynamics, and physics that would have required knowledge we now associate with modern science. Their ability to design effective solutions for surviving in one of the most extreme environments on Earth suggests that the Inuit possessed a wealth of advanced knowledge, passed down from generation to generation, that may date back to a much earlier and more developed time than is usually recognized.

Inuit astronomical knowledge and ancestral navigation

One of the Inuit's most outstanding skills was their ancestral navigation, which enabled them to orient themselves and move accurately through vast territories of ice and snow. Although the Inuit had no tools such as compasses or maps, their knowledge of the sky, stars, and constellations was critical to their survival and navigation in environments without immediate visual references.

The Inuit developed their own celestial map, which used constellations to determine directions and predict seasons. Prominent among the major constellations used for navigation were Orion, Taurus, Great Bear and Pleiades, all of which are visible in the Arctic sky. The stars and planets thus became fixed landmarks, used to calculate position and determine the path to follow while traveling across the ice expanses. The position of the Sun, which in the Arctic extremes does not set for weeks or months, was also crucial for navigation. The Inuit knew how to read solar movements to determine time and direction. Their knowledge of the sky went beyond simple orientation, however, it was also cyclical knowledge, which allowed them to predict seasonal changes or adapt to extreme weather conditions.

A fascinating example of this astronomical wisdom is their use of the position of the moon. The Inuit observed its phases and movements in the sky, associating each lunar cycle with certain animal behaviors and changes in climate. In fact, the lunar cycle was also used as a system for measuring time, correlating with the natural rhythms of the Arctic world. Changes in the sky and variations in light were indicators of impending weather events. The Inuit knew how to predict storms and wind changes based on the position of the Sun and stars, knowledge that seems incredible today considering that it was based on observations made without telescopes or scientific instruments.

Another remarkable element is the system of directions and orientation. The Inuit not only oriented themselves in relation to the sky, but also used natural references such as wind directions, the shape of the ice, and the behavior of sea animals. Elders, custodians of the traditions, taught younger people how to read these signals, imparting knowledge that enabled them to tackle journeys across frozen seas and endless glaciers, often for tens of kilometers.

These abilities are not simply the result of practical adaptation, but reflect a deep connection between the Inuit and their environment, a scientific and spiritual understanding of the laws of nature that met daily survival needs, but also suggests knowledge that may date back to a much older and more sophisticated tradition. If the Arctic peoples possessed such knowledge of heaven and earth, there may be a link between their traditions and ancient vanished civilizations, which perhaps had observed the same interaction between the Earth and the cosmos, without the knowledge ever having been written down, but only passed down orally over the centuries.

Today, many of these ancient navigation methods are studied by modern science, but the fact that a culture without the use of technology can predict weather events and navigate in impossible conditions challenges our conception of human knowledge and its roots. The question that arises is whether this extraordinary ability to read nature and the sky is the result of millennia of adaptation or a legacy of knowledge tied to an ancient and forgotten civilization.

THE SECRET CULT OF THE POLES

Hidden gods in the ice: forgotten polar deities

The polar regions, inhospitable and seemingly desolate, have always evoked a sense of mystery and reverence in the peoples who inhabited or ventured there. The Inuit, Sami and other Arctic peoples have for centuries passed down stories of deities and spirits hidden in the ice, powerful beings dwelling beneath the earth's surface or emerging during storms to manifest their presence. In Nordic and Scandinavian traditions, too, tales are found about supernatural beings bound to the poles, capable of influencing human destiny and controlling the forces of nature.

Among the Inuit, one of the most enigmatic figures is Sedna, the goddess of the sea and the deep, who, according to legend, resides in the icy depths and rules the sea animals. Sedna is often described as a semi-human creature with long dark hair and missing fingers, cut off by a cruel father who had betrayed her. According to Inuit mythology, Sedna can punish hunters who disrespect animals, triggering sudden storms and mysterious disappearances in the ice. Some scholars have speculated that Sedna's myth may have older roots and connect to legends about submerged civilizations or cults of deities linked to the underground.

Another spirit feared by the Inuit is Mahaha, a creature said to live in the eternal ice and who enjoys tormenting humans with his sinister laughter. Described as a tall, skeletal figure with blue skin, Mahaha is associated with the disappearances of people in the Arctic, and some accounts speak of wayfarers found dead in the ice with an expression of terror and an eerie grin on their faces. Although the myth may seem folkloric, it is interesting to note that many stories of Arctic peoples speak of beings hidden in the ice, silent observers living on the border between the human and spirit worlds.

The Sami, an indigenous people of northern Scandinavia, also believe in deities and spirits related to the frozen lands. Among them, Jábmeáibmo, the lord of the underworld, is one of the most enigmatic gods. According to the Sami, there is an invisible realm beneath the earth's surface inhabited by the spirits of the dead and supernatural creatures, who sometimes emerge to communicate with shamans. These beliefs, similar to those of other polar cultures, suggest an ancient worship of subterranean beings, perhaps inspired by real contact with something unknown.

What is striking is that many of these deities and spirits are not considered abstract entities, but real, tangible beings that physically dwell in the ice or beneath the earth's crust. Some researchers have speculated that these tales may stem from real experiences with unexplained phenomena, such as mysterious lights, subterranean sounds or encounters with unknown creatures. If so, we may be looking at one of the oldest accounts of contact with beings that may not belong to the human world.

Norse legends and the realm of underground beings

Scandinavian and Germanic cultures have for centuries passed down legends about beings inhabiting the underground, powerful and ancient creatures living hidden beneath mountains, in caves and even under polar ice. These tales find many similarities with those of the Inuit and Sami, suggesting a link between the traditions of peoples thousands of miles apart, perhaps based on common experiences or shared knowledge of realities now forgotten.

One of the most famous myths in Norse mythology is that of Niflheim, the realm of mist and ice, considered one of the primordial worlds in the universe of Norse cosmology. According to the sagas, Niflheim was a land shrouded in eternal cold, inhabited by mysterious creatures and ancient primordial forces. This realm connected to Hel, the world of the dead, but also to Yggdrasil, the cosmic tree that connected all the realms of the universe. Some scholars have speculated that Niflheim might represent an ancient reminder of an underground civilization hidden beneath the ice, an echo of a time when the north was inhabited by beings other than ordinary humans.

Another fascinating element of Norse mythology is the figure of the frost giants, called Jǫtnar. These creatures were described as huge and powerful, inhabitants of inaccessible lands, particularly of Jötunheimr, an icy realm separated from the human world. According to accounts, the frost giants were ancient inhabitants of the world, predating even the gods, and possessed secret knowledge that only a few could understand. Some alternative theories suggest that the frost giants may represent the mythological memory of a vanished civilization, perhaps a population of nonhuman beings who inhabited the Arctic before the arrival of humans.

Germanic myths also speak of subterranean beings, such as the Nibelungs, mysterious creatures who lived in cities hidden under mountains and guarded incredible treasures. According to some tales, these entities had built secret passages that led to the world of men, but only those with the right knowledge could find them. The concept of underground cities also recurs in Icelandic sagas, where they speak of tunnels hidden under the ice and entire kingdoms lost in the depths of the Earth.

Another enigmatic figure in Norse mythology is that of Surtr, the fiery giant who, at the end of time, will emerge from the depths to bring destruction during Ragnarok. The description of Surtr and his underground army has led some to speculate that the myth may represent a reminder of a catastrophic geological event, such as a volcanic eruption or sudden climate change. If Surtr represents an energy hidden underground, could it be a reference to something that actually exists deep within the Earth, waiting to be awakened?

Nordic and polar legends have a common thread: the belief that a hidden world exists beneath the earth's surface, populated by ancient, powerful, and mysterious beings. The question is: Are these tales merely symbolic, or could they be based on real experiences?

When we consider the constant reports of luminous phenomena, magnetic anomalies and unexplained sounds from polar ice, it becomes possible that Nordic and Arctic myths are not just made-up stories, but fragments of ancient knowledge that has been passed down for generations. Could it be that what the ancients called ice gods and subterranean giants was actually an unknown civilization, hidden in the poles for millennia?

The implications of these stories are enormous. If the myths contain hidden truths, we may be confronted with evidence that there are realities beneath the ice that we do not yet understand, and that perhaps the lost knowledge of ancient civilizations has not entirely disappeared, but is just waiting to be rediscovered.

The mysterious inhabitants of the frozen caves

Indigenous cultures in the polar regions have for centuries passed down stories about mysterious beings who would live deep in the ice, in underground caves and hidden cities. According to these tales, the inhabitants of the underground would not simply be spirits or mythological creatures, but real beings with their own society and secret knowledge of the world. Inuit, Sami and Siberian peoples speak of sporadic encounters between humans and these beings, often described as keepers of ancient knowledge or as creatures who prefer to remain hidden from modern civilization.

One of the most fascinating tales concerns Inuit legends about the Tuniq, a mysterious and reclusive people who reportedly lived in remote parts of the Arctic and were known for their great physical strength and extraordinary ability to build underground shelters. The Tuniq, described as very tall and silent beings, would be able to suddenly disappear into the ice, as if they knew secret passages hidden in the depths of the polar ice cap. Some accounts claim that the few Inuit who came into contact with them were warned never to seek out their underground cities because secrets too dangerous to be revealed to ordinary humans were hidden there.

The peoples of Siberia and the Russian Arctic tell similar stories about the Chud, an underground people who allegedly lived in the frozen lands for millennia. According to ancient legends, the Chud were an advanced civilization who knew technologies and secrets of the underground and who, to escape a great cataclysm, would have retreated into the depths, sealing their cities to avoid contact with the outside world. Some Siberian hunters still speak today of strange glows from crevasses in the ice and underground metallic humming, which local beliefs claim are signs of their presence.

The Sami of northern Scandinavia also speak of beings inhabiting the depths of ice and mountains, entities often associated with nature spirits, but which in some accounts seem more like physical beings, able to communicate and interact with humans. Some Sami shamans claim to have received visions of passages hidden beneath glaciers, which would lead to an underground world where the ancient spirits of the North would live.

Tales of ice cave dwellers are repeated with striking similarity in different polar cultures, which raises a fundamental question: are these mere myths, or distorted memories of real encounters with unknown beings? If there really are hidden passages under the poles, it could be possible that these beings have found refuge in an as yet unexplored subterranean ecosystem. Modern remote sensing technologies have revealed the existence of immense cavities under the ice of Antarctica and the Arctic, some of which may be large enough to house man-made structures. If these legends have a kernel of truth, it is possible that a network of tunnels and underground cities exist beneath the poles, just waiting to be discovered.

The connection with the hollow earth theory

The idea that a hidden world exists beneath the earth's surface is not a recent theory, but has deep roots in the traditions of many civilizations. Stories of subterranean beings, buried cities, and secret passages to an inner world are found in the myths of cultures around the world, from Indian Vedas to Native American legends. In the poles, these legends take on an even more mysterious significance as they are intertwined with modern theories of the Hollow Earth, according to which our planet may be hiding an inner ecosystem inhabited by intelligent beings.

According to this hypothesis, immense voids would exist beneath the Earth's crust, with entire regions still unexplored. Some theorists claim that the poles could harbor giant openings leading to the underworld, a hypothesis fueled by alleged magnetic anomalies detected in past decades in some polar areas. Explorers such as Admiral Richard E. Byrd have reported tales of strange formations in the heart of Antarctica and sightings of unexplained phenomena, leading some to speculate that the U.S. government may have discovered secret underground entrances while keeping the information confidential.

The Hollow Earth theory suggests that advanced cities may exist beneath the Earth's crust, powered by unknown energy sources, and that some of the sightings of lights and glows at the poles may be manifestations of this energy. Some researchers speculate that the beings described in Inuit, Sami and Siberian legends may actually be the descendants of a very ancient civilization that would have fled underground to escape global cataclysms, perhaps during a prehistoric era when the Earth was very different from today.

If this theory were true, it would explain why so many polar cultures have such similar tales of underground beings emerging sporadically to interact with humans, then returning to their hidden cities. It could be that some ancient peoples discovered these passages and had contact with those living beneath the Earth, but that, over time, this knowledge was turned into myth and legend.

Modern explorations have revealed that the polar subsurface is not an impenetrable block of ice, but is crisscrossed by natural caves, underground rivers and vast empty spaces. Some scientists have discovered that under the Antarctic ice are large lakes of liquid water, kept warm by geothermal heat. One of the most mysterious is Lake Vostok, a huge subglacial basin buried under 4 km of ice, which may harbor completely unknown life forms. According to some researchers, these conditions could also exist in other polar regions, providing a perfect environment for a civilization that took refuge beneath the surface thousands of years ago.

If the legends of the Inuit and Nordic peoples about the presence of subterranean beings at the poles had a kernel of truth, it would mean that Earth's history is much more complex than we think. There may have been a time when humanity shared the planet with another intelligent race, which for some reason chose (or was forced) to hide in the depths of the Earth. The continuing magnetic and geological anomalies detected in the polar regions could be the traces of a still-active subterranean civilization, observing the surface world without revealing itself openly.

If one day the existence of an entrance to this underground world is discovered, it would change forever our understanding of the planet and of our own existence. Ancient myths, far from being mere stories, could prove to be the keys to unlocking Earth's greatest secret: the existence of a world hidden beneath the ice, populated by beings who know truths that humanity has forgotten.

Polar peoples ritual practices for communicating with hidden beings

Polar peoples, such as the Inuit, Sami and indigenous tribes of Siberia, have always lived in symbiosis with nature, developing a spirituality based on connection with the elements and with the spirits that, according to them, inhabit the ice, the sky and the depths of the earth. To get in touch with these entities, shamans in these cultures perform complex ritual practices, which seem to have the purpose not only of honoring spirits, but also of establishing a real dialogue with beings hidden in the underground worlds.

Inuit shamans, known as angakkuq, are considered the mediators between the human and spirit worlds. According to tradition, certain spirits inhabit the underground and the ice, and to make contact with them the shaman must enter a trance-like state induced by sacred drumming and the repetition of rhythmic chants and sounds. During these ceremonies, the angakkuq may receive visions and messages from unseen entities, who reveal to him secrets about nature, seasons and future events. Some accounts speak of shamans who are said to have learned from these entities knowledge about navigation, igloo construction, and even animal behavior, suggesting that this knowledge is not only the result of observation but also knowledge transmitted by mysterious beings.

Another ritual practiced by the Inuit to communicate with underground spirits is the "wind invocation", a ceremony performed before long and dangerous journeys across the ice. According to belief, certain underground entities are storm keepers and can influence winds and weather. The shaman, after fasting and chanting for hours, enters a trance-like state and asks the spirits to reveal to him whether the journey will be safe or if there will be danger. In some cases, there are stories of shamans who would receive specific warnings, such as the sudden appearance of lights in the sky or sounds from the ice, which would signal an impending climate change.

The Sami of northern Scandinavia also have similar traditions. Their shamans, called noaidis, perform rituals in which they use drums decorated with mysterious symbols, representing the map of the cosmos and connections between the human and spirit worlds. Some of these symbols seem to represent entrances to the underground, sacred places where the ancient entities of the earth dwell. During ceremonies, the noaidi may fall into a trance and claim to have traveled to the underworld, encountering beings who impart secret knowledge to them.

There are also accounts of rituals practiced by Siberian peoples, in which shamans go to caves or crevices in the ice, considered portals to the spirit world, and there perform ceremonies involving offerings of bones and sacred objects. Some accounts handed down by older shamans speak of occasions when offerings were accepted and gifts, such as stones engraved with strange symbols or messages received in dreams, were received in return.

These ritual practices, repeated over centuries, seem to indicate a deeply held belief: that intelligent forces exist beneath the poles with which it is possible to interact. The entities with which these peoples believe they communicate could be simple spiritual manifestations or, according to a more radical hypothesis, distorted accounts of actual encounters with subterranean beings, passed down through the centuries in the form of myth and ritual.

What can archaeology tell us about the legends of the poles?

Official archaeology has always regarded the poles as places devoid of ancient human settlements because of extreme climatic conditions that would have made it impossible for advanced civilizations to survive. However, in recent decades, surprising findings have emerged that could overturn this idea and provide evidence to support legends about subterranean peoples and ancient polar civilizations.

One of the most discussed findings is that of geometric structures buried under the Antarctic ice, detected by ground-penetrating radar. Some of these structures, detected in the Queen Maud Land region, appear to have a symmetrical and artificial appearance, with formations resembling walls and corridors. Although official scientists speak of simple geological anomalies, some independent researchers argue that these formations could be the remains of ancient cities submerged by ice thousands of years ago.

In Greenland in 2018, archaeologists discovered an underground site buried under layers of ice, containing stone tools that should not be found in those regions, dating back to a time before the first Inuit migrations. This suggests that someone may have inhabited the Arctic much earlier than previously thought, perhaps at a time when the climate was very different from today.

One of the most mysterious findings is the one made in Lake Vostok, Antarctica. This subglacial lake, located 4 km below the ice surface, has been isolated for millions of years, and when scientists drilled into the ice to analyze it, they found unknown microorganisms and unexplained thermal anomalies. Some researchers believe Lake Vostok may be hiding something much larger, perhaps a hidden ecosystem or even the traces of an ancient civilization submerged beneath the ice.

Another interesting feature is the rock carvings found in some polar areas, which depict humanoid figures and symbols that do not seem to belong to traditional Inuit or Sami culture. Some of these petroglyphs seem to show strange creatures, beings with nonhuman proportions, and representations of underground passageways, which has led some alternative researchers to suggest that they may be evidence of contact with beings not belonging to our known civilization.

If legends about subterranean peoples had a kernel of truth, these archaeological findings could be the first tangible evidence of the existence of an ancient civilization hidden beneath the poles. The possibility that some of the caves and subglacial formations are man-made structures or remains of lost settlements would completely change our understanding of human history.

Connections between the ritual practices of polar shamans and archaeological discoveries suggest that there may be answers under the ice that humanity has not yet fully explored. If there are indeed beings hidden beneath the poles, as ancient legends tell us, it is possible that past civilizations were aware of them and left clues scattered among myths, carvings, and buried structures. The question that remains is: who or what really lurks beneath the ice? More importantly, why has this knowledge been forgotten or concealed?

THE HIDDEN PYRAMIDS OF THE POLES

TRUTH OR FICTION?

Satellite discoveries: pyramidal structures at the poles

In recent decades, satellite images have revealed anomalous structures at the poles, particularly in Antarctica, that strikingly resemble geometrically perfect pyramids. These formations have attracted great interest and speculation, as some appear to have sharp edges and 60-degree angles, features that are difficult to explain by simple natural geological processes.

The most striking discovery dates back to the 2000s, when satellite images of the Queen Maud Earth region showed a triangular formation with three symmetrical sides, silhouetted between the surrounding mountains. The precision of its shape led some independent researchers to speculate that it may be an artificial structure buried under the ice for thousands of years.

Another anomaly has been identified in the Wilkes Land region, where other pyramid formations have been observed, some of them partially submerged in ice. The arrangement of these structures has led some scholars to speculate on a possible alignment with constellations, as is the case with the pyramids of Giza in Egypt and other ancient structures around the world. If this were true, it would mean that someone built these pyramids in a remote era when Antarctica was not yet covered by ice.

Official scientists claim that many of these structures are the result of normal geological processes, such as erosion caused by wind and frost. However, some researchers have pointed out that some of the pyramids have proportions and orientations that are too precise to be simple natural formations. In addition, their distribution closely resembles that of other pyramids discovered in different parts of the world, which has fueled the hypothesis that they may belong to a forgotten ancient civilization that lived in Antarctica before the continent was covered by ice.

Some theorists suggest that the Antarctic pyramids could be related to similar structures found on other continents, such as the submerged pyramids off the coast of Japan or the mysterious pyramids of Bosnia and Egypt, suggesting a possible global pattern of construction, perhaps carried out by an advanced civilization that existed in the distant past.

One of the most intriguing elements concerns the restrictions placed on expeditions to the area, which have made it difficult to explore these structures directly. Some independent explorers who have attempted to approach the alleged pyramids have reported magnetic interference and anomalies in electronic devices, which has led to theories that these structures may be covered by a layer of ice but still contain man-made materials or even sealed rooms.

If these structures were indeed man-made, it would mean that an ancient, technologically advanced civilization inhabited Antarctica at a time when the continent was ice-free, a theory that is reflected in some ancient maps, such as the Piri Reis map, which show the Antarctic coast without the ice sheet.

Possible geological explanations: mountains or man-made constructions?

The official scientific community has tried to explain pyramidal structures at the poles with conventional geological theories. The most accepted explanation is that these formations are the result of natural processes of erosion, due to the action of the strong winds and extreme temperatures that characterize Antarctica. According to this hypothesis, over millions of years, the combined action of ice and wind would have shaped some mountains into triangular shapes, giving them the appearance of pyramids.

One of the examples cited by scientists is the Pyramid of the Ellsworth Mountains, a rock formation found in the Antarctic region that has an almost perfectly pyramidal shape, but according to experts is the result of a combination of geological fractures and selective erosion processes. This type of formation is also known in other parts of the world, such as in Mount Kailash in Tibet and Mount Belukha in Siberia, which have pyramid-like shapes but are considered natural phenomena.

However, some features of Antarctic pyramids challenge this explanation. In particular, some of the formations identified in satellite images have perfectly symmetrical angles and precise alignments with astronomical points, features that can hardly be attributed to simple erosional processes. In addition, some of the alleged pyramids appear to have secondary structures nearby, as if they were part of a larger architectural complex, leading some researchers to speculate that they may be remnants of buildings submerged under the ice.

Another interesting item concerns measurements made by some scientists through georadar techniques and gravitational analysis, which have revealed the presence of subsurface anomalies near these structures. Some of these measurements suggest that there may be cavities or gaps under the pyramids, which has fueled the hypothesis that these are man-made constructions buried under miles of ice.

Scientists most open to the hypothesis of an Antarctic civilization argue that if indeed in the distant past Antarctica was ice-free and home to an advanced civilization, the pyramids could be the last visible remains of a submerged city, preserved for millennia under the polar ice cap. This theory also relates to the possibility that some ancient maps, such as that of Piri Reis, were based on cartographic knowledge of a lost civilization that was able to explore the Antarctic continent long before modern times.

Some alternative scholars have advanced the hypothesis that the pyramids may be energy structures, similar to what some theories attribute to the Egyptian pyramids. According to this view, the pyramids were not simply tombs or monuments, but energy collection and distribution centers, perhaps used for scientific or spiritual purposes. If so, the pyramids of Antarctica could be part of an ancient global system built to harness natural energies still unknown today.

The debate about Antarctic pyramids remains open. While the traditional geological explanation seems plausible, some details, such as geometric precision and anomalies detected in the subsurface, suggest that there may be more than just a natural formation. If one day these structures are fully explored, we may be faced with a discovery that would completely change our understanding of ancient history, showing that unknown civilizations inhabited the poles much earlier than official science recognizes.

The mystery of the polar pyramids is still far from being solved, but if satellite images and geophysical data continue to provide clues, we may be closer to discovering whether these structures are indeed man-made constructions, traces of a forgotten past and of a civilization that may have left signs of its existence in the remotest places on Earth.

Links with pyramids of other ancient civilizations

The hypothesis that Antarctic pyramids and other similar structures in the poles may have a connection with the pyramids of ancient civilizations such as those of Egypt, Mesoamerica and China is one of the most fascinating aspects of the mystery. If it is shown that these polar formations are not of natural origin but rather man-made structures, it would open up a fundamental question: was there an ancient global civilization capable of building pyramids on different continents, including the poles?

Pyramids were built by numerous ancient cultures, often with similar geometric proportions, precise astronomical alignments and a possible energetic or spiritual purpose. If Antarctic pyramids shared some of these features, it would imply that ancient civilizations were far more advanced and interconnected than official history acknowledges.

Egyptian pyramids, such as the Great Pyramid of Giza, are famous for their extraordinary precision engineering and alignment with the constellation Orion. Some alternative researchers speculate that the pyramids of Giza were not simply tombs, but part of an ancient system of energy collection and transmission, based on advanced knowledge of sacred geometry and electromagnetic waves. If the pyramids of Antarctica were confirmed as man-made structures, their location could be part of an ancient global scheme in which all the pyramids on Earth were connected by a system of forgotten knowledge.

Mesoamerican pyramids, such as those at Teotihuacan in Mexico or Mayan structures in Guatemala and Belize, are known for their connection to astronomy and the cyclical calendar of time. Some Mesoamerican pyramids were built with multiple levels and contained hidden chambers and underground tunnels, which may have a connection to the subglacial structures detected in Antarctica.

Another interesting comparison involves the lesser-known but equally enigmatic Chinese pyramids. The pyramids of Shaanxi Province, China, bear similarities to Egyptian and Mesoamerican pyramids and are associated with legends about divine emperors and advanced astronomical knowledge. Some ancient Chinese texts speak of "visitors from the sky" who allegedly passed on knowledge of pyramid construction, a narrative that is echoed in the stories of many other civilizations.

If the pyramids at the poles followed a similar pattern to these structures, one might speculate that an ancient civilization had a definite plan for building these structures around the planet, perhaps for purposes of navigation, energy or even communication. The fact that many of the world's pyramids were built on points of strong geomagnetic energy suggests that these civilizations had a much more advanced knowledge of the Earth than was thought possible.

One of the most enigmatic aspects is the possibility that the Antarctic pyramids are older than the known ones, and that later civilizations imitated a preexisting pattern, passed down through time as a legacy of lost knowledge. If so, the pyramids of Giza, Teotihuacan, and Xi'an may not be the first of their kind, but only the last survivors of an ancient construction pattern spread globally.

Theories of ancient polar civilizations advanced

The idea that an advanced civilization existed at the poles in the distant past is based on various indirect evidence, including ancient maps, geological anomalies, and mythological accounts from different cultures that speak of a time when the world was very different from today.

Some researchers suggest that Antarctica, now covered by miles of ice, was once habitable, and that an ancient civilization thrived there before a global cataclysm changed Earth's geography. One of the most fascinating theories is that of crustal displacement, proposed by Charles Hapgood, that Antarctica had not always been at the poles, but due to a rapid movement of the Earth's crust, shifted to its present location, freezing all traces of civilization beneath the ice cap.

This theory ties in with tales about Atlantis and Mu, two legendary continents described in ancient texts as the abodes of extraordinarily advanced civilizations capable of navigating the oceans and building monumental structures. According to some scholars, if Atlantis existed, it could have been in Antarctica before the continent was covered by ice, and the Antarctic pyramids may be the last remnants of this lost civilization.

The connection between the poles and ancient civilizations is also present in the myths of indigenous peoples. Some Inuit legends speak of "lost lands under the ice", where powerful beings with superior knowledge lived. Tibetan lore also speaks of Shambhala, a legendary city hidden under the ice and mountains, which would hold secret knowledge. If these stories had a kernel of truth, it could be that the ancient myths do not speak of imaginary places, but of civilizations that really existed and then disappeared.

Magnetic anomalies detected under Antarctica, particularly in the Wilkes Land region, have led some researchers to speculate that there may be man-made structures under the ice that are still intact, perhaps sealed for thousands of years. Modern sensing technologies have revealed immense cavities under the ice, which could house buried cities, tunnels or as-yet unexplored structures.

Some theorists argue that if an advanced civilization had inhabited the poles, it may have developed technologies to adapt to extreme conditions, perhaps using forms of energy unknown to modern science. If the world's pyramids were designed to collect or distribute energy, it is possible that the polar pyramids played a special role in this ancient system, exploiting the geomagnetic uniqueness of the poles for unknown purposes.

If this theory were true, it would mean that human history is much older and more complex than we think today, and that our planet may have been home to extraordinary civilizations capable of building monuments that still defy modern understanding. The presence of pyramids at the poles could be proof that there was a time when Antarctica was not a wasteland, but a center of knowledge and advanced technology, the memory of which has been erased by a global cataclysm.

If one day these structures are explored and analyzed in depth, we may be faced with a discovery that will rewrite our understanding of the past, proving that polar civilizations were not just a myth, but a forgotten reality in the millennia-old ice.

The role of science missions and restrictions on research

Despite Antarctica being considered a continent dedicated to science and international cooperation, many areas remain inexplicably inaccessible to independent scientists. Officially, the restrictions are justified on grounds of safety and environmental protection, but several researchers suspect that behind these restrictions are secrets that governments and large institutions want to keep confidential.

A key element is the Antarctic Treaty, signed in 1959, which expressly prohibits all military, mining and commercial activity on the continent, allowing only regulated scientific missions. However, this treaty has often been interpreted as a means of maintaining control over what is discovered at the poles. Some private expeditions that have attempted to explore poorly documented regions of Antarctica have been denied permission to land or have been turned away by authorities, with vague and unconvincing justifications.

The most interesting areas from the point of view of geological anomalies and alleged pyramid structures, such as Queen Maud Land and the Wilkes Land region, are among the most heavily guarded and difficult to explore. Some reports indicate that government expeditions are equipped with highly advanced instrumentation for remote sensing and monitoring of forbidden areas, suggesting that there is a strong interest in controlling who can access certain information.

A particularly controversial case is that of Vostok Base, a Russian research station located above the mysterious Lake Vostok, a huge subglacial basin that has remained sealed under more than 4 km of ice for millions of years. When Russian scientists drilled through the ice to reach the lake, they detected unexplained thermal anomalies and unknown microorganisms. However, details of the research have been kept secret, and much information has never been publicly disclosed. Some speculate that at the bottom of Lake Vostok may lie submerged man-made structures, or even a unique ecosystem that could reveal ancient and possibly non-terrestrial life forms.

Another incident that has fueled suspicions concerns the NASA and National Science Foundation (NSF) mission to Antarctica in 2016, during which a team of scientists visited a remote area of East Antarctica to conduct atmospheric surveys. Officially, the mission was intended to study cosmic ray emissions, but the choice of site and absolute secrecy about the findings led to speculation about a possible cover-up of geological or archaeological anomalies.

Many independent researchers ask: If the pyramids in the poles were really just mountains eroded by time, why would governments and scientific institutions prevent access to these areas? Some argue that authorities may have found evidence of an ancient civilization, and that their goal is to prevent this information from becoming public knowledge, upsetting our understanding of history.

If man-made structures under the ice were confirmed, this would imply that an advanced civilization inhabited the poles long before the beginning of official human history. This would challenge not only academic theories of prehistory, but also the way we view our planet's past.

What might melting ice reveal?

Climate change is accelerating the retreat of the ice sheet at the poles, exposing territories that have remained sealed for tens of thousands of years. This transformation could reveal hidden structures and artifacts, finally providing tangible evidence of a lost Antarctic civilization.

In recent years, satellite images have already shown geological anomalies in regions where the ice has thinned. In some areas of Queen Maud Land, rock formations have been detected that appear to be geometrically arranged, which has led some researchers to speculate that they may be ancient buried structures that have remained hidden under the ice for millennia.

If global warming continues, new archaeological evidence may emerge in the coming decades, including remains of buildings, inscriptions, tools or even bodies preserved in permafrost, similar to discoveries made in Siberia, where mammoths and other animals have been found perfectly preserved in the ice.

One of the most intriguing aspects is that the Antarctic pyramids may be only the upper part of much larger structures buried under layers of ice. As the ice melts, we may discover entire architectural complexes, connected by tunnels or inner rooms, similar to the secret chambers found in the pyramids of Giza.

Some scientists suggest that climate change may also unearth unknown artifacts or technologies belonging to an advanced civilization that inhabited the poles in ancient times. If this happens, the scientific community and governments may be forced to reconsider entirely the history of human civilization and the role of Antarctica in our past.

Another interesting possibility involves energy buried beneath the ice. If an ancient civilization inhabited the poles, it may have harnessed forms of energy unknown today, and the remains of their technologies could provide clues to new renewable energy sources or even advanced propulsion systems.

However, there is also the possibility that if concrete evidence of an ancient polar civilization is discovered, governments and scientific institutions will try to hide this information, as seems to have happened with other controversial archaeological discoveries in different parts of the world. If the Antarctic pyramids are indeed artificial, their existence could disrupt the current historical paradigm, leading to questions about who built them, when, and for what purpose.

The melting of the ice could thus represent a turning point for archaeological research at the poles. If concrete evidence of man-made structures emerges, we could be facing the greatest discovery in modern history: the existence of an ancient, technologically advanced civilization that inhabited the poles long before known humanity. The question is not whether we will discover anything, but when and especially whether the information will ever be released to the public or will remain a secret guarded by a select few.

ANOMALOUS GENETICS

TRACES OF AN UNKNOWN SPECIES IN ICE SAMPLES

Findings of unknown DNA in polar ice

In recent years, analyses of ice samples taken from the polar regions have uncovered mysterious genetic sequences that do not correspond to any known species on Earth. These discoveries have raised crucial questions about the possibility that unknown, or even non-terrestrial, life forms may exist under the ice, or that they may be the remains of a lost civilization whose DNA has been preserved for thousands or millions of years.

One of the best-known studies was conducted at Lake Vostok in Antarctica, a huge subglacial lake sealed under more than 4 kilometers of ice for millions of years. When Russian scientists drilled into the ice to take water samples, they found genetic sequences that did not match any current life forms, suggesting the existence of unknown microorganisms. Some bacteria isolated in the samples had completely new characteristics, with mutations that could not be explained by known evolution.

Another interesting finding was made in 2017, when a team of researchers took samples from underwater ice caves in Antarctica and discovered DNA that was not related to any of the species catalogued so far. Some scientists suggest that these could be ancient bacterial strains that have remained isolated for millions of years and survived in extreme conditions. However, an even more intriguing aspect is that some of the genetic sequences seem more complex than would be expected from microbial organisms, leading some to speculate that they may belong to more evolved life forms, perhaps unknown to official science.

Some researchers have begun to wonder whether the unknown DNA found in the ice could be the trace of a vanished advanced civilization whose biological remains were preserved in the permafrost. If so, these sequences could belong to an ancient humanoid species or a group of beings that evolved separately from humanity at a time when the poles were still habitable.

The implications of these findings are extraordinary: if traces of DNA are found in polar ice that do not belong to any known species, it means that the history of life on Earth may be much more complex than we think. Some scientists have also speculated that these sequences could be of extraterrestrial origin, arriving on Earth via meteorites or comets that impacted the poles in ancient times. This theory ties in with the panspermia hypothesis, according to which life on Earth might have been seeded by organisms from space.

If the unknown DNA found in the ice was confirmed as belonging to an evolved species and not to mere bacteria, then we would be faced with a discovery that would completely change our understanding of evolution and human history. If, on the other hand, these were the remains of an advanced civilization, then the more disturbing question would be: what happened to these beings and why did they disappear?

Unknown DNA in polar ice: a genetic secret to be deciphered

The fact that unexplained genetic sequences have been found in polar ice has prompted scientists to question the nature of these anomalies. Why was the unknown DNA sealed for millennia in the poles? And if it belonged to more complex creatures, what were their characteristics?

One of the most controversial cases involves genetic mutations found in some biological samples taken from Arctic permafrost. A team of researchers found DNA fragments that appeared to be hybrids between different species, as if they were the result of nonlinear evolution or ancient genetic manipulations. Some of these samples had DNA coding sequences that had never been seen before, leading some to speculate that they might be traces of an intelligent species other than Homo sapiens, perhaps a humanoid population that lived at the poles in ancient times.

One of the most fascinating possibilities is that the unknown DNA could belong to a species completely distinct from humans, developed under extreme conditions and perhaps endowed with superior genetic characteristics, such as greater resistance to cold or an ability to survive in environments with little oxygen. If so, we may be looking at evidence of a vanished race that once inhabited the poles before being wiped out by a catastrophic event.

Another, even bolder theory suggests that some of the mutations observed in polar DNA could be the result of ancient genetic manipulations, perhaps carried out by an advanced civilization. If these hypotheses were confirmed, it would mean that advanced genetics may have existed long before our modern era, and that some humans or humanoids may have been genetically modified to adapt to polar conditions.

The implications of such a discovery would be enormous. If it were proven that there was another intelligent species on Earth, our entire understanding of human evolution would change dramatically. Some scientists have speculated that the genetic anomalies found in the ice could be linked to legends of mysterious beings who inhabited the poles, such as the "Snow Men" of Inuit lore or the Tornit, legendary creatures described as humanoid but different from humans.

If the unknown DNA found in the polar ice was connected to these tales, it could mean that the ancient myths were not just fantasies, but memories of encounters with a different race, which may have been forced to take refuge in the depths of the Earth or went extinct due to as yet unknown causes.

As ice continues to melt due to climate change, new genetic evidence may emerge, revealing even more extraordinary details about the nature of species that once inhabited the poles. If these findings are analyzed without bias, they could provide answers to fundamental questions about evolution and the possibility that humanity was not the first intelligent species on Earth.

One question still open concerns the fate of these studies. Why are some DNA samples taken from the poles never fully disclosed? Are there government restrictions on genetic research in Antarctica? And if so, why? Some independent researchers suspect that information about these findings is being kept secret, perhaps because it could rewrite the history of human evolution and reveal inconvenient truths about the origins of life on our planet.

If the unknown DNA found in the ice was really a trace of an ancient civilization or a species other than humans, it could be the greatest scientific discovery in history, capable of changing the way we view the past and our place in the universe. But the real question is: Is the world ready for such a revelation? Or will this information remain buried in ice, just like the secrets they have been guarding for millennia?

Unknown creatures in the ice: accounts of mysterious beings

For centuries, explorers, scientists and indigenous peoples have reported accounts of unknown beings allegedly living among the polar ice. These tales, initially considered legends or the result of suggestion, are receiving new attention due to recent advances in biology and the discovery of unknown life forms in ice samples taken in the polar regions.

Inuit peoples speak of mysterious creatures emerging from icy waters or hiding in the depths of the ice. According to some tales passed down orally, there are beings that look half human and half animal, endowed with superhuman cold resistance and abilities that defy scientific understanding. Some tales speak of humanoid figures observed in snowstorms, moving with unnatural speed and leaving no visible traces, suggesting that they may have a connection to the ice itself or unknown technology.

But it is not only the Inuit who have reported disturbing accounts. During the polar expeditions of the 19th and 20th centuries, some European and American explorers wrote in their diaries of sightings of creatures not catalogued by science. For example, members of British missions to the Arctic reported seeing large dark figures moving silently across the ice, disappearing as soon as they were followed. Some reports speak of seal-like beings, but with vaguely humanoid features, sighted near crevices in glaciers.

One of the most mysterious episodes occurred in the 1950s, when a Soviet expedition to Antarctica reported strange bluish lights emerging from under the ice, accompanied by deep sounds and unexplained vibrations. Some crew members spoke of moving shapes beneath the ice surface, as if something was observing their movements. This event was quickly classified, and much information was kept secret by the Soviet government.

Another interesting account concerns Operation Highjump, a 1946-47 U.S. military expedition led by Admiral Richard E. Byrd. According to some unofficial reports, unexplained phenomena were observed in the polar skies during this mission and even strange objects emerged from frozen water, moving at speeds impossible for any known technology at the time. Although these accounts have often been considered speculation, the continued secrecy around certain mission data suggests that there may be more to it than just random sightings.

Another fascinating aspect is the possibility that as yet unknown life forms, surviving in extreme environments and completely isolated from the rest of the planet, may be found in polar ice. In recent years, scientists have discovered ancient microorganisms and bacteria in the subglacial lakes of Antarctica that seem capable of surviving without oxygen or sunlight, challenging current theories of terrestrial biology. If there are organisms capable of surviving in such extreme conditions, there may be a possibility that larger, more complex creatures have remained hidden in the poles for millennia.

If these stories and discoveries are confirmed, it would mean that the Earth is not yet fully explored and that there are life forms that escape current scientific classification. These could be species unknown to conventional biology, ancient life forms that have survived global climate change, or even beings that are not terrestrial in origin but may be biological relics from a time when Earth was very different from today.

Analysis of old polar biological specimens and the surprises of modern sequencing

Using modern genetic sequencing technologies, researchers are reanalyzing biological samples that have been frozen for decades, and the results are revealing anomalies that had not previously been identified. These studies are showing that some life forms discovered at the poles may belong to entirely new biological categories, or even suggest the existence of ancient and unknown biodiversity.

One of the most interesting examples involves the re-examination of ice samples taken from Lake Vostok, a subglacial basin sealed for millions of years. Scientists, using advanced genetic analysis techniques, have found microorganisms with DNA sequences never seen before, suggesting that the lake may harbor an entire ecosystem unknown to modern science. Some of the genetic sequences found appear to belong to multicellular organisms, implying that there may be more complex life forms hidden beneath the ice.

Another study re-examined biological samples taken in 1959 by a Soviet expedition to the Arctic. When DNA from these samples was sequenced using the latest technology, researchers found unusual mutations and genetic sequences that did not match any known organisms. Some scientists speculate that these anomalies could be the result of evolution that occurred in isolation over thousands or millions of years, while others suggest the possibility of unknown hybridizations between different species.

Another field of research that is providing surprising results is the study of frozen tissues found at the poles, including remains of prehistoric mammals and fragments of marine organisms trapped in ice. Some of these samples have revealed unusual biological structures, such as tissues with properties that appear to resist decomposition for long periods or cells capable of regenerating under extreme conditions.

Scientists are also studying Siberian permafrost, which has preserved animal remains and, in some cases, tissues of unknown origin for thousands of years. In 2018, research uncovered DNA fragments that appeared to belong to an uncatalogued mammalian species, suggesting the existence of an unknown evolutionary branch. Some researchers speculate that it could be an archaic humanoid species or an ancient life form adapted to extreme polar temperatures.

Sequencing technologies are revealing that our planet may have harbored far more diverse life forms than previously believed, and that some of them may have gone extinct or survived in isolated ecosystems at the poles. If this is true, it would mean that DNA preserved in ice could hold the key to solving some of the greatest mysteries of evolution and even suggest that unknown life forms may still exist today in the depths of the ice.

If this research continues and is conducted with the utmost transparency, it could lead to a revolutionary discovery: proof that life forms exist, or have existed, that challenge our understanding of Earth's biology and natural history. The question that remains open is: what are the depths of the ice hiding from us? And most importantly, are we ready to discover the truth?

Scientific censure on some genetic discoveries

Over the years, numerous studies on biological findings in the poles have revealed genetic anomalies and unknown organisms, but many of these findings have been hidden, downplayed or even secreted. Why? If science has a duty to explore and disclose new discoveries, how come some research is inexplicably ignored or restricted in its dissemination?

One of the first indications of this scientific censorship concerns Lake Vostok, a subglacial basin that had been sealed for millions of years under more than 4 kilometers of ice. When Russian researchers finally succeeded in drilling through the ice and taking samples in 2012, it was discovered that the water contained traces of unknown DNA. However, after an initial official announcement, details about the genetic sequences were withdrawn or not published in full, fueling suspicions that there might be something too relevant to be made public. Some independent sources say that life forms were found that did not correspond to any of the known biological categories, and that part of the research was classified for national security reasons.

Another disturbing example involves research on Siberian permafrost, where DNA fragments belonging to unknown organisms have been found, some of which exhibit characteristics that are extremely resistant to extreme environmental conditions. Again, initial studies were published with great enthusiasm, but later many data were withdrawn, and some of the teams involved found themselves unable to continue their research due to lack of funding or unspecified pressures. Some scientists stated anonymously that certain findings might have implications too great to be made public without political or social consequences.

Restrictions on biological research in the poles seem to follow a definite pattern: whenever anomalous organisms or genetic sequences are found, the official narrative tends to downplay the discoveries or shift attention to conventional explanations. Some independent scientists suspect that governments and influential scientific institutions may be aware of the existence of uncatalogued life forms and are trying to manage the release of this information carefully.

Another possibility is that some of these discoveries have implications beyond the simple realm of biology. If traces of nonterrestrial DNA, or of an extinct civilization with advanced genetic characteristics, were found in the polar ice, the impact on our understanding of history and science would be devastating. This may explain why some findings are covered up, to prevent difficult questions about the origins of life on Earth and possible connections with extraterrestrial life forms from emerging.

Scientific censorship could also be related to biosafety issues. If some of the organisms discovered in the poles were highly resistant to extreme conditions or possessed unique properties, they might be considered risky to the environment or to humanity itself. There could be ancient viruses hibernating in ice, capable of awakening under global warming, or microorganisms with extraordinary genetic and biochemical capabilities that could potentially be used in biotechnology or the military.

If indeed some of these discoveries have been deliberately hidden, this means that there is secret knowledge about the biology of the poles, guarded by a select few groups. And if this information were accessible to the public, it could revolutionize not only science, but also our concept of life and evolution.

What are the implications for the future of humanity?

Genetic discoveries in the poles are not just an academic matter, but could fundamentally change our future. If unknown life forms were found, the impact on biology, medicine, technology and even geopolitics would be enormous.

One of the most immediate implications concerns biotechnology. If organisms found in the poles possess abilities to withstand extreme cold, low pressure or oxygen deprivation, we could study their biological mechanisms to create new medical treatments, genetic therapies and technologies for adaptation to extreme conditions. For example, some microorganisms discovered in ice possess enzymes that can function at extremely low temperatures, which could be used for new applications in cryogenic medicine or human tissue preservation.

Another fascinating possibility involves space exploration. If life forms exist at the poles that can survive without sunlight and under extreme conditions, this could provide vital clues about how to search for life on other planets, such as Mars or the icy moons of Jupiter and Saturn. Studies of bacteria and organisms found in the subglacial lakes of Antarctica could help us understand how life might exist in extraterrestrial environments, and may even suggest that some of the life forms at the poles have a nonterrestrial origin.

However, there are also serious biosafety concerns. If some of the organisms found in the ice are ancient viruses or bacteria with unknown properties, their accidental release into the environment could pose a global health risk. With global warming and melting ice, we are already seeing the reappearance of viruses and bacteria that had been hibernating for thousands of years. Some scientists fear that we may be facing pathogens for which humanity has no defense.

Moreover, the ethical and geopolitical implications of genetic discoveries in the poles cannot be ignored. If some nations had access to life forms with unique properties, they might seek to exploit them for military or economic purposes, keeping this knowledge secret for strategic advantage. Antarctica is already an area under strong international control, and if evidence of genetically advanced organisms or a lost civilization emerged, it is likely that the management of such discoveries would be centralized and not disclosed to the public.

The most fascinating aspect concerns the philosophical and historical implications. If DNA traces belonging to an unknown civilization were found in the ice, we would have to rewrite the history of humanity and our origins. It could mean that we were not the only intelligent species to develop on Earth, or that our evolution was influenced by yet unknown external factors.

If this information were to be openly disclosed, it could change the way we view humanity's past, present and future. But the risk is that, for reasons of power and control, these discoveries will be kept hidden, leaving the world in the dark about one of the greatest revelations in history.

The final question is: What secrets still lurk in the ice? And who will decide when and how they are revealed?

UFO SIGHTINGS IN THE ARCTIC AND ANTARCTIC

Official reports on UFO sightings in the poles

Sightings of Unidentified Aerial Phenomena (UFOs or UAPs) in the poles have been reported for decades by pilots, scientists, military personnel and explorers. Despite the extreme climate and limited access to these areas, numerous reports indicate that unexplained phenomena occur in the polar skies, often accompanied by electromagnetic interference, radar anomalies, and flight behavior inconsistent with known technologies.

One of the best known cases dates back to the 1940s, when the famous Admiral Richard E. Byrd, during Operation Highjump (1946-47), claimed to have observed flying objects at incredible speeds in the skies over Antarctica. According to some unofficial reports, Byrd reported that the objects could perform maneuvers impossible for land-based aircraft, and that they appeared to emerge from openings in the ice. Some declassified U.S. Navy documents confirm that polar expedition crews recorded anomalous phenomena, although details have been largely omitted from official reports.

In the 1960s and 1970s, the phenomenon continued to be reported by military pilots and scientists on missions to the poles. Several reports from the former Soviet Union describe spherical or discoidal objects flying at extremely high speeds over Antarctic bases. Some Russian documents speak of "spheres of light" that moved intelligently, changing course suddenly and exhibiting instantaneous acceleration and deceleration capabilities, phenomena that still defy the laws of known physics.

In 1985, a team of researchers at the Soviet Mirny base in Antarctica reported seeing a huge glowing structure emerge from icy water and then quickly disappear into the sky. This incident, known as the Mirny Case, was dismissed by Soviet authorities without further public investigation. However, in later years, declassified documents suggested that the Soviet military had an active interest in UFO sightings at the poles, and that there were entire classified files on the subject.

More recently, in 2018, a National Science Foundation (NSF) scientific expedition engaged in studying the polar atmosphere reported unexplained radar anomalies in the Queen Maud Land region. According to the expedition's report, several atmospheric detection instruments recorded unidentified objects moving at speeds exceeding Mach 10 (more than 12,000 km/h), performing sudden turns that would have destroyed any conventional aircraft. Although the report was initially made public, it was quickly withdrawn without explanation, fueling theories that some findings about UFO phenomena at the poles are covered by government secrets.

A common feature of many of these sightings is the complete absence of sound emissions and propulsion trails, features typical of modern UAPs recorded elsewhere in the world. If these objects do not use conventional propulsion methods, it could mean that they are employing anti-gravitational technologies or other systems as yet unknown to human science.

Many UFO researchers and analysts ask: Why do the poles seem to be a focal point for UAP activity? Is it possible that these objects have bases hidden beneath the ice? Or do the poles hide portals or space-time anomalies that attract such phenomena?

UAP submarine bases in the poles: myth or reality?

One of the most fascinating hypotheses about UFOs at the poles is that there are secret undersea bases used by both terrestrial forces and nonhuman entities. These bases could be hidden in the ocean floor or under the ice caps, and could serve as starting points for flying objects observed in the polar regions.

The idea that UAPs can emerge from underwater bases is not new. For decades, reports of UFO sightings in oceanic areas have suggested that these objects can travel through water as easily as they move through the air. According to some theories, the oceanic depths of the poles may offer ideal conditions for hiding bases of unknown origin that are inaccessible to most human technologies.

One of the most emblematic cases involves the Mystery of Lake Vostok, a subglacial lake located under 4 km of ice in Antarctica. In 2001, when a Russian expedition began drilling through the ice to reach the lake, anomalous signals and unexplained electromagnetic variations were recorded. Some independent researchers have speculated that Lake Vostok may harbor an artificial submerged structure, perhaps an underground base capable of operating under both ice and water.

In 2012, a mysterious break in contact with the Russian drilling team in Lake Vostok further fueled theories about possible undisclosed discoveries. When the mission resumed, it was announced that the lake contained unknown microorganisms, but many scientific details remained classified, suggesting that undisclosed elements may have been found.

Some alternative sources speculate that Antarctica might host underground UAP bases, used by nonhuman entities or terrestrial governments that have discovered advanced technologies in recent times. According to some theories, these bases could exploit the geomagnetic properties and gravitational anomalies of the poles, which would explain why UFO sightings are so frequent in these areas.

The Arctic is also the focus of speculation about UAP submarine bases. In recent decades, numerous military ships and submarines have reported unidentified objects moving at impressive speeds under water, much faster than any known submarine. These objects, often called USOs (Unidentified Submersible Objects), appear to dive and re-emerge rapidly, as if using passages or structures hidden in the polar seabed.

If UAP bases exist in the poles, crucial questions arise: who built them? How long have they existed? Are they terrestrial or extraterrestrial in origin? Some researchers suggest that they may be installations dating back to ancient times, perhaps related to lost civilizations such as Atlantis or other unknown cultures that may have inhabited Earth before our recorded history.

If the existence of UAP bases in the poles were confirmed, it would be one of the greatest revelations in modern history. However, the possibility that governments and institutions know about these facilities but have chosen to keep them secret remains a real possibility. The question that remains is when will the truth about UAPs in the poles finally be revealed? More importantly, what lies beneath the ice?

Sightings during military missions

In the course of the many military operations conducted in the poles, sightings of unexplained phenomena have been recorded that, despite strict secrecy policies, have emerged through the testimony of members of the armed forces. These accounts, ranging from flying objects that defy the laws of physics to unexplained electromagnetic interference, paint a disturbing picture of UFO activity in the polar regions.

One of the best known episodes dates back to Operation Highjump (1946-47), one of the largest U.S. military expeditions to Antarctica, led by Admiral Richard E. Byrd. Officially, the mission was intended to test the capabilities of the armed forces under extreme conditions, but according to alternative sources, unknown aircraft were sighted during operations moving at incredible speeds, performing maneuvers impossible for the technologies of the time. According to some unofficial accounts, Byrd reported seeing flying saucers emerge from the ice sheets and attack U.S. forces, forcing the expedition to be halted prematurely.

In later years, numerous military pilots reported close encounters with unidentified flying objects in the polar skies. During the Cold War, when the United States and Soviet Union constantly monitored the poles for possible missile launches, several reports described spherical objects flying at very high speeds, far exceeding any known aircraft. Some pilots claimed to have tracked these objects with radar, only to see them suddenly accelerate and disappear from the monitors without a trace.

One of the most controversial cases involves a secret mission of the British Royal Air Force in the 1960s, during which a group of airmen on a reconnaissance mission over the Arctic reported that they were followed for several minutes by a bright light that zigzagged above the clouds, avoiding all attempts at interception. When the crew tried to approach, the object instantly disappeared, as if it had vanished into another dimension. The official incident report was classified and never made public in its entirety.

In the 1980s, the Soviet Union conducted a series of military tests in the Arctic to study the effect of polar conditions on new radar technologies. During these operations, more than once monitoring systems detected unidentified objects moving at speeds above Mach 10, with instantaneous accelerations and no signs of propulsion. Records of these events remained secret until the collapse of the USSR, when some former Russian officers revealed that the Red Army was aware of the presence of unknown objects at the poles and had devoted entire intelligence units to their study.

One of the most recent cases occurred in 2018, when a U.S. Navy research vessel off Antarctica reported the appearance of a metallic object emerging from icy waters and hovering above the ocean before disappearing at extreme speed. The crew report mentioned clearly non-terrestrial technology, but the incident was quickly dismissed without further public investigation.

The military's interest in UFO phenomena in the poles suggests that there is a broader awareness of the phenomenon than officially admitted. If these objects do exist and are able to operate undisturbed in the most remote regions of the planet, the question becomes inevitable: what are they looking for in the poles? Is it possible that UFOs are monitoring particular human activities, or has the poles always been a prime access point for their presence on Earth?

The connection between UFOs and polar magnetic anomalies

One of the most intriguing aspects of UFO sightings at the poles is their connection to the strange magnetic anomalies that characterize these regions. Scientists have long known that Earth's poles are subject to intense magnetic field fluctuations, phenomena that could influence the behavior of unidentified flying objects or even be the key to understanding their origin and technological capabilities.

East Antarctica, in particular, is home to an electromagnetic anomaly of great interest: the so-called Wilkes Land anomaly, a huge region where the Earth's magnetic field exhibits an anomalous and unexplained intensity. Some scientists have speculated that it may be a structure buried under the ice, perhaps an ancient meteoritic impact, but some alternative theories suggest that it may be a hidden base or energy portal used by UFOs to enter and exit Earth's atmosphere.

Another point of interest is the magnetic anomaly of the Arctic, a region over Siberia and the North Pole where navigation instruments and tracking systems often experience unexplained interference. During the Cold War, several Soviet and American nuclear submarines reported guidance system malfunctions in these very areas, as well as sightings of submarine objects moving at incredible speeds in polar waters.

Many UFO researchers speculate that these anomalies may represent access points to parallel dimensions or advanced underground facilities, explaining why so many sightings are concentrated in precisely these regions. The idea that UFOs may exploit the Earth's magnetic field for their movements is not new and is reflected in the many cases where UAPs seem to disrupt radar and electronic instruments whenever they appear.

Another interesting element is the correlation between intense solar activity and increased UFO sightings at the poles. During periods of strong geomagnetic activity, such as solar storms and solar wind variations, several scientific observers have recorded a spike in light phenomena and unidentified objects in the Arctic and Antarctic skies. This suggests that UFOs may be attracted to or influenced by these magnetic fluctuations, or even using these energies to power their technology.

A further connection between UFOs and magnetic anomalies at the poles involves the concept of electromagnetic portals, or points where the Earth's magnetic field could create natural gaps in space-time. Some scientists have speculated that invisible magnetic tunnels exist that could act as travel corridors for advanced vehicles, allowing them to move instantaneously from one point to another on the planet. If this theory were true, it could explain why UFOs are often observed to suddenly disappear without a trace, as if they were passing through some kind of "dimensional window".

If UAPs are indeed using the polar magnetic field to move or communicate, then the poles would not simply be remote areas of the planet, but could be strategically crucial areas for their activity on Earth. This might explain why governments around the world have always taken a strong interest in polar anomalies, keeping much data about UFO sightings in these regions secret.

The real question is: Are we observing an unknown natural phenomenon or a higher intelligence operating through mechanisms we do not yet understand? If UFOs and polar magnetic anomalies are connected, then we may be facing a phenomenon that goes beyond simple extraterrestrial technology, but concerns the very nature of the reality we know.

The hypotheses on the presence of dimensional portals in the poles

One of the most fascinating and controversial concepts related to UFO sightings at the poles is the possibility that these objects do not come from space, but from other dimensions, exploiting gaps located in the polar ice caps to enter and exit our world. This theory, known as the interdimensional hypothesis, suggests that energy portals or space-time anomalies may exist in the poles, which would allow advanced entities to traverse our plane of existence.

The idea that the poles may host dimensional gateways is not new and is rooted in ancient traditions and myths from different cultures. Many Inuit and Siberian legends speak of passages between worlds, located in the most remote and inaccessible regions of the Arctic and Antarctica. According to some tales, shamans of Arctic tribes believed that certain places in the ice were gateways to hidden realms inhabited by powerful and mysterious beings.

Modern science has also begun to explore the idea that the Earth's magnetic field may create "connecting corridors" between different realities, particularly in the polar regions, where the geomagnetic field is most intense and unstable. Some astrophysicists speculate that the anomalous magnetic distortions detected at the poles may be clues to the presence of quantum tunnels or natural wormholes, through which some life forms or advanced technologies might move between parallel dimensions.

A possible indirect confirmation of this hypothesis comes from unexplained events recorded during military and scientific missions to the poles. Numerous reports speak of objects suddenly disappearing without a trace, anomalies in navigation systems and interference in radar and satellites, as if something was altering the very structure of space-time.

One of the most discussed episodes concerns Operation Deep Freeze, a series of missions conducted by the United States to Antarctica in the 1950s and 1960s. According to some confidential sources, strange electromagnetic phenomena were detected during these missions, including unexplained radiation spikes and areas where compasses and electronic instruments stopped working properly. Some independent researchers suggest that the U.S. government may have discovered a zone of space-time anomaly in Antarctica, which may have been secretly monitored or even exploited in later years.

In recent decades, a number of satellites have detected strange energy emissions from Antarctica, particularly from the Queen Maud Land region and the mysterious Wilkes Land Anomaly, an area where the Earth's gravitational field has unexplained irregularities. Some physicists have speculated that these emissions could signal the presence of a point of contact between our world and another dimension.

If these theories were confirmed, it would mean that UFOs observed at the poles would not be extraterrestrial spacecraft in the classical sense, but manifestations of civilizations or entities operating on a different level of reality than ours. This would explain why many sightings describe objects that seem to defy the laws of physics, moving at impossible speeds, changing shape or even disappearing into thin air.

If the poles are indeed access points to parallel dimensions, a crucial question arises: who or what uses them? Is it possible that these portals were discovered by ancient Earth civilizations, and were exploited for interdimensional travel in ancient times? Or could they be natural, and thus used by entities outside our reality to observe or interact with us?

What are space agencies and governments hiding?

If UFO sightings in the poles represent a real and documented phenomenon, why do the scientific community and governments seem to avoid discussing them openly? There is evidence to suggest a cover-up of information, with classified documents and official reports being censored or downplayed.

One of the most obvious clues is the amount of declassified government documents revealing the interest of world powers in UFOs at the poles. Reports from the FBI, CIA and Pentagon show that, as early as the 1940s, the United States was carefully monitoring unidentified aerial phenomena in the polar regions, often associated with magnetic anomalies and electromagnetic interference. Some of these documents, such as those published in Project Blue Book, clearly indicate that the UFO phenomenon in the poles was considered a national security issue.

The Soviet Union had a similar interest. During the Cold War, numerous Russian intelligence reports mentioned unknown objects in the Arctic skies, often observed by submarine crews and military bases. Some declassified files after the fall of the USSR reveal that the Soviet government had collected data on more than 300 UFO sightings in the polar regions between the 1960s and 1980s, with instances in which objects appeared to submerge under the ice and re-emerge at enormous distances within seconds.

Space agencies, such as NASA and Roscosmos, also appear to have classified information about UFOs at the poles. Several former astronauts, including Edgar Mitchell and Gordon Cooper, have publicly stated that governments are aware of the presence of UFOs on Earth but are keeping many details secret to avoid global panic. Some conspiracy theorists claim that satellite images of Antarctica taken by space missions may have captured evidence of anomalous structures or dimensional portals, but that these data are edited or concealed before being released to the public.

A case in point concerns a series of images taken in 2012 by the Landsat-8 satellite, which showed strange light emissions in the Queen Maud region of Earth. These images were available for a short time before being removed from NASA's public databases, without any official explanation.

If governments and space agencies know more than they reveal, the key question is why hide the truth? Some researchers suggest that the discovery of advanced technologies at the poles could be a strategic and military asset, and that world powers are trying to study and replicate these phenomena before disclosing them to the world.

Another possibility is that the UFO phenomenon in the poles is too complex and upsetting to be publicized without serious social consequences. If it turns out that intelligent entities are using dimensional portals in the poles to travel to Earth, this could upset our view of reality, challenging the foundations of science and human spirituality.

If one day the truth about UFOs in the poles is revealed, it is likely to radically change the way we understand the cosmos, the nature of space-time and our role in the universe. But until then, we will continue to ask: Who really controls what we know about UFO sightings in the poles? And what are they hiding from us?

MYSTERIOUS CRATERS IN THE POLES

Impacts or Man-Made Structures?

Craters discovered in Antarctica and the Arctic: unexplained features

The polar regions, with their vast expanses of ice and geographic isolation, harbor as yet little-explored geological secrets. Among the most fascinating anomalies are the circular craters discovered under the Antarctic and Arctic ice, structures whose origin is still debated among scientists. While some of them may be the result of ancient meteoritic impacts, other formations exhibit features that do not align with traditional models of impact craters, raising alternative hypotheses, including the possibility that some cavities may have artificial origins or even have been excavated by intelligent entities in ancient times.

One of the most well-known craters is the Wilkes Land anomaly, located under the ice of East Antarctica. This huge crater, stretching more than 300 km in diameter, was discovered through gravitational anomalies detected by satellites. According to some scientists, this formation could be the result of a catastrophic impact that occurred about 250 million years ago, which may have contributed to the largest mass extinction in Earth's history. However, despite this theory, no meteorite fragments have been found, and the structure of the crater has unexplained magnetic anomalies, suggesting that it may be hiding more than just an impact.

Another interesting case is that of the Hiawatha crater, discovered in 2018 under the Greenland ice. This crater, about 31 km in diameter, lies under nearly a kilometer of ice and shows signs of a relatively recent impact, which probably occurred less than 12,000 years ago. If this dating is confirmed, the event may have had direct implications for human history, perhaps linking to major climate change or global myths about an ancient catastrophe, such as the Great Flood.

In addition to these better-known craters, other circular structures have been detected in the polar regions in recent years, some of which exhibit features that distinguish them from classic impact craters. Some of them have strangely regular walls, resembling man-made geometric structures, while others appear to contain unexplained underground cavities detected by ground-penetrating radar.

Another curious element is the presence of strong electromagnetic anomalies recorded in some of these craters. In particular, in Antarctica, some scientific expeditions have reported interference in electronic devices and strange readings in magnetic sensing sensors, as if something under the ice was emanating an unknown energy field. These phenomena have fueled speculation that some of these cavities may be more than just natural formations.

If these structures were not traditional impact craters, what might be the alternatives? Some independent researchers speculate that they could be remnants of ancient underground installations, perhaps built by advanced civilizations that lived on Earth in ancient times, or even by non-terrestrial intelligences. If so, the ice would have acted as a natural cover, protecting these structures for millennia and preventing their discovery until the modern era.

Theories of meteoritic impacts hidden by ice

The most widely accepted hypothesis to explain the origin of most polar craters is that they are the result of meteoritic impacts that occurred in Earth's geological past, events that could have had dramatic effects on the history of the planet and even the evolution of life. However, the main problem is that many of these craters are buried under layers of ice miles thick, making it difficult to study them directly and verify their origin with certainty.

One of the most fascinating possibilities is that the poles hide craters from impacts that have never been documented in human history, perhaps dating back to times when the planet was inhabited by ancient civilizations, or even that some of these impacts occurred in more recent times, altering Earth's climate and contributing to catastrophic events described in the myths of many cultures.

If Hiawatha Crater was formed during the last ice age, it may have had a direct impact on human populations of the time, triggering drastic climatic cooling and forcing ancient civilizations to migrate or adapt to extreme conditions. Some researchers have suggested that this event could be related to the so-called Younger Dryas Hypothesis, a period of abrupt climatic cooling that occurred about 12,800 years ago, coinciding with the disappearance of many megafaunal species and a possible decline of prehistoric civilizations.

Another interesting hypothesis is that meteoritic impacts at the poles may have created underground caverns, isolated environments in which some life forms may have survived for millennia. If these craters were much deeper than we imagine, they could hide entire networks of tunnels or caverns that might contain biological remains, fossils or even traces of intelligent activity.

Another aspect to consider is the role these craters may have played in the evolution of life on Earth. Some scientists hypothesize that meteoritic impacts at the poles, combined with the unique conditions of these regions, may have favored the formation of new life forms or the preservation of ancient microorganisms, which could represent a missing link in the history of Earth's evolution.

Some theorists argue that some of these impacts may not have been entirely natural. If it turns out that some of the circular structures under the ice have a geometry that is too regular to be random, one might speculate that they are the traces of something man-made, perhaps related to advanced technologies of unknown epochs or cosmic events of non-terrestrial origin.

If subglacial exploration technologies someday allow us to analyze these craters more closely, we may get answers about what really lies beneath the polar ice. We might discover not only evidence of ancient catastrophic impacts, but perhaps also evidence of lost civilizations or phenomena that challenge our current understanding of Earth's history.

The question that remains open is why are these discoveries still not being fully disclosed? If remnants of unknown cosmic events or even clues to man-made structures lie beneath the ice, who might have an interest in keeping the secret? More importantly, what might the gradual melting of the ice reveal in the coming decades?

Artificial structures buried under craters?

The idea that some cavities in the poles may hide man-made structures is one of the most controversial, but also among the most intriguing hypotheses. Modern ground-penetrating radar and satellite imaging technologies have revealed the existence of immense cavities beneath the polar ice, many of which are located at craters or gravitational anomalies. This raises a fundamental question: are these cavities the result of natural geological processes, or could they be the remnants of ancient constructions or underground bases, made in past ages?

One of the most speculative but fascinating theories holds that some of these formations may be abandoned underground bases, perhaps built by an advanced civilization that existed in prehistoric times or by non-terrestrial entities that used the poles as an access point to Earth. This hypothesis is based on scientific data showing anomalies beneath some of the craters, such as the presence of materials with anomalous densities or the presence of regular geometric structures detected by some radar studies.

An interesting example is the cavities discovered under the East Antarctic Ice Sheet, where satellite images have shown strange symmetries, which some researchers believe are not compatible with simple natural formations. Some of these underground spaces appear to have smooth walls and sharp edges, features that suggest an artificial origin. If this is confirmed, it would mean that someone built structures under the ice before Antarctica became the frozen desert we know today.

The hypothesis of hidden bases in the poles is not new. During World War II, the Nazis showed extraordinary interest in Antarctica, with alleged secret missions to the Queen Maud Land region. According to some theories, the Germans allegedly searched for entrances to underground cavities, believing that ancient cities or advanced technologies were hidden beneath the ice. Some accounts even speak of expeditions searching for underground passages to an inner world, an idea linked to the controversial Hollow Earth theory.

Modern scientific expeditions have also detected similar anomalies in the Arctic, where some explorers and military scientists have reported the presence of strange formations under the ice, some of which look like tunnels or interconnected rooms. If these structures were man-made, we would be looking at one of the most extraordinary discoveries in history: proof that an advanced civilization inhabited the poles long before our time.

Another possibility is that some of these cavities have been reused in modern times by secret military programs, taking advantage of their strategic location and natural isolation for advanced research operations or to hide technologies not disclosed to the public. If so, it would explain why access to certain areas of the poles remains tightly controlled and why some geological anomalies are not openly studied.

If the gradual melting of the ice continues in the coming decades, it could reveal hitherto hidden structures, bringing to light tangible evidence of an intelligent presence at the poles at a much earlier time than official history acknowledges.

The mystery of Wilkes Land crater: an ancient global catastrophe?

Wilkes Land Crater, located beneath the East Antarctic Ice Sheet, is one of the most enigmatic geological anomalies ever discovered. This huge basin, about 500 km in diameter, was first detected by measurements of the Earth's gravitational field, which revealed a massive gravitational anomaly, as if something extremely dense was buried under kilometers of ice.

Scientists believe the crater may have been formed by an impact that occurred about 250 million years ago, a time coinciding with the Permian-Triassic mass extinction, the most catastrophic in Earth's history, during which more than 90 percent of marine species and 70 percent of terrestrial species disappeared. If this hypothesis is confirmed, it would mean that Antarctica may have been the epicenter of an event that changed the history of life on Earth, perhaps even setting the stage for the evolution of dinosaurs.

What makes the Wilkes Land crater even more mysterious is that it has never been possible to analyze it directly because it is buried under miles of ice. However, radar images have revealed that the area contains circular-shaped structures and other anomalies not commonly found in traditional impact craters. Some researchers speculate that it may hide remnants of extraterrestrial material, such as fragments of an asteroid or an object of unknown origin.

An even bolder hypothesis is that the crater is not only the result of a meteoritic impact, but may hide underground structures connected to ancient civilizations or even unknown technologies. Some theorists argue that the gravitational anomaly detected in Wilkes Land could be evidence of a large metallic mass buried under the ice, perhaps an artificial construction or the remains of an ancient technological structure.

In 2006, some scientists proposed that the Wilkes Land crater might hide a huge buried city, possibly belonging to a civilization that disappeared long before the arrival of modern humans. This theory was fueled by the discovery of curious geometric formations in the region, which appear to be arranged too regularly to be the simple result of random geological phenomena.

Another fascinating theory is that the Wilkes Land crater may have been the site of a non-natural impact, perhaps a collision between a spacecraft and Earth millions of years ago. Some independent researchers have suggested that the magnetic anomalies in the area could be the remnants of advanced technologies buried under the ice, perhaps belonging to an extraterrestrial civilization or a human society much older and more technologically advanced than we think.

If the Wilkes Land crater were fully explored, it could provide revolutionary answers about past catastrophic events, the possibility that lost civilizations inhabited Antarctica, and perhaps even larger mysteries concerning human history and its origins. However, technical difficulties and political restrictions prevent a true large-scale investigation, leaving the mystery still unsolved.

What is really lurking beneath the ice of Antarctica? Is the Wilkes Land crater just the result of a natural impact, or is it evidence of even more extraordinary events that could change our understanding of the past forever? Time and future exploration may reveal unexpected truths, if only humanity is ready to accept them.

The connections between polar craters and the Hollow Earth theory

One of the most fascinating and debated hypotheses about the craters found at the poles is that some of them might not be simple depressions caused by meteoritic impacts, but real openings to vast subterranean environments, related to the so-called Hollow Earth Theory. According to this controversial hypothesis, our planet may contain huge interior spaces, with entire underground regions still unexplored, perhaps even inhabited by unknown life forms or forgotten ancient civilizations.

The Hollow Earth theory has ancient roots. Many traditional cultures, from Norse legends to Inuit myths, speak of hidden worlds beneath the earth's surface, accessible through secret openings located at the poles. Some millennia-old Sanskrit texts mention a place called Agartha, an underground realm of advanced beings, while accounts of past explorers describe strange atmospheric and magnetic anomalies near the poles, which could indicate the presence of entrances to Earth's inner regions.

Some argue that the poles are the most plausible locations for the existence of such openings, as the Earth's magnetic field is significantly more unstable in these regions, creating interference in navigation systems and gravitational anomalies. Some craters discovered at the poles, particularly deeper craters with electromagnetic anomalies, could be natural or man-made passageways leading to vast unexplored underground systems.

One of the most debated elements concerns satellite images of the polar ice caps, which on several occasions have shown strange visual anomalies, such as dark openings that seem to suddenly appear and disappear in photographs taken from space. Some Hollow Earth theorists argue that these openings could be temporary entrances, hidden by atmospheric phenomena or advanced technologies. Some NASA and ESA satellite images have been controversial because, in some cases, they appeared to show unexplained circular openings in the poles, which were later removed or censored in public databases.

Wilkes Land crater is often cited as possible evidence for this theory. Located under the Antarctic ice sheet, this crater has a very intense gravitational anomaly, suggesting that it may be hiding a huge cavity or structure not yet identified. If it were indeed an entrance to an underground world, this would imply that our planet has a much more complex internal geography than previously believed.

Another possible connection between polar craters and the Hollow Earth theory involves light phenomena and magnetic interference reported near some of these structures. Explorers and military personnel have repeatedly reported unexplained lights emerging from icy regions or electronic instruments suddenly failing near some cavities. If these anomalies were related to unknown natural phenomena or unknown forms of energy, they could provide further evidence of access to undiscovered underground areas.

The question remains: are craters at the poles simply geological formations, or do they represent accesses to a hidden world beneath the ice? The answer may lie in data from modern subsurface survey technologies, which are gradually revealing details never seen before.

What do the most recent radar and geological studies reveal?

In recent decades, thanks to advances in ground-penetrating radar (GPR), georadar and geophysical satellite technologies, science has begun to unravel what lies beneath the polar ice. These instruments have made it possible to map vast areas of the Earth's crust hidden for millennia, leading to the discovery of enigmatic structures and unexplained anomalies.

One of the most surprising studies was conducted using gravitational satellites, which revealed unexplained variations in the gravitational field of Antarctica, especially in areas that host large craters and underground cavities. In particular, in the Wilkes Land region, the data showed a dense, compact mass located several kilometers beneath the ice, the origin of which remains unknown. It could be a remnant of an ancient meteoritic impact, or an artificial structure buried under the ice for millions of years.

Ground-penetrating radar (GPR) has revealed extraordinary details. In 2019, a NASA-led study used this technology to examine the depths of the Antarctic ice sheet, discovering huge hollow cavities in areas where, theoretically, such vast voids should not exist. Some of these cavities appear to have smooth, regular walls, suggesting that they may not be the simple result of natural geological processes.

One of the most groundbreaking studies was conducted in 2018 by an international team of scientists who explored Subglacial Lake Mercer, buried under more than a kilometer of Antarctic ice. When they took water and sediment samples, they discovered traces of biological organisms dating back more than 100,000 years, suggesting that Antarctica may have hosted complex life forms in the distant past.

Other studies have revealed the presence of huge tunnel systems and caves under the ice, some of which extend for hundreds of kilometers. Some researchers have speculated that these cavities may be remnants of ancient underground rivers, but their conformation also suggests that they may have been used by past civilizations or even modern secret programs to hide advanced structures and technologies.

The most recent satellite images also show unusual geometric formations, with straight lines and angles that are difficult to explain by natural phenomena. Some of these structures have been spotted in the Queen Maud Land region, an area that has always been considered strategically sensitive and accessible only to selected government missions.

If radar and geological studies continue to explore the mysteries beneath the ice, they could unearth discoveries that challenge our understanding of

Earth's history. It is possible that evidence of buried man-made structures, remains of ancient civilizations or even entrances to unknown subterranean worlds will emerge in the coming decades.

If these technologies finally reveal what lies beneath the poles, it could completely change our view of Earth's past and geology. The real question is, what will be the reaction of the scientific community and governments if concrete evidence of something extraordinary emerges? Most importantly, how long will it be before the public is informed of these discoveries?

THE IMPOSSIBLE TECHNOLOGY HIDDEN IN THE POLES

Unexplained devices found in ice

In recent decades, the gradual melting of polar ice and increasingly advanced scientific missions have unearthed anomalies and artifacts that challenge our understanding of history and science. On several occasions, fragments of unknown materials, objects with unexplained technological features, and structures that seem too advanced to belong to known past civilizations have been found under kilometer-thick layers of ice.

One of the most puzzling findings was reported in 2012 by a Russian expedition to Lake Vostok, a body of water located under about 4 km of ice in Antarctica. During drilling operations, researchers reported anomalies in the samples they took, including a metal object with unusual properties, initially described as a circular structure partially buried in the lake sediments. After the initial disclosure of the discovery, details of the find were classified, and some members of the expedition stated that their reports were modified before being made public.

Another enigmatic case concerns a U.S. Antarctic Program (USAP) mission in 2001, in which a team of scientists who were analyzing gravitational anomalies in Antarctica suddenly stopped their search without giving official explanations. According to some informants, the team reportedly found regular metal structures buried under the ice, similar to the remains of an ancient technological construction. Some undisclosed radar data suggested the presence of geometric underground chambers, but no further study was made public.

In 2018, an expedition to Greenland reported the discovery of metal fragments with anomalous composition near Hiawatha crater. The samples, analyzed in independent laboratories, showed traces of alloys unknown on Earth and magnetic properties that cannot be explained in conventional materials. The scientists involved talked about a possible meteoritic impact that could have brought exogenous material to the planet, but some researchers raised another hypothesis: what if these materials belonged to a lost technology buried by ice thousands of years ago?

Even more puzzling is the report of an alleged "machine buried in the ice", reported by anonymous sources linked to U.S. and Russian military missions. This device, if it really existed, would have features unrelated to known human technology, and some argue that it could be part of an ancient power source or an advanced navigation device. However, because of the secrecy imposed on many expeditions to the poles, there is no official confirmation of these findings.

If these devices were authentic, their existence would imply that advanced civilizations inhabited the poles long before modern humanity, leaving behind traces of their technological knowledge. This could explain why many governments restrict access to certain polar areas, preventing certain secrets from being discovered or disclosed.

Strange energy emissions and unexplained phenomena

In addition to physical findings, the poles appear to be the scene of anomalous energy and magnetic phenomena that elude conventional explanations. Several scientific missions have recorded unexplained energy emissions, sudden alterations in the Earth's magnetic field, and electromagnetic signals from the depths of the ice.

One of the most famous examples involves the electromagnetic anomaly of Wilkes Land, an area in Antarctica with an anomalous concentration of gravitational energy. This phenomenon was first detected by NASA's GRACE satellite, which showed a massive gravitational distortion under the ice, as if an object of exceptional density were buried in the region. Some scientists suggested that it might be the remains of an ancient meteoritic impact, but others speculated that it might be something artificial, perhaps an ancient technological installation that is still active.

Another case concerns a phenomenon recorded in 2004 in the Queen Maud Land region, where a Norwegian mission detected a sudden emission of high-frequency radio waves from a completely uninhabited area with no human installations. This signal, which seemed modulated and not random, was never officially explained. Some independent researchers speculated that it might be an artificial transmission, perhaps a remnant of a vanished civilization or a signal emitted by a technology still active under the ice.

Magnetic interferometers used to monitor the South Pole have often detected unexplained energy spikes, with fluctuations that appear to have no natural origin. Some of these signals have been compared to those produced by advanced propulsion devices, suggesting that something at the poles may be able to generate energy in ways we do not yet understand.

Experiments conducted by the High-Frequency Active Auroral Research Program (HAARP) in Alaska have also raised questions. Some researchers believe that the interference detected at the poles may be related to secret tests of manipulation of the Earth's electromagnetic field, while others speculate that the energetic emissions recorded at the poles may be of natural origin, but related to phenomena as yet unknown to science.

In 2016, a study conducted by NASA and the National Science Foundation (NSF) detected a strange source of energy from beneath the Antarctic ice sheet that seemed to rise and fall cyclically, almost as if it were an artificial signal regulated by some kind of intelligent system. Although no official explanation has been given, some scientists have suggested that these emissions could be clues to the presence of a still-active structure beneath the ice.

If these energy anomalies were linked to unknown technologies, they could represent a revolutionary discovery for humanity, paving the way for new sources of energy and even advanced theories about manipulating the Earth's electromagnetic field. However, most of these discoveries are quickly dismissed or downplayed, fueling suspicions about a possible desire to keep what really lies at the poles a secret.

If climate change continues to melt the polar ice caps in the coming years, we may see the revelation of artifacts and technologies that could rewrite human history. But the real question is: Will governments and scientific institutions allow these discoveries to be disclosed? Or will they try to cover them up to protect secrets that could shock the entire world?

The role of secret missions in the search for advanced technologies

In recent decades, numerous expeditions to the poles, both official and undeclared, have raised questions about the possibility that major world powers are searching for advanced technologies, perhaps of extraterrestrial origin or belonging to lost civilizations. Many declassified documents, whistleblower testimonies, and anomalies recorded in the polar regions indicate that the United States, Russia, and other nations have been conducting secret missions in the ice with goals beyond simple scientific research.

One of the best known examples is Operation Highjump, a military mission led by Admiral Richard E. Byrd in 1946-47. Although officially the expedition was intended to test military equipment under extreme conditions, many independent researchers believe the United States was looking for something far more significant. Some unofficial reports suggest that unknown flying objects were sighted during the mission, and that U.S. forces were forced to withdraw prematurely after encountering advanced non-terrestrial technology.

Another item of interest concerns the Soviet Antarctic Program, active during the Cold War. Declassified documents indicate that Soviet expeditions in the 1950s and 1960s were focused on searching for magnetic anomalies and underground structures, particularly in the Queen Maud Land region. Some secret reports, which emerged after the collapse of the USSR, suggest that the Soviets had discovered huge cavities under the ice, some of which contained traces of man-made structures. However, these discoveries were immediately classified and kept secret.

In the 1990s, after the end of the Cold War, the U.S. government intensified its presence in Antarctica, funding ostensibly scientific projects but with limited access only to selected personnel. One of the most mysterious episodes concerns a 2001 U.S. expedition that allegedly discovered a strange formation under the ice of East Antarctica. According to an anonymous source, the team allegedly found a metallic artifact with unconventional properties, but the discovery was quickly covered up, and the details of the mission remained secret.

NASA has also conducted several missions to the poles, officially to study polar climate and geology, but some researchers speculate that space scientists are interested in possible energy anomalies and buried structures. The fact that many of the remote sensing technologies used in Mars missions are being tested in Antarctica has fueled speculation that the space agency may be looking for more than just geological data.

Another element that raises suspicion is the sudden closure of some scientific research stations at the poles. In 2018, the National Science Foundation (NSF) ordered the sudden closure and evacuation of the Amundsen-Scott South Pole Station, without providing detailed explanations. Some researchers suggested that the closure might be related to an anomalous discovery made in the region, perhaps an ancient technology or device that is still active.

These events indicate that major powers may be competing for control of advanced technologies buried in the ice, which could have incalculable strategic value. If secret missions to the poles are indeed searching for lost devices or technology of unknown origin, the question becomes: how much of what has been found has been made public? And how much has been hidden for military or geopolitical purposes?

Links with ancient civilizations and assumptions about their advanced knowledge

Evidence from the poles suggests that ancient civilizations may have inhabited or exploited these regions in ancient times, leaving behind traces of advanced technology that we are only beginning to discover today. If Antarctica had been ice-free in the distant past, as some ancient maps suggest, it may have been home to a sophisticated culture with technological knowledge superior to that attributed to prehistoric civilizations.

One of the most enigmatic clues is the Map of Piri Reis, a document from 1513 that shows Antarctica without ice and with inexplicable geographic precision for the time. Some historians believe that this map is based on much older documents from civilizations that knew Antarctica when the continent was still habitable. If this is true, it would mean that an ancient advanced culture had mapped the entire world long before our documented history.

The legends of many ancient civilizations speak of lost lands at the edge of the world, places where superior beings would have lived or left behind secret tools and knowledge. According to some alternative scholars, these legends may refer to Antarctica, which may once have been the center of a technologically advanced civilization, later destroyed by a global cataclysm or covered by ice as a result of a shift in the Earth's crust.

Another interesting connection involves pyramids discovered at the poles. Some satellite images have shown pyramid structures in Antarctica, whose alignment seems to coincide with other great pyramids of the world, such as those at Giza in Egypt and Teotihuacan in Mexico. If these structures were indeed artificial, they could be remnants of a highly advanced global culture capable of building large-scale monuments with technologies unknown today.

Some of these theories are reflected in anomalous artifacts found in the ice, such as metal objects with unusual properties or mysterious energy emissions recorded in remote polar regions. If ancient inhabitants of the poles possessed advanced technologies, they may have left behind energy devices, navigational tools or even superior scientific knowledge, now buried under miles of ice.

Radar studies have revealed huge cavities under the ice, some of which appear to have smooth walls and geometries that suggest intentional construction. If these cavities were ancient underground bases or part of a forgotten technological infrastructure, their discovery could revolutionize our understanding of human history.

If ancient civilizations really did inhabit the poles and develop advanced technologies, the question becomes inevitable: what happened to them? Is it possible that they were destroyed by catastrophic events, or that they left Earth using knowledge that still eludes us? What if some governments were already aware of these discoveries and were trying to recover these technologies for secret purposes?

The implications of these theories are enormous. If definitive evidence of a technologically advanced civilization at the poles emerges in the next few years, it would be the greatest discovery in modern history. However, it remains to be seen whether the world will ever be ready to accept the truth about what lies beneath the ice.

Hypotheses on extraterrestrial origins of technology hidden in ice

The idea that technologies of extraterrestrial origin may be buried at the poles is one of the most controversial and fascinating theories in the field of Antarctic and Arctic mystery research. According to some researchers, energy anomalies, unexplained geometric structures, and metallic artifacts with unknown properties could be traces of ancient interaction between alien civilizations and our planet. If this hypothesis is correct, it would mean that Earth's history was influenced by external intelligences long before the advent of human civilization.

One of the most debated evidences supporting this theory is the presence of gravitational and magnetic anomalies at the poles, particularly in the Queen Maud Earth region and Wilkes Land crater. Some researchers argue that these phenomena could be the result of the presence of huge buried man-made structures, perhaps remnants of ancient crashed spaceships or alien bases built in the remote past. Anomalous energy emissions recorded in the depths of the ice sheet have led some to speculate that there may be devices still active, perhaps powered by an unknown energy source.

Some declassified documents suggest that the governments of the major powers have long been aware of these anomalies and conducted secret expeditions to investigate them. During the Cold War, both the United States and the Soviet Union sent missions to Antarctica and the Arctic, officially for scientific purposes, but according to some confidential sources, their real goals were to search for non-terrestrial technologies. Some reports mention fragments of unknown metal alloys found under the ice, similar to those studied in U.S. defense laboratories after the famous UFO sightings of the 20th century.

Extraterrestrial hypotheses also find support in the ancient legends of various cultures, which describe deities or higher beings descending from the sky to the remotest places on Earth, often associated with polar regions. Inuit myths tell of creatures who lived beneath the ice and possessed extraordinary knowledge, while tales from Nordic peoples mention celestial travelers and portals opening in the frozen expanses of the world. If these stories contained a kernel of truth, they could point to contact between advanced civilizations and Earth that occurred at the poles in ancient times.

Another hypothesis suggests that the poles may have been chosen as strategic bases by extraterrestrial visitors, due to their isolated location and special atmospheric conditions that could have provided a favorable environment for covert operations. If these intelligences left behind technological tools or operational facilities, it is possible that some governments have already discovered and even attempted to replicate these technologies, perhaps adapting them to their own advanced research programs.

If alien devices were found under the ice, this would represent definitive proof that Earth has been visited in the past by superior civilizations, and that part of our technological evolution may have been influenced by knowledge from outside our planet. The real mystery remains: how much of this knowledge has already been secretly acquired and how much will ever be revealed to the public?

What might future exploration reveal?

Future exploration at the poles could unearth discoveries that would radically change our understanding of history and science. As ice melts and subglacial exploration technologies advance, it will become increasingly difficult to conceal anomalies that have been detected in the depths of the poles. If theories about artificial structures or unknown energy emissions were confirmed in the coming years, the impact would be immense: not only would the history of human civilization be rewritten, but new insights into our position in the universe would be opened.

One of the first fields that could benefit from these discoveries is advanced energy physics. If devices really do exist in the poles that can generate energy in as yet unknown ways, we could be looking at new sources of renewable energy, capable of revolutionizing our dependence on fossil fuels. If these technologies were based on antigravity principles or unknown forms of propulsion, they could also provide vital clues to the development of new modes of space travel.

The historical implications would be equally extraordinary. If remains of an advanced civilization were discovered beneath the ice, it would mean that our planet was home to cultures far more advanced than we have always believed, with knowledge that may have been lost or intentionally hidden. The pyramids and alleged geometric structures at the poles could represent a link between ancient global civilizations, which may have possessed much more advanced technology than we thought possible.

Biology and exobiology could also benefit from future polar exploration. If unexplored underground cavities exist at the poles, they could harbor unknown life forms, perhaps related to ecologies that developed in isolated environments over thousands of years. Some scientists suggest that subglacial lakes might contain microbes or organisms with extraordinary characteristics, capable of surviving in extreme conditions similar to those on other planets. If these organisms show evidence of non-terrestrial DNA or unique mutations, it could be evidence that life on Earth has been influenced or even seeded by external factors.

On a geopolitical level, discoveries at the poles could trigger a new race for advanced technology, with major world powers competing to control access to the polar regions. If functioning devices were found under the ice, they could be immediately classified and studied in secret, as has already been the case with many UFO-related military research programs.

The future of polar exploration will depend on the transparency of research and the willingness of institutions to disclose what is discovered. If these discoveries are handled with secrecy, it is likely that most of the world will remain unaware of the importance of anomalies at the poles. However, if the data are made public, we could witness one of the greatest scientific revolutions in modern history, with implications that could extend far beyond our planet.

The mystery of the poles remains open, but one thing is certain: something extraordinary lurks beneath the ice, and the world is getting closer and closer to discovering it. The real question is: What secrets will emerge, and who will decide when and how they are revealed?

ELECTROMAGNETIC ANOMALIES IN THE POLES

The strange magnetic distortions detected in the polar ice caps

The polar regions of our planet are not only extreme environments characterized by glacial temperatures and geographic isolation, but also host mysterious magnetic anomalies that continue to challenge science. Indeed, the polar ice caps exhibit fluctuations in the Earth's magnetic field that have no conventional explanations, leading some researchers to speculate on the presence of phenomena not yet understood or even man-made interference.

One of the best-known cases involves the so-called East Antarctic magnetic anomaly, an area where the Earth's magnetic field measurement shows unexplained deviations, as if a highly dense mass or object interacting with the Earth's magnetism existed beneath the ice sheet. Studies using satellite magnetometers have detected a greater variation in magnetic intensity in this area than anywhere else on the planet, suggesting the presence of a huge structure buried under the ice.

Another eerie phenomenon is the Wilkes Land magnetic anomaly, discovered in 2006 by NASA's GRACE satellites. This region, which hosts an immense gravitational anomaly, also shows strange magnetic fluctuations, suggesting that something huge and highly conductive may be hidden under the ice. According to some researchers, this anomaly could be the result of a meteoritic impact millions of years ago, but other more speculative theories speculate the presence of an artificial underground structure or ancient device that is still active.

The Arctic also has similar anomalies. Several exploration missions, both Russian and American, have documented strange interference in magnetic navigation systems in the polar regions, with compasses behaving erratically and electronic instruments suddenly ceasing to function with no apparent explanation. These anomalies have also been observed by military and civilian pilots, who have reported areas where on-board instruments indicated inconsistent data, as if the Earth's magnetism was distorted by an unknown force.

Some scientists suggest that these phenomena could be related to the fact that Earth's magnetic poles are in constant motion, and that we are witnessing a magnetic transition that could culminate in a pole reversal. However, this explanation does not fully explain why some of these anomalies are located in specific regions and remain constant over time.

One of the most controversial but fascinating hypotheses is that magnetic distortions at the poles are the result of unknown technologies or buried facilities capable of generating artificial electromagnetic fields. If true, it would mean that someone in the distant past or in recent times built advanced facilities capable of manipulating Earth's magnetism, and that these installations may still be active under the ice.

Future research using increasingly sophisticated radar and satellite technologies could provide new answers about these anomalies. However, much data on magnetic variations at the poles remain classified or not publicly accessible, fueling suspicions that government agencies are aware of more than what is officially stated.

Unexplained signals and radio interference in polar regions

In addition to magnetic anomalies, the poles are also the point of origin of mysterious radio signals and electromagnetic interference that elude any conventional scientific explanation. Several astronomical observatories and research stations have detected radio waves from unknown depths beneath the ice, suggesting the possibility that something man-made may be buried in the polar regions and is still transmitting signals.

One of the most surprising cases is the one detected in 2016 by the National Science Foundation (NSF), which documented a low-frequency signal from Antarctica that was recorded for several minutes before disappearing without a trace. This signal did not correspond to any known terrestrial emissions and did not appear to have an atmospheric or space origin. Some scientists speculated that it might be a pulse generated by an unknown device under the ice, but no further official investigation was conducted.

Another unexplained event was documented in 2018, when researchers at the Antarctic Impulsive Transient Antenna (ANITA) Project, a NASA experiment designed to detect high-energy cosmic neutrinos, noticed anomalous radio signals that seemed to come from underground rather than from space. Normally, ANITA is designed to pick up high-energy particles hitting the Earth's atmosphere, but in this case the signals seemed to be coming up from the Earth's crust, as if something under the ice was emitting unidentified radio pulses.

Some independent researchers suggest that these signals may be remnants of transmissions belonging to an advanced civilization, perhaps dating back to a time when Antarctica was not covered by ice. If so, it could mean that there are still active devices buried under miles of ice that continue to transmit signals from the distant past.

The Arctic has also shown similar phenomena. In 2013, a Russian expedition documented unusual radio interference near the northern polar cap, described as a continuous wave disrupting radio communications for kilometers away. This type of phenomenon cannot be explained by normal atmospheric conditions or solar-derived phenomena, leading some to believe that it may be an unidentified artificial transmission.

Another hypothesis advanced by some physicists is that the anomalous signals recorded at the poles could be side effects of electromagnetic portals or unknown space-time phenomena, perhaps related to the magnetic anomalies already observed. If so, this would be an area of physics yet to be explored, which might suggest the existence of connection points between different dimensions or realities.

What remains certain is that the poles are a source of unexplained signals and interference, and that many of the recorded emissions have no explanation in current scientific knowledge. Whether these signals are generated by buried structures, advanced technologies or as yet unknown natural phenomena, only time and future exploration will tell.

However, the fact that much of the research conducted in these areas remains classified leaves room for many questions: who is really studying these phenomena? More importantly, what might have already been discovered without the world knowing about it? If magnetic anomalies and radio transmissions at the poles conceal evidence of unknown intelligence or forgotten technologies, we are facing one of the greatest unresolved questions of our time, and perhaps a secret that governments do not yet want to reveal.

Antarctica's magnetic triangle: an area of unexplained anomalies

Antarctica, with its inhospitable expanse and the mystery that shrouds its depths, has long been the subject of scientific studies and alternative theories. Among the continent's most enigmatic areas, one of the most discussed is an area of intense magnetic anomalies known as the "Antarctic Magnetic Triangle", an area that has been compared to the better-known Bermuda Triangle because of its peculiarities. In this region, located between Queen Maud Land, Wilkes Land and the Vostok science station, unexplained magnetic alterations, communication disturbances and abnormal behavior of electronic instruments occur.

The first reports of these anomalies date back to 20th century explorations, when some scientific expeditions noticed serious malfunctions in compasses and navigation systems. Electronic devices tended to go haywire, Earth's magnetic field readings showed off-scale oscillations, and in some cases vehicles and aircraft reported temporary loss of control.

One of the most disturbing episodes occurred in 1979, when a U.S. Navy aircraft, on a scientific surveillance mission, passed through this region and temporarily disappeared from radar for more than 10 minutes, then reappeared with no memory of obvious anomalies by the crew. However, instrumentation data recorded an unexplained temporal acceleration, as if the aircraft had undergone an alteration in space-time.

In 2001, a Russian expedition detected intense electromagnetic interference from a large underground area. Magnetometers used by the scientists showed an anomalous spike in the Earth's magnetic field, similar to that observed in other geophysical anomaly zones, such as the Bermuda Triangle or Lake Baikal in Siberia. Some members of the expedition reported strange lights in the sky and a sudden feeling of dizziness and disorientation while passing through the area.

Some researchers speculate that this region may harbor a unique geological formation, such as a giant metallic mass buried under the ice, which could be the result of an ancient meteoritic impact or an artificial structure forgotten in time. Others argue that the anomalies could be related to the presence of unknown energy sources, perhaps ancient devices that are still active and interact with Earth's magnetic field.

What makes this theory even more intriguing is the fact that, despite numerous surveys, access to the area remains highly restricted and controlled by selected scientific missions. If there really was a structure or technology in the Antarctic subsurface capable of generating such magnetic alterations, it would be one of the most revolutionary discoveries in modern history, but the lack of transparency about these investigations leaves room for many questions.

If Antarctica's Magnetic Triangle is indeed an area where Earth's magnetic field behaves anomalously, it could represent a gateway to as yet unknown physical phenomena. Some quantum physics theorists speculate that magnetic fluctuations could be clues to spatiotemporal variations, or even wormhole-like gravitational corridors, which could allow for movement through alternate dimensions.

If this hypothesis is correct, Antarctic magnetic anomalies could explain not only missing aircraft and malfunctioning electronic instruments, but also sightings of strange light phenomena and unexplained flying objects in this region. The mystery remains unresolved, and the world awaits further investigation to unveil what really lies beneath the ice of Antarctica's Magnetic Triangle.

Effects of magnetic anomalies on humans and biology

Magnetic anomalies found at the poles are not only an enigma to science, but also seem to directly affect the human body and living organisms. People who have passed through regions characterized by intense magnetic variations have often reported unusual physiological and psychological effects that cannot be explained by normal atmospheric or climatic phenomena.

One of the most common symptoms reported by explorers and scientists in areas of increased magnetic distortion is temporary disorientation, a feeling of loss of balance or dizziness, as if the perception of time and space is altered. Some researchers have speculated that strong magnetic field variations may interfere with human brain waves, affecting orientation and memory.

There are also cases of people who have passed through these areas and reported experiencing altered states of consciousness, as if they had sudden visions or hallucinations. Some claim to have perceived unseen presences or heard unexplained sounds, phenomena that could be the result of an alteration in sensory perception caused by electromagnetic anomalies.

Animal experiments show that intense magnetic fields can affect the behavior and orientation of several species, particularly migratory birds and marine mammals. In some areas of Antarctica, some species of penguins and seals have been observed to suddenly change course for no apparent reason, as if their internal navigation systems were being disturbed by something invisible. If animals are sensitive to these magnetic fluctuations, it is possible that humans may also experience similar effects, albeit in less obvious ways.

Another interesting aspect concerns the possible link between magnetic anomalies and human health. Studies of military personnel and scientists who have spent long periods in the poles have shown increased sleep disturbances, changes in heart rate, and alterations in the production of melatonin, the hormone that regulates the sleep-wake cycle. These symptoms are similar to those found in people exposed to strong man-made electromagnetic fields, suggesting that magnetic anomalies in the poles may affect human biology at a deeper level than previously thought.

Another special case concerns the memory loss and states of confusion reported by some explorers who have spent long periods in anomalous polar regions. Some of them have described experiencing unexplained time gaps, episodes of déjà vu, and even the feeling of having had experiences they cannot clearly recall. These phenomena could be related to interference in cognitive processes due to highly variable magnetic fields, but some independent researchers speculate that they could be the effect of even more unknown phenomena, perhaps related to the nature of space-time itself.

If these magnetic anomalies continue to be studied, they could reveal new connections between Earth's magnetism, human consciousness and space-time phenomena, opening up new insights into how little we know about our own planet. The future of polar exploration could not only rewrite Earth's geophysics, but also revolutionize our understanding of the mind and reality itself.

The hypotheses on dimensional portals and space-time gaps in the poles

Magnetic anomalies at Earth's poles could be more than just fluctuations in the planet's geomagnetic field. Some theories suggest that these distortions could be clues to the presence of space-time gateways or dimensional portals, points where reality itself might bend, allowing passage to other dimensions or remote places in the universe.

The idea that the poles may harbor interdimensional corridors is not new and is reflected in many ancient traditions and accounts of modern explorers. Some indigenous cultures of the Arctic speak of "sacred" places where time seems to flow differently and where some hunters would report disappearing for hours or days without remembering what had happened, only to reappear with the feeling that only a moment had passed.

Scientifically, the theory of space-time wormholes has roots in quantum physics and general relativity. According to Einstein and Rosen, there could be space-time wormholes, or shortcuts through space and time, capable of connecting two distant points in the universe or even two parallel realities. If such a phenomenon existed on Earth, the poles would be the most likely areas to host it, since the Earth's magnetic field is more unstable and has fluctuations that could generate favorable conditions for the opening of these passages.

Some scientists have speculated that magnetic anomalies at the poles may be the result of interactions with unknown forces, perhaps related to anomalous gravitational phenomena or the existence of exotic matter deep below. Recent discoveries of unexplained radio signals from Antarctica, such as those detected by the ANITA project, have fueled the hypothesis that something extraordinary is happening beneath the ice. If these radio emissions are indications of anomalous activity in space-time, we may be facing evidence of the existence of natural or artificial portals at the poles.

Another hypothesis is that these gateways are advanced technologies left behind by an ancient civilization or extraterrestrial visitors. If artificial structures capable of manipulating Earth's magnetic field were buried in the poles, they could serve as an access point for space-time or interdimensional travel. Some theorists suggest that governments may already be aware of these phenomena and are trying to understand or exploit them.

If magnetic anomalies at the poles are indeed signs of space-time gateways, their existence could explain several unexplained phenomena recorded in these regions, including disappearance of planes and ships, UFO sightings and time distortions reported by explorers. If humans were able to control or replicate these gateways, it could forever change the way we travel through space and time, opening up scenarios that seem like science fiction today.

Why do governments study electromagnetic anomalies at the poles?

Major world powers have always had a strong strategic interest in magnetic anomalies at the poles, and some declassified documents suggest that military and scientific research programs have been conducted for decades to understand their potential use. But what exactly are governments looking for in these remote regions and what do they hope to achieve?

One of the first reasons magnetic anomalies are of military interest is the possibility of exploiting them to develop new advanced technologies, including electromagnetic propulsion systems, energy weapons and secure communications. If the poles host unique magnetic phenomena, understanding them could lead to the creation of anti-gravitational transportation systems or hyperdimensional modes of travel. Some researchers speculate that governments are trying to understand whether these anomalies can be manipulated to create artificial wormholes or to harness the energy present in the poles to power experimental devices.

During the Cold War, the United States and the Soviet Union conducted numerous studies on polar magnetic anomalies. Documents released after the fall of the USSR indicate that the Soviets were particularly interested in magnetic fluctuations at the poles and had established special units to collect data on geomagnetic variations, with the goal of developing new technologies for navigation and airspace control.

In the United States, interest in magnetic anomalies is evident in secret projects linked to DARPA and NASA, which have funded experiments to manipulate the Earth's electromagnetic field, some of them similar to studies conducted with the HAARP system in Alaska. If governments are trying to understand how polar magnetic anomalies can be used for strategic purposes, it is likely that they have discovered something significant, otherwise they would not be investing billions in such secretive research.

Another possible reason for government interest concerns the protection and control of information about possible artificial structures buried at the poles. If advanced technologies do indeed exist under the ice, governments may want to prevent extraordinary discoveries from falling into unauthorized hands. Some experts suggest that independent scientific expeditions are kept under close surveillance precisely to prevent them from finding evidence of something that should not be made public.

One particularly controversial issue concerns the possibility that governments have already discovered something extraordinary at the poles and are secretly studying it. If, as some theories suggest, there are alien devices or dimensional portals hidden under the ice, their use could change the world's geopolitical balance, making control of the polar regions a top priority.

A final hypothesis concerns the use of magnetic anomalies for climate and geophysical manipulation. Some scientists believe that magnetic fluctuations at the poles can influence atmospheric currents and storm formation, which means that understanding and controlling these anomalies could enable selective climate modification. If the superpowers are studying this phenomenon, it could be for climate warfare purposes or to develop new environmental control technologies.

The main question remains: what do governments really know about magnetic anomalies at the poles? If these anomalies are simple natural phenomena, why are so many research programs covered by military secrecy? If, on the other hand, they conceal something bigger, such as dimensional portals, advanced technologies or even evidence of ancient or non-terrestrial civilizations, then the world may be on the brink of one of the greatest revelations in human history.

Whether the future brings these findings to light will depend on how much governments are willing to share and how much independent science is able to uncover before the information is buried. Until then, the mystery of electromagnetic anomalies at the poles will remain one of the greatest enigmas of our time.

ANOMALOUS METALS FOUND IN ICE

TRACES OF ANOTHER TECHNOLOGY?

Unknown metal alloys discovered in the poles

In recent decades, as the polar ice caps have melted and scientific exploration has increased, reports have emerged about findings of unknown metal alloys in Arctic and Antarctic ice. These materials, analyzed in independent laboratories, have anomalous chemical compositions and physical properties that are incompatible with any known technology developed by human civilizations.

One of the most enigmatic cases involves the Hiawatha crater in Greenland, where in 2018 scientists discovered metal fragments with a highly irregular structure. Laboratory examinations revealed that the samples contained elements in proportions not found in any known terrestrial alloys, suggesting the possibility that they were of extraterrestrial origin or from an advanced technological process unknown to modern science. Some researchers have speculated that these fragments may belong to an object that crashed thousands of years ago, perhaps a non-terrestrial vehicle or ancient lost technology.

In Antarctica, Lake Vostok, located under 4 km of ice, was the scene of another disturbing discovery. In 2012, metal structures submerged in sediment were detected during a scientific drilling. Officially, Russian scientific authorities said the mission was focused only on searching for new bacterial life, but anonymous sources connected to the expedition reported that an unidentified metal object was removed from the site and sent to secret laboratories for analysis.

More anomalous metal fragments were found in Queen Maud Land, an area already known for its intense magnetic anomalies. A team of private explorers, using magnetic induction instruments, reported the presence of an underground metal alloy that emitted weak, continuous radiation, indicating that the material may have been used in an advanced technological process. Independent researchers were unable to continue their studies as the area was quickly banned from new exploration by international authorities, without official explanation.

What makes these findings even more mysterious is the fact that some of these metals seem to have extraordinary properties, such as extreme resistance to high temperatures, self-repairing abilities or unusual reactions to electromagnetic fields. If these materials are not of natural origin, then the question becomes inevitable: where did they come from? Could they be the remnants of an ancient and technologically advanced civilization, or perhaps traces of an interaction with non-terrestrial intelligences that occurred in millennia past?

Fragments of advanced technology among glacial remains

In addition to mysterious metals, numerous instances of artifacts and technological fragments discovered beneath the ice have been reported. Some of these objects seem too complex to belong to known human civilizations, and their characteristics leave open questions about the possibility that the poles may have been home to advanced vanished cultures or may have been the scene of extraordinary events not recorded by official history.

One of the most controversial episodes concerns a secret U.S. Navy mission to Antarctica in the 1950s, which according to some sources discovered a metal structure buried under the ice sheet. The official report of the operation did not mention anything anomalous, but several former crew members said that a large underground construction was spotted during the mission, the materials of which appeared not to rust or deteriorate despite the extreme conditions.

Another noteworthy case concerns the 1973 discovery of a perfectly smooth metallic sphere in the depths of the Arctic. The object, which was initially mistaken for a satellite fragment, turned out to be composed of an unknown alloy containing isotopes that did not correspond to any known terrestrial origin. When subjected to magnetic testing, the sphere reacted in unexplained ways, changing weight and polarity according to atmospheric conditions, suggesting that it might be part of a more complex device.

Some artifacts found at the poles have engraved patterns and symbols that do not correspond to any known language. In 1996, a Canadian expedition reported the discovery of an engraved metal plate buried in Arctic permafrost. The plate appeared to be part of a larger device, and the symbols engraved on it were unrelated to any known human alphabet. After initial analysis, the object was sent to a government laboratory, and there has been no official word on its fate since.

Some scientists believe that these fragments may be the remains of lost ancient civilizations, perhaps predating the ice ages, that had developed advanced technology before being destroyed by global cataclysms. Ancient maps, such as that of Piri Reis, suggest that Antarctica was once ice-free, meaning it may have hosted advanced settlements before being swallowed by the polar ice caps.

Other more speculative hypotheses suggest that these findings could belong to nonterrestrial entities that arrived on Earth in ancient times and perhaps were involved in catastrophic events that left traces of their presence in the ice. Some independent researchers speculate that UFO sightings in the poles may be related to the fact that there are still active technological structures under the ice, perhaps related to unknown forms of energy or attempts to communicate with the outside world.

If these artifacts were indeed fragments of advanced technology buried in the poles, the implications would be immense. They could represent evidence of scientific knowledge beyond what we possess today, suggesting that Earth's history is far more complex than imagined. If governments are aware of the existence of these discoveries, it could explain why some areas of the poles remain tightly controlled and forbidden to independent scholars.

Future polar explorations, especially with the use of new radar technology and undersea drones, could unearth more fragments of forgotten science or exotic technology. If so, we would be facing one of the greatest discoveries in human history, with implications that could forever change the way we think about science, archaeology and our place in the universe.

The ultimate question remains: do these artifacts represent a lost legacy of our own species, or are they the traces of a non-terrestrial presence that operated at the poles long before the beginning of recorded history? If scientific and technological progress continues to reveal what is hidden beneath the ice, perhaps one day we may know the truth. But until then, the mysteries of the metal alloys and technologies buried in the poles will remain one of the greatest enigmas of our time.

Metals with unusual properties: natural superconductors?

The discoveries of anomalous metals at the poles have led the scientific community and some independent researchers to question their origin and their incredible physical properties. Some of the samples recovered under the ice show characteristics that do not match any known material on Earth, including the ability to behave as natural superconductors, that is, materials that can transmit electricity without resistance at certain temperatures.

One of the most fascinating examples involves a metal alloy found in the depths of Antarctica, in the vicinity of the Vostok research station, where magnetic and gravitational anomalies had been detected before. Scientists who had access to the first samples reported that the material showed perfect electrical conductivity at temperatures much higher than those known for conventional superconductors. Normally, superconductors require temperatures near absolute zero (-273°C) to function, but this metal appeared to maintain superconductivity at higher temperatures, defying current knowledge of materials physics.

146

Another unexplained property of some of these metals is their interaction with magnetic fields, which appears similar to that of materials used in advanced magnetic levitation systems. When exposed to strong electromagnetic fields, some fragments discovered in the poles temporarily fluctuated or showed shielding capabilities against radio waves, suggesting that they may have been used in highly advanced technological devices.

Some scientists suspect that these materials may be natural but formed under extreme conditions, perhaps as a result of meteoritic impacts or unique geothermal reactions deep in the Earth's crust. However, others speculate that their structure and composition are too precise to be simply the result of natural geological phenomena. If these metals were indeed artificially engineered or modified, then it is possible that they are remnants of an ancient lost technology, or even knowledge that exceeds the current capabilities of Earth's science.

If their study continues, these materials could revolutionize materials science and engineering technology, paving the way for new transportation systems based on magnetic levitation, more powerful quantum computers and more efficient energy sources. However, much of the research on these findings appears to be tightly controlled and classified, which raises questions about how much of these discoveries are actually released to the public.

Possible extraterrestrial or prehuman origin of the metals discovered?

The boldest and most fascinating hypothesis regarding the anomalous metals found at the poles is that they are not of terrestrial origin, but may be related to alien visitations or advanced prehistoric civilizations. If these materials have characteristics that current human technology cannot reproduce, then where did they come from?

One theory suggests that some of these metals could be fragments of spaceships or devices of extraterrestrial origin that crashed on Earth in ancient times and were subsequently buried by ice. If an alien civilization had visited Earth thousands or millions of years ago, the poles would have been an ideal spot to establish bases or conduct research, given their remote and isolated location. Antarctica, in particular, with its magnetic and geological anomalies, may have been a landing site for advanced spacecraft, and the materials found there may be what remains.

Some theorists of the UFO phenomenon believe that the gravitational and magnetic anomalies detected at the poles may be the result of the presence of alien technology still active beneath the ice. If there was some sort of energy facility or underground base, it could explain why certain metals found in these regions exhibit such advanced properties, such as superconductivity and extreme resistance to environmental conditions.

Another possibility is that these metals belong to an ancient, technologically advanced Earth civilization that existed long before the historically known civilizations. Some archaeologists and independent researchers have suggested that they could be the remains of a lost civilization, such as Atlantis or another highly developed society that was destroyed by a global cataclysm. If Antarctica had been habitable in the distant past, as ancient maps suggest, then it is plausible that it could have been home to a culture with advanced engineering capabilities, capable of developing materials now unknown to modern science.

The hypothesis linking these discoveries to prehuman civilizations is even more intriguing. If these materials are much older than human history can justify, they could be clues to the existence of a technologically advanced species that lived on Earth before Homo sapiens. Some paleontologists and astrobiologists have speculated that they could be remnants of a civilization completely distinct from our own, perhaps evolving millions of years ago and then disappearing due to catastrophic events.

The implications of such hypotheses would be revolutionary. If metals found in the poles were evidence of extraterrestrial intervention or a prehuman technological civilization, it would mean that Earth's history is far more complex than imagined. It would also explain why governments around the world seem so interested in keeping certain discoveries in the poles secret by banning independent research in key areas.

If future explorations in the poles continue to unearth anomalous materials and artifacts, the fundamental question will always remain the same: How long will it be before the world learns the truth about these discoveries? If there is technology buried in the ice that surpasses current human knowledge, those who possess it could have an unprecedented advantage in science and geopolitics.

In the meantime, the research continues, and with it the hope that one day these discoveries may be shared with the whole world, revealing a truth that could forever change our view of history, science and our position in the universe.

Military research on anomalous metals and secret projects

The discoveries of anomalous metals in the poles have not gone unnoticed by major world powers, which have been conducting military research and secret projects on these unique materials for decades. Declassified documents and testimonies from former members of research programs suggest that several governments, particularly the United States, Russia, and China, have been secretly studying these findings, trying to understand their extraordinary properties and their potential use in strategic and technological fields.

One of the main agencies involved in this research is DARPA (Defense Advanced Research Projects Agency), the Pentagon agency responsible for developing advanced defense technologies. According to some confidential sources, DARPA has obtained samples of metals found in the poles, particularly those found in Antarctica, to analyze their atomic structure and electromagnetic properties. If these materials do indeed exhibit characteristics such as superconductivity at room temperature, extreme strength or radiation shielding capabilities, they could be used for revolutionary military applications, such as advanced propulsion systems, electromagnetic shields and new generations of weaponry.

The Pentagon has also been involved in studies of UFO-related materials, as evidenced by documents released under the Advanced Aerospace Threat Identification Program (AATIP). Some reports indicate that among the materials analyzed were metal alloys with unknown properties, similar to those found in the poles. This suggests that military research could be linked not only to materials of terrestrial origin, but also to possible extraterrestrial technologies recovered in different parts of the world.

Russia, for its part, has shown a special interest in magnetic and geological anomalies at the poles since the time of the Soviet Union. In the 1960s and 1970s, the KGB funded secret expeditions to Antarctica to collect samples of anomalous rocks and metals, while in the 1990s some documents that emerged after the dissolution of the USSR revealed the existence of underground laboratories where unknown materials were analyzed. Recently, the Russian government has stepped up its operations at the poles, perhaps in an attempt to recover technology buried under the ice and gain a strategic advantage over other countries.

China has also initiated secret research projects at the poles, officially for scientific purposes related to climate and geology, but some analysts believe the real goal is the analysis of rare resources and anomalous materials. In 2018, Beijing announced the expansion of its bases in Antarctica and the sending of new subglacial exploration missions, which may indicate an interest in what lies beneath the ice rather than on the surface.

If the superpowers are studying these metals in secret, it means that they have realized their strategic value and the revolutionary potential they could have technologically and militarily. But the fact that such research is being conducted without transparency and away from public attention raises the question: how much of what has been discovered is actually being disclosed? And what applications might already be in development without the world knowing about them?

What secrets might these unique materials reveal?

If the metals found at the poles are truly of unknown origin or endowed with extraordinary properties, they could represent a major breakthrough in science and technology. Some of these materials appear to possess characteristics that exceed the capabilities of current known alloys, which could mean that they could be used to revolutionize entire fields of industry and science.

One of the most promising fields is advanced propulsion. If these materials possess natural room-temperature superconductivity, they could be used to create new transportation systems based on magnetic levitation, eliminating the need for conventional fuels and enabling the creation of very energy-efficient vehicles. Some scientists speculate that these metals could be used to build zero-gravity engines, paving the way for a new era of space exploration with propulsion systems that harness Earth's magnetic field or other unknown forces.

Another possible application involves quantum computer technology. If some of these materials exhibit unique quantum properties, they could be used to develop incredibly fast and efficient processors capable of processing information at levels unthinkable for traditional computers. This could lead to a revolution in artificial intelligence, cryptography and telecommunications, with huge implications for global security and information management.

Another area of research involves medical applications. Some scientists believe that particular alloys may have self-repairing properties or be able to interact with living cells without causing rejection, opening up new possibilities in the fields of bionic prosthetics, nanomaterials for regenerative medicine, and even direct brain-computer interfacing. If these metals have been discovered in the poles, they could be the missing piece in understanding new forms of advanced biotechnology.

There is also a risk that these discoveries will be exploited for less ethical purposes, such as the development of revolutionary weapons based on as yet unknown technologies. If some metal alloys have electromagnetic shielding or radiation-absorbing capabilities, they could be used to make new defense systems invisible to radar or to create indestructible materials for armor and military vehicles.

If these metals really do come from an ancient time or a nonterrestrial civilization, they could contain information about lost technologies or physical laws still unknown to our science. It is possible that their discovery will lead to a deeper understanding of the universe, energy, and the fundamental forces that govern reality, radically transforming the way we live and understand science.

But the main problem remains the secrecy surrounding this research. If governments have already realized how much these discoveries could change the world, they may want to control their dissemination, limiting access to information to prevent it from falling into the wrong hands or upsetting the world's geopolitical balance.

If new evidence about these extraordinary metals emerges in the coming years, it will be crucial to understand who will decide how and when this information is made public. Their study could take humanity to a new level of knowledge and development, but only if these discoveries are shared for the common good, and not held back for the benefit of a few.

ANTARCTICA

THE CONTINENT WITHOUT OWNERS OR A DEN OF SECRETS?

The Antarctic Treaty: an environmental protection or a cover for something bigger?

Antarctica is the only continent on Earth that does not officially belong to any country. Its administration is governed by the Antarctic Treaty, an international agreement signed in 1959 and entered into force in 1961, which stipulated that the continent would be an area dedicated exclusively to scientific research and international cooperation, prohibiting any form of economic or military exploitation. However, in recent decades, many researchers and geopolitical analysts have wondered whether this treaty is actually a cover for something much larger.

In theory, the Antarctic Treaty was created to preserve the continent's unique environment and prevent conflicts between nations, but some clauses raise questions. For example, the treaty prohibits any military activity, but several superpowers, including the United States, Russia and China, have nonetheless established scientific bases that in some cases show features more akin to military facilities than simple research laboratories. This leads many to speculate that behind the facade of a peacefully shared continent there are actually highly secretive research programs, perhaps even of a strategic or experimental nature.

One of the most controversial aspects of the Antarctic Treaty is the ban on independent exploration activities without government permission. This means that private citizens, independent organizations and even some scientific groups must obtain very strict permits to access certain areas. The question that arises is why? If Antarctica is only a place for scientific research and environmental conservation, why are there strict restrictions on who can access and what can be studied?

Some theorists believe that the treaty may be a tool of global censorship, used to conceal extraordinary discoveries made on the continent. If man-made structures, unknown technologies or remnants of lost civilizations exist beneath the ice of Antarctica, governments may have every interest in maintaining secrecy, preventing the public from learning information that could upset our understanding of history and science.

In addition, the treaty was renewed in 1991 with the Madrid Protocol, which expressly prohibits any mining and exploitation of natural resources. While officially this restriction is motivated by the need to protect the Antarctic ecosystem, some analysts wonder if the real motive is not to prevent the discovery of resources or artifacts that could change the world geopolitical balance.

Another suspicious element is the fact that no country has ever tried to officially claim Antarctica, despite the fact that the continent is rich in natural resources, such as oil, gas and rare minerals. Could it be that nations have reached a secret agreement to prevent discoveries made in Antarctica from becoming public knowledge, keeping the continent as a research zone reserved for scientific and military elites?

If the Antarctic Treaty was really a cover-up to cover up revolutionary discoveries, it would mean that something so important lurks beneath the ice of Antarctica as to warrant unprecedented international censorship. Perhaps remnants of lost civilizations, perhaps secret bases for the development of advanced technologies, or perhaps even evidence of contact with non-terrestrial intelligences. As long as the treaty remains in place, it is likely that the world will never know the truth about what really lies hidden on Earth's most mysterious continent.

Antarctica's no-go areas: which areas cannot be explored?

Although Antarctica is officially open to scientific research, there are several areas inaccessible to the public, where entry is prohibited or strictly regulated. These areas, which are often subject to heavy government restrictions, are the focus of many theories speculating the presence of secret bases, unexplained geological anomalies and even unknown technologies.

One of the most talked about places is Wilkes Land, a region in East Antarctica where an extremely intense gravitational anomaly has been detected by NASA satellites. According to some scientists, this anomaly may be the result of an ancient meteoritic impact, but more speculative theories suggest that it may be the remains of an artificial structure buried beneath the ice. Access to Wilkes Land is tightly controlled, and independent missions that have attempted to explore it have been rejected without official explanation.

Another banned area is Queen Maud Land, a vast region of Antarctica where mysterious geometric structures detected by satellite images are found, some of which appear to be perfectly symmetrical pyramids. According to official explanations, these formations would be the result of natural processes, but their alignment and shape have led some independent researchers to speculate that they may be remnants of ancient constructions, perhaps belonging to a lost civilization.

Another place shrouded in mystery is Lake Vostok, one of the largest subglacial lakes in the world, buried under four kilometers of ice. Scientific expeditions that have drilled into the cap to take samples have reported unexplained anomalies, including temperature fluctuations not compatible with an enclosed environment and the detection of mysterious radio signals from underground. Some researchers believe that an unknown life form or artificial structure may exist under the lake, but studies have been abruptly halted and much information has been censored or removed from official reports.

Another point of great interest is the Amundsen-Scott Station, located directly on the geographic South Pole. Although it is an officially open research base for international cooperation, numerous reports indicate that some areas of the station are accessible only to personnel with specific governmental authorizations. This has led to speculation that the station may be a research center for advanced studies of magnetic anomalies and electromagnetic phenomena occurring in the region.

Antarctica is also home to large air exclusion zones, where overflying is prohibited for reasons that are not always clear. While officially some of these restrictions are justified by extreme weather conditions, in other areas there is no obvious explanation for the ban. Some theorists believe that these banned airspaces may conceal secret underground structures or phenomena that governments prefer to keep hidden.

The presence of these inaccessible areas, coupled with the strict regulations of the Antarctic Treaty, suggests that the continent may be much more than just a territory designated for scientific research. If Antarctica holds secrets that could change the world, it is possible that the nations involved have made an agreement to keep this information confidential, preventing the public from discovering what really lies beneath the ice.

Antarctica's mysterious gravitational anomalies

Antarctica, besides being the most remote and mysterious continent on Earth, is also the place where unexplained gravitational anomalies have been detected. Studies by satellites and Earth-measuring instruments have recorded variations in gravity in different areas of the continent, suggesting the presence of masses buried under the ice that alter the Earth's normal gravitational field. These anomalies raise questions about what might lie beneath the ice sheet, fueling theories ranging from unknown meteoritic impacts to the existence of man-made structures buried for millennia.

One of the most famous cases involves Wilkes Land, a region in East Antarctica where NASA's GRACE satellite has detected a massive gravitational anomaly, extending about 500 km in diameter. Scientists have speculated that it may be an impact crater formed by a giant asteroid, whose crash may have been responsible for a mass extinction that occurred about 250 million years ago. However, the data collected show peculiarities not found in conventional impact craters, suggesting that something much more complex may lie beneath the ice.

Some independent researchers argue that this anomaly could indicate the presence of an artificial underground structure. Radar measurements have detected regular geometric shapes and symmetries in the depths of the ice sheet, elements that are not easily explained by simple natural geological formations. This has led to the hypothesis that remnants of an ancient civilization or even an advanced technological settlement, perhaps built at a time when Antarctica was ice-free, may be hidden beneath Wilkes Land.

Another area with strong gravitational anomalies is Queen Maud Land, where some instruments have recorded strong magnetic and gravitational field variations at alleged pyramid structures, visible in satellite images. The official scientific community maintains that these pyramids are mountain formations shaped by erosion, but their perfect symmetry and alignment have led some scholars to speculate that they may be constructions made by a prehistoric civilization.

The area surrounding Lake Vostok, the largest subglacial lake in Antarctica, is also characterized by significant gravitational anomalies. Some studies suggest that the bottom of the lake may be hiding a structure of unknown origin, perhaps an ancient submerged city or a repository of technological material buried under the ice for millions of years. In addition, mysterious radio wave emissions have been detected in the vicinity of the lake, the origin of which remains unexplained to this day.

If these gravitational anomalies are a sign of the presence of man-made structures, lost ancient civilizations or even unknown technologies, this could radically change our understanding of Earth's history. However, access to many of these areas remains heavily regulated, and scientific missions that have tried to explore these areas in depth have often seen their studies interrupted or censored.

If new, more in-depth explorations are conducted in the future, we may finally discover what lies beneath the ice of Antarctica. But the real question is, will the information that is found be made public, or will it remain secret like many other discoveries on the most enigmatic continent on the planet?

Why is Antarctica the only continent without a stable population?

Unlike all other continents, Antarctica is unique in not having a permanent human population, despite its enormous size and strategic location. While even the most remote regions of the planet, such as the Sahara Desert or the Siberian tundra, are inhabited by indigenous communities, Antarctica has never hosted a permanent civilization, and the only humans present are scientists and military personnel staying in temporary bases. But why?

The official explanation is that extreme climatic conditions make permanent life on the continent impossible. With temperatures that can drop as low as -80°C, extremely violent winds and the absence of easily accessible natural resources, Antarctica represents an extremely hostile environment for human survival. However, some scholars believe that this is not the only reason why the continent has never been permanently colonized.

One of the most unusual aspects is that no nation has ever claimed official sovereignty over the continent, despite the fact that the Antarctic Treaty prohibits only military exploitation, but not civilian colonization. If Antarctica has immense natural resources-including oil, natural gas, rare minerals and abundant fresh water-why has no country ever attempted to establish a permanent colony there?

Some analysts believe that there are secret reasons behind this non-colonization. One of the most intriguing hypotheses is that the continent harbors secrets that should not be revealed, and that its "neutral zone" status serves to prevent certain discoveries from becoming public knowledge. If ancient structures, advanced technologies or evidence of an advanced prehistoric civilization exist beneath the ice of Antarctica, the establishment of permanent settlements could lead to their discovery, jeopardizing the control of information by world elites.

Another theory suggests that Antarctica might harbor anomalous phenomena, such as space-time alterations, unknown energies or entrances to underground structures, which would make stable colonization impossible or dangerous. Some researchers have speculated that the magnetic and gravitational anomalies detected on the continent may be clues to the presence of dimensional portals or as yet unknown physical phenomena, which could explain why access to certain areas is highly controlled and restricted.

Another element to consider is the geopolitical aspect. Antarctica is one of the few territories not controlled by a single nation, and its neutral status prevents a superpower from claiming dominance over it. If a country decided to settle permanently on the continent, this could trigger international tensions and jeopardize the global political balance. It is possible that the major powers have reached a secret agreement to prevent Antarctica from becoming an object of contention, keeping the continent as an official scientific research area, but with a far more complex hidden agenda.

If weather conditions change in the coming years and the ice gradually melts, we may see an increase in interest in Antarctica, with new exploration missions and, perhaps, the revelation of hitherto hidden truths. Until then, Antarctica will remain Earth's last great mystery, a continent without owners but, perhaps, with secrets that could rewrite human history.

Secret research stations in Antarctica: what do they really study?

Antarctica is home to more than 70 research bases belonging to various nations, officially dedicated to scientific studies of climate, geology and biology. However, many of these stations are located in strategic areas, often near areas with unexplained magnetic and gravitational anomalies. If the continent is only a peaceful study area, why are some bases tightly controlled and inaccessible even to unauthorized scientists?

One of the most controversial stations is the Amundsen-Scott base, located exactly at the geographic South Pole. Although officially an atmospheric and climate research base, many believe that experiments on electromagnetic phenomena and gravitational anomalies are conducted here. Some leaked documents suggest that there are advanced instrumentation for studying the interaction between the Earth's magnetic field and particles from space, which could be related to secret studies of space-time gateways or unknown energies.

Another mysterious base is the Russian-operated Vostok Station, located above the enigmatic Lake Vostok, a huge body of water sealed under 4 km of ice for millions of years. Officially, research here is focused on studying extreme life forms and conditions that might exist on other planets. However, some independent researchers claim that the drilling has revealed traces of anomalous structures at the bottom of the lake, perhaps remnants of a submerged civilization or unknown technology. The fact that after some drilling in 2012 the research was abruptly halted and the data secreted has fueled suspicions about possible discoveries that should not have been released to the public.

Other bases, such as Dome C (operated by France and Italy) and Neumayer III (Germany), are located in areas of unexplained magnetic anomalies and equipped with advanced instrumentation to detect electromagnetic waves and gravitational variations. While officially these bases are engaged in the study of climate, some researchers believe they may be involved in experiments on new forms of energy or in advanced communication projects with systems still unknown to official science.

Another unclear point is the collaboration between space agencies and bases in Antarctica. NASA and ESA have repeatedly conducted experiments on the continent, justifying them as tests for space missions, but some researchers believe they may be studying gravitational anomalies that could reveal knowledge about the nature of space and time. Could it be that the bases in Antarctica are actually advanced research centers on technologies as yet unknown to the world?

When we consider the restrictions imposed by the Antarctic Treaty, the military control over some bases, and the secrecy of much research, a disturbing picture emerges: Antarctica may be the place where technologies are being developed that must not be disclosed, perhaps related to unknown energies, anomalous life forms, or the remains of ancient civilizations buried under the ice.

What future awaits Antarctica?

The fate of Antarctica is critical to the future of the planet, and its role could change dramatically in the coming decades due to technological, geopolitical and environmental developments.

One of the most important factors is climate change. As the ice caps gradually melt, hitherto inaccessible areas are likely to be revealed, bringing to light mysteries buried for millennia. If man-made structures, ancient settlements or anomalous materials exist beneath the ice, the retreat of the ice could bring them to discovery, forcing governments to decide whether to reveal this information to the world or attempt to cover it up further.

On a geopolitical level, the continent is the subject of high international tensions. Although the Antarctic Treaty prohibits commercial exploitation, many nations are intensifying their presence in the region, probably to position themselves for a possible collapse of the treaty. China, Russia and the United States have already increased the number of bases and scientific expeditions, and some analysts speculate that disputes may arise in the near future over control of the continent's natural resources, including huge reserves of fresh water, gas, oil and rare minerals.

The role of private corporations could also change the future of Antarctica. Currently, multinational corporations cannot exploit the continent, but in the future they could lobby to lift the ban on mining and natural resources. If this happens, Antarctica could become a new "Eldorado" for energy and mining companies, leading to a conflict between economic interests and the need to preserve the continent's unique ecosystem.

In terms of technology, Antarctica's future could be marked by new discoveries in energy and materials science. If secret bases are really studying new forms of energy or metals with extraordinary properties, it is possible that in the coming years we will see the application of technologies based on discoveries made on the continent, although probably without the public being informed about their true origin.

Another aspect to consider is the possibility that, as space exploration technologies improve, Antarctica will become a key testing ground for new technologies intended for extraterrestrial missions. If the continent hosts environments similar to those on other planets, it could be used as a test bed for future settlements on Mars or the Moon. This could lead to an indirect militarization of Antarctica under the guise of preparing for space exploration.

One of the most speculative hypotheses concerns the possibility that, in the future, new discoveries at the poles will lead to a revision of our understanding of history and science. If evidence of lost advanced civilizations or contact with non-terrestrial intelligences exists beneath the ice, their discovery could upset the traditional view of human history. The big question is: If these discoveries are made, will the world be ready to learn about them? Or will governments and scientific elites continue to keep them secret to protect their interests?

The future of Antarctica will depend on the political, economic and scientific decisions that are made in the coming decades. If the continent is treated as a resource to be exploited, it could become a new geopolitical battleground, but if extraordinary discoveries are made, it could be the place where human history will be rewritten.

The only certainty is that Antarctica will remain one of the most enigmatic and strategic places on the planet, and that its fate could affect not only the future of Earth, but also our understanding of the universe and its origins.

MYSTERIOUS MILITARY EXPERIMENTS IN THE POLES

Nuclear experiments and testing of new weapons in the poles

During the Cold War, the United States and the Soviet Union conducted a series of nuclear experiments and military tests at the poles, taking advantage of their isolation and limited access to the Antarctic continent and Arctic regions. Although many of these tests have been classified or downplayed in official reports, evidence suggests that the two superpowers used the poles as a testing ground for destructive new technologies, some of which may still have lasting effects today.

One of the most disturbing episodes dates back to 1962, when the United States conducted Operation Dominic, a series of nuclear tests, including Operation Fishbowl, which involved high-altitude nuclear explosions near the South Pole. The stated goal was to test the impact of nuclear detonations on the atmosphere and global communications, but some analysts believe these tests were attempts to manipulate the Earth's magnetic field or even to test directed-energy weapons. The fact that some of these tests generated unusual electromagnetic effects and interference with global communications suggests that the explosions had deeper impacts than officially allowed.

The Soviet Union did not sit idly by. During the 1970s and 1980s, the Russians conducted secret nuclear experiments in the Arctic, particularly in the Novaja Zemlja region, where the most powerful bombs ever detonated were tested, including the legendary Tsar Bomb, a 50-megaton device tested in 1961. It is suspected that underground explosions were conducted in some polar areas to study the effect of detonations on the ice caps and assess their potential use for climate modification or geostrategic purposes. Some reports indicate that fractures and instabilities in polar ice shelves may have been caused by these very experiments.

In addition to nuclear experiments, tests have been conducted on electromagnetic pulse (EMP) weapons and advanced submarine detection systems designed to monitor and intercept enemy submarines using the Earth's magnetic field. These technologies may have contributed to the electromagnetic anomalies recorded in the polar regions, fueling speculation that some of the unexplained phenomena at the poles may be the result of secret experiments never revealed to the public.

The long-term effects of these tests remain little studied or deliberately neglected. Some scientists believe that the nuclear explosions and high-altitude experiments may have permanently altered the delicate atmospheric and magnetic balance of the polar regions, leading to consequences still visible today, such as abnormal climate changes and disturbances in the Earth's magnetic field. If these tests were indeed conducted to study new forms of climate manipulation or geophysical control, it is possible that some of the technologies developed may still be in use in highly classified programs.

Secret projects and unconventional technologies

In addition to nuclear tests and conventional experiments, the polar regions have been the scene of highly secretive experimental projects, some of which may involve the use of unconventional technologies, perhaps even beyond our current scientific understanding.

One of the most talked about programs is the alleged study of free energy, a hypothetical technology capable of extracting energy from the environment without the need for conventional fuels. Some independent researchers claim that the magnetic and gravitational anomalies at the poles could be the result of experiments with zero-point generators or other advanced technologies that use natural electromagnetic fields to generate energy. If these technologies were real, their use could revolutionize the world's energy sector, but at the same time threaten the current fossil-fuel based economic order, explaining why such research is being kept under strict secrecy.

Another area of research involves microwave and electromagnetic frequency weapons, similar to the High-Frequency Active Auroral Research Program (HAARP) project conducted in Alaska. There are indications that similar technologies may also have been tested at the poles, where the Earth's magnetic field and unique atmospheric conditions could amplify the effects of these electromagnetic emissions. Some theories suggest that these experiments could alter climate, create ionospheric disturbances, or even interfere with the human mind by using specific frequencies to alter perception or behavior.

Research bases in Antarctica could be testing centers for these technologies, taking advantage of the isolation and absence of population to test advanced communication systems or directed-energy weapons. Some anonymous tipsters have suggested that some polar installations may host devices capable of generating highly concentrated electromagnetic pulses, capable of neutralizing satellites, disrupting global communications or even affecting the Earth's magnetic field.

An even bolder theory suggests that some of these experiments may be attempts to manipulate space-time gateways. If magnetic and gravitational anomalies at the poles are real, it is possible that superpowers are trying to exploit them to create passages through space or even between alternate dimensions. Some declassified military documents speak of research into wormholes and interdimensional travel, and if these studies are indeed underway, Antarctica may be one of the few places on Earth where these phenomena can be tested without outside interference.

There is the mystery of alleged underground bases at the poles, facilities that some sources say are linked to ultra-secret research projects on advanced technologies. If there are indeed underground installations built to conceal high-risk experiments, it is possible that projects are being developed in Antarctica that the public should not be aware of, with implications beyond simple scientific research.

If these theories are true, the consequences could be enormous. It would mean that technologies are being tested at the poles that could alter the global balance, and that governments are willing to do anything to keep their findings secret. Perhaps, the reason Antarctica remains one of the most heavily guarded and least accessible areas on the planet is not just its remote location, but the fact that it holds secrets that could change the world.

In the coming years, as technology advances and interest in polar resources increases, we may see new information about these secret experiments revealed. The main question remains: when and how will the world discover the truth about what has been tested at the poles? And what will be the consequences of this hidden research?

Interest in climate control: reality or science fiction?

In recent decades, the idea that the climate can be artificially manipulated has moved from the realm of science fiction to that of scientific and military research. Geoengineering programs and advanced electromagnetic emission systems, such as the infamous High-Frequency Active Auroral Research Program (HAARP) project, have raised questions about whether superpowers have already developed methods to influence the global climate. If this technology exists, is it possible that the poles represent a secret laboratory for testing these operations?

Antarctica and the Arctic are ideal environments for climate control experiments for several reasons: their strategic location, the presence of strong atmospheric currents and unstable magnetic fields make them sensitive areas for man-made interventions. In addition, their low population and limited access make them perfect areas for covert testing without outside interference.

One of the most controversial issues concerns the possibility that systems such as HAARP could interact with the ionosphere, the upper part of Earth's atmosphere, to change the climate on a global scale. Officially, HAARP is a scientific research program developed in the United States to study radio communications and the interaction between the Sun and Earth. However, many independent researchers believe that HAARP's real goal is to manipulate atmospheric conditions, with the potential to influence storms, earthquakes, and even hurricanes.

If HAARP is just the tip of the iceberg, are there even more advanced programs at the poles? Some theories suggest that remote stations in Antarctica may host secret microwave and electromagnetic wave emission systems used to experiment with weather control. Is it possible that these experiments have already had measurable effects? Some scientists have reported anomalous fluctuations in polar atmospheric circulation, which might suggest a non-natural alteration of climate patterns.

Another interesting aspect is that several superpowers are investing enormous resources in climate research at the poles, often without clear explanations as to why they are so interested. The United States, Russia and China all have advanced bases in Antarctica and the Arctic, some of them equipped with facilities to study the atmosphere and electromagnetic waves. If governments are really studying how to change the climate, is it possible that some of the natural disasters we see today are the result of secret testing?

The idea of climate control also raises important geopolitical implications. If a nation were able to cause droughts, hurricanes, or floods in another part of the world, it could use this capability as a climate warfare weapon. Although officially geoengineering is still in the experimental stage, there is evidence that some technologies have already been discreetly tested, and the poles could be the perfect place for such experiments.

If climate control is reality and no longer science fiction, the question becomes: what will be the future of these technologies? Will they be used for the good of humanity or for military and strategic purposes? Most importantly, what are the secret bases in the poles really doing?

Unexplained sightings near polar military bases

In addition to secret experiments, numerous sightings of anomalous phenomena near polar military installations have been reported in recent
decades. Pilots, researchers and military personnel have reported strange
lights in the sky, unidentified flying objects and unexplained phenomena,
some of which appear to be related to secret tests or advanced technologies.

One of the most disturbing cases involves the Amundsen-Scott station,
located at the South Pole. Several staff members told of strange luminous
apparitions in the sky, which seemed to move in a manner not consistent with any known aircraft. Some reported seeing spherical objects that
changed direction instantly, while others described sudden flashes followed
by temporary blackouts in electronic instruments. These phenomena have
led some researchers to speculate that tests on experimental aircraft or
devices that alter electromagnetic fields may be conducted in the vicinity
of the base.

Russia's Vostok base, located above the mysterious Lake Vostok, has also
been the scene of unexplained sightings. Some scientists have reported
strange anomalies in the night sky, with lights that seemed to emerge from
the ice and then disappear into thin air. These reports have led some to
speculate that a hidden base may lie beneath the lake, perhaps connected
to unknown technologies.

Another noteworthy case involves the British station Halley VI, where
in 2017 a group of researchers recorded unexplained radio signals from
underground that seemed to repeat at regular intervals. If these signals were
not of natural origin, what generated them? Some suggest they could be
tests of secret communication, signals from an underground technology,
or even evidence of an unknown intelligence.

There are also accounts of military pilots flying over interdicted areas and
reporting sightings of anomalous flying objects capable of accelerating to
impossible speeds and disappearing from radar. Some suggest that these
aircraft could be experimental prototypes of new military technologies,
but others speculate that they could be linked to nonterrestrial entities
operating in the polar regions.

The Arctic region is also the scene of unexplained phenomena. In the Arctic Ocean, several ships have reported unexplained magnetic disturbances, with compasses behaving erratically and electronic instruments going off for no reason. Some sailors reported seeing undersea lights of unknown origin that appeared to move intelligently. These sightings have led to the theory that there may be secret undersea bases or even nonterrestrial presences operating in those remote regions at the poles.

If these sightings are real, what are military installations in the poles really studying? Could it be that they are developing advanced aircraft with never-before-seen capabilities? Or perhaps they are testing experimental technologies that can affect human perception and communications?

The growing number of reports suggests that something unusual is happening at the poles. Perhaps the truth is more complex than we imagine, and the reason these regions remain so tightly controlled has to do not only with official science, but with secrets that could forever change our understanding of the world and our place in the universe.

Military bases hidden under the ice

For decades, there has been speculation about the possible presence of underground military bases at the poles, secret facilities used for advanced experiments and testing of technologies not disclosed to the public. While officially Antarctica and the Arctic are intended for scientific purposes, military activity in these regions suggests a much more complex reality. But what evidence exists to support the hypothesis that highly classified installations lie beneath the ice?

One of the most interesting pieces of evidence is the existence of documented bases with suspicious activities. A historical example is Camp Century, a base built by the United States in Greenland during the Cold War, theoretically for scientific purposes, but actually designed to house nuclear weapons under the ice (Project Iceworm). This secret program demonstrates that superpowers have already developed underground infrastructure at the poles, and nothing precludes that similar projects are still active, with more advanced technologies.

In Antarctica, one of the most enigmatic bases is Vostok Station. Located above the mysterious Lake Vostok, this Russian installation is surrounded by absolute secrecy. According to some sources, drilling under the station has revealed the presence of non-natural structures, which could be remnants of a lost civilization or an underground technological base. The fact that data on research in Lake Vostok is often classified and not released to the public has fueled speculation that the Russians have found something extraordinary and are studying it in secret.

There is also indirect evidence suggesting the presence of advanced underground structures at the poles. Magnetic and gravitational anomalies recorded in some areas, such as Wilkes Land and Queen Maud Land, could indicate the presence of artificial masses hidden beneath the ice. Some satellites have detected unusual electromagnetic emissions from underground, a phenomenon that could be associated with active technologies or underground experimental devices.

Some theories suggest that underground bases at the poles could be used to test new forms of advanced propulsion, studies on climate manipulation, and even research on space-time phenomena. If these hypotheses are correct, it means that governments are exploiting the isolation of the poles to pursue research that would be impossible elsewhere without attracting attention.

There are also rumors that large technology companies are collaborating with governments in these programs, developing new forms of energy and testing materials with properties not yet understood by conventional science. If revolutionary technologies are really being studied in the poles, those who control these discoveries could have an unprecedented advantage in global technological and military domination.

What is the ultimate purpose of these experiments?

Interest in the poles is not just a matter of scientific research or military strategy. If superpowers are investing enormous resources to keep certain activities at the poles secret, it means that the ultimate goal may be something much larger and more impactful for the future of humanity. But what?

One of the most likely purposes is the race for future technologies. If experiments on free energy, anti-gravitational propulsion systems or new forms of quantum communication are conducted in the poles, the first country to develop these technologies could dominate the world for centuries to come. Some sources suggest that the experiments could be linked to research on wormholes or space-time gateways, trying to figure out whether our planet has access points to alternate dimensions or cosmic shortcuts.

Another hypothesis is that the poles are being used for large-scale climate manipulation experiments. If climate control were to become a reality, it could be used as a strategic weapon to destabilize enemy nations, control global agricultural production, or alter weather conditions at certain points on the planet. If HAARP and other similar systems are already testing climate control, Antarctica could be the perfect laboratory for more advanced experiments away from the public eye.

Some independent researchers speculate that bases at the poles are being used to study gravitational and magnetic anomalies, trying to understand whether there are areas on Earth where the laws of physics behave differently. This could be related to the possibility that structures or devices of non-terrestrial origin, perhaps ancient remnants of forgotten technology or evidence of extraterrestrial visitations in the distant past, may be found at the poles.

Another theory suggests that secret bases at the poles may be intended to prepare the planet for a major future event, such as a global catastrophe or contact with nonhuman civilizations. If governments are aware of information that the public ignores-such as the possibility of a catastrophic change in Earth's climate, an inversion of the magnetic poles or an impending interaction with an outside force-they may be secretly preparing underground shelters and technologies to deal with the event.

One of the most disturbing scenarios is that the poles are where new forms of advanced weapons are being developed, such as directed energy weapons, seismic weapons, or devices that interfere with the Earth's magnetic field. If underground bases are indeed operational, it is possible that they are experimenting with technologies with effects that could change the very structure of reality as we know it.

If all this is true, the more important question is: When will these technologies be made public? Or will they remain secret to be used only by a small power elite?

The isolation and secrecy surrounding activities at the poles indicate that what is happening there is not meant to be shared with the rest of the world. The future of humanity may already be decided in the hidden depths of Antarctica and the Arctic, and the day these secrets are revealed could mark an unprecedented turning point for our civilization.

If these poles do indeed exist, it is possible that they hold the keys to a new global order, a new technological era, or even proof that our history and understanding of science are far more limited than we have always believed. Until then, the poles will remain the greatest mystery on the planet, an enigma that only time-or a sudden revelation-can unravel.

SECRET LAKES UNDER THE ICE AND THE MYSTERY OF LAKE VOSTOK

The mystery of subglacial lakes

Hidden under miles of ice, subglacial lakes represent one of Antarctica's most fascinating discoveries. These bodies of water, sealed by ice for millions of years, constitute extreme and isolated environments that could contain unique life forms and even provide clues as to how life might exist on other planets or icy moons in the Solar System. But why are these lakes so important and, more importantly, what could they really be hiding?

Subglacial lakes have been discovered thanks to advanced technologies such as ground-penetrating radar and satellite imagery. It is estimated that more than 400 exist under Antarctica, distributed in different regions of the continent. These lakes do not freeze despite extreme temperatures due to two main factors: geothermal heat from underground and the enormous pressure of the overlying ice, which prevents the water from solidifying.

The scientific importance of these lakes is immense. They represent pristine ecosystems that have been separated from the rest of the world for millions of years. Any life forms found in these waters could offer valuable information about biological adaptation to extreme conditions and could even provide clues as to how life might exist beneath the ice of Europa (Jupiter's moon) or Enceladus (Saturn's moon). However, some scientists believe that subglacial lakes could hold even more surprising secrets, perhaps related to anomalous geological phenomena or non-natural structures.

If we consider the possibility that Antarctica was once ice-free, these lakes may have harbored much more complex life forms in past ages, and some of them may have adapted to the isolation, developing unique characteristics. This opens up a number of fascinating questions: are there unknown life forms that have remained hidden under the ice for millions of years? If so, what kinds of organisms might they have evolved?

Some more speculative theories suggest that some subglacial lakes may contain traces of lost civilizations or even man-made structures buried by ice. This hypothesis is based on gravitational and magnetic anomalies detected in some Antarctic regions, which could indicate the presence of underground structures of unknown origin.

But the most enigmatic of all the subglacial lakes is undoubtedly Lake Vostok.

Lake Vostok: a time capsule sealed in ice

Lake Vostok is the largest subglacial lake in Antarctica, and it is also the one that has sparked the most speculation at the scientific and theoretical level. Located under about 4 km of ice, it has been isolated for at least 15 million years, making it a veritable natural laboratory for the study of extreme life and conditions that might exist on other worlds. But Lake Vostok may be hiding more than just ancient bacteria.

Its discovery dates back to the 1950s, when the Soviets established the Vostok base, located just above the lake. However, the true extent of the lake was only understood in the 1990s, thanks to satellite images and radar data, which revealed a body of water about 250 km long and 50 km wide, with a depth exceeding 1,000 meters.

What makes Lake Vostok so mysterious is the amount of scientific anomalies detected in its area. For example, data show that the lake's water is surprisingly warm compared to expectations, suggesting the possible presence of an underground heat source, perhaps related to geothermal activity, hydrothermal springs or yet unknown processes. In addition, studies of variations in the Earth's magnetic field have revealed a significant magnetic anomaly beneath the lake, which could indicate the presence of a large underground structure buried beneath the lake sediments.

In 2012, a team of Russian scientists managed to drill through the ice and reach the waters of Lake Vostok, but their expedition ended with a sudden cessation of communication and very vague official statements. Samples taken showed traces of unknown microorganisms, proving that the lake harbors unique life forms, but some researchers believe that the most extraordinary discoveries have never been revealed to the public.

According to unofficial sources, some samples reportedly contained traces of bacteria with uncatalogued DNA, raising questions about the possibility that never-before-seen life forms may exist in Lake Vostok, perhaps evolving separately from the rest of the planet.

But the real enigma concerns the aforementioned magnetic anomaly beneath the lake. Some independent researchers speculate that it could be the trace of an artificial structure, perhaps an ancient submerged city or technological installation buried for millions of years. If so, it would mean that Antarctica once hosted an advanced civilization, the ruins of which are now hidden under the ice.

Another theory links Lake Vostok to UFO sightings recorded in Antarctica, suggesting that it may be a point of interest for nonterrestrial activity. Some argue that the electromagnetic anomalies could be the result of still active technologies, perhaps left behind by a past civilization or even entities outside our planet.

If Lake Vostok really hides more than just microorganisms, why is information about it so tightly controlled? Why has Russia, which has exclusive control of the base, restricted access to drilling data? Is it possible that they have discovered something extraordinary and are trying to understand and exploit this knowledge before revealing it to the world?

The implications of such a discovery would be enormous. If an artificial structure exists beneath Lake Vostok, it would mean that Earth's history is much older and more complex than we have ever imagined. If unknown life forms exist, they could provide a bridge to understanding the origin of life itself and perhaps offer clues to other life forms in the universe.

The reality is that no one knows for sure what is really in Lake Vostok, but the interest that scientists and governments are showing in this region suggests that it may be hiding one of Earth's greatest secrets.

In the coming years, if new exploration is conducted and if the ice continues to melt, we may finally discover what lies beneath the depths of Lake Vostok and other subglacial lakes. The big question is: Will the truth be made public, or will it be kept hidden like so many other Antarctic mysteries?

Genetic mutations in polar fossils: unexplained anomalies

In recent decades, the gradual melting of polar ice has revealed fossils of ancient life forms that offer an unprecedented glimpse into Earth's biological history. However, some of these remains have shown unexplained genetic mutations, raising questions about their origin and the conditions that might have led to such alterations.

Among the most surprising discoveries are fossils of prehistoric animals found in Antarctica, a continent that millions of years ago was home to lush forests, lakes and a temperate climate. Scientists have identified remains of amphibians, dinosaurs and ancient mammals, some of which show DNA anomalies never found elsewhere in the world. Some of these fossils show unusual bone structures, variations in limb morphology, and genetic features that cannot be explained by current evolutionary theories.

A prime example is the discovery of ancient marine reptiles, such as ichthyosaurs and plesiosaurs, whose fossilized soft tissues have revealed evidence of mutations in their genes, suggesting that these animals may have undergone accelerated forms of evolution or extreme adaptations to unique conditions. Some scientists speculate that these anomalies may have been caused by radiation from underground, interactions with unknown chemicals, or even a currently unknown energy source.

Another enigmatic case concerns the discovery of fossil plants with anomalous genetic sequences. Fossil tree fragments with cell structures highly resistant to cold and pressure have been discovered in Antarctica, suggesting that some species may have adapted to extreme conditions long before the continent became an expanse of ice. This has led some researchers to speculate that life forms with extraordinary characteristics may still exist in isolated environments under the ice, such as subglacial lakes.

But the most controversial finding concerns some biological remains found near Lake Vostok, which appear to belong to an unknown organism, with DNA traces that do not correspond to any known species on Earth. If this discovery is confirmed, it would mean that there are life forms in Antarctica that are completely distinct from the rest of the planet, having evolved in isolation for millions of years.

These anomalies raise fascinating questions: could these organisms be the result of natural experiments in accelerated evolution? Or are there unknown forces at the poles that have influenced the development of life in ways we do not yet understand? Some theorize that the unstable magnetic field and gravitational anomalies recorded in Antarctica may have created a unique environment, fostering mutations and adaptations impossible elsewhere on Earth.

If further research were to confirm these genetic anomalies in polar fossils, our understanding of evolution could undergo an unprecedented revolution. Would we be faced with evidence that Antarctica hosted unique life forms, or perhaps confirmation of interactions with unknown forces that left traces in the genetic makeup of ancient organisms?

Possible presence of submerged structures under Lake Vostok?

One of the most fascinating aspects of Lake Vostok is the presence of geological and magnetic anomalies that suggest the possible existence of submerged structures beneath its surface. This has led many researchers to speculate that the lake may be hiding something much more mysterious than just natural formations.

Radar data obtained from exploration missions have shown unusual geometric structures in the sediments beneath Lake Vostok, some of which appear too regular to be natural formations. In particular, some satellite images have revealed symmetrical and linear patterns, suggesting the possibility of man-made constructions buried under the ice.

One of the most controversial theories suggests that Lake Vostok may be the site of an ancient submerged city, built millions of years ago before Antarctica was covered by ice. According to some researchers, the continent may have been home to an unknown civilization whose remains were sealed by ice and protected for millions of years. If this theory is true, Lake Vostok could represent one of the most extraordinary archaeological sites ever discovered, containing technologies and knowledge of a forgotten civilization.

Other hypotheses suggest that advanced technological structures, perhaps of non-terrestrial origin, may lie beneath the lake. Some independent scientists have theorized that the electromagnetic anomalies detected in the area may be signs of an energy source still active under the ice, perhaps an ancient device that continues to function despite the passage of millennia.

Another possibility is that Lake Vostok hides an underground base built by modern nations, used for secret experiments and research into unknown phenomena. Russia, which has sole control of the Vostok base, has restricted access to scientific data and suddenly stopped some of the deeper drilling, fueling suspicions that they have found more than just bacteria in the lake's waters.

In addition, some accounts speak of anomalous sightings in the Lake Vostok region, including strange lights in the sky and unexplained electromagnetic phenomena. If these reports are real, they could be related to technologies still active underground, or to presences operating in the region for unknown reasons.

If Lake Vostok does indeed contain submerged structures, this could completely change our understanding of Earth's history. It would mean that Antarctica has not always been an isolated and uninhabitable continent, but at one time may have hosted advanced civilizations, or been the point of contact with non-terrestrial entities.

The main problem remains the secrecy surrounding the research in Lake Vostok. If the nations involved have discovered something extraordinary, why restrict access to information? Is it possible that the world is not yet ready to know the truth about what lies beneath the ice of Antarctica?

As the polar ice caps melt and exploration technologies advance, the day may come when the mystery of Lake Vostok will finally be revealed. The real question is, will we be ready to accept the implications of what might be found there?

Why were some findings censored?

Discoveries related to Lake Vostok and other subglacial lakes in Antarctica are surrounded by an aura of secrecy and censorship, raising questions about what was really discovered and why some information was withheld from the public.

One of the main discrepancies in official reports concerns the results of drilling in Lake Vostok, which took place in 2012. Initially, Russian researchers claimed to have reached the lake's waters and taken sterile samples, but the information was released months late and with little explanation of the actual results. When some data were finally published, only the presence of extremophilic microorganisms was mentioned, ignoring rumors that genetic anomalies or traces of unknown materials were found in the samples.

Some independent scientists have speculated that the reason for censorship may be related to discoveries that challenge the current scientific paradigm. If organisms with completely unknown DNA were found under Lake Vostok, the implications would be enormous: it could be an evolutionary lineage separated by millions of years, or it could be life forms with such unusual characteristics that Earth's biology would have to be rewritten.

Another theory suggests that Lake Vostok may contain traces of an ancient civilization, perhaps buried under the ice millions of years ago. Some researchers have advanced the hypothesis that magnetic anomalies recorded in the area may be clues to the presence of man-made structures beneath the lake, which would explain why search operations were suddenly halted and the information classified.

Russia, which has sole control of the Vostok base, has maintained a policy of silence on the findings, limiting access to scientific data and preventing foreign researchers from conducting independent exploration. Some leaked documents suggest that Russian missions may have found something far more interesting than just bacteria, and that the government may have decided to study it in secret before revealing it to the world.

But censorship is not just about Russia. The United States and other powers have also imposed restrictions on research at the poles, banning access to certain areas and limiting the publication of data on anomalous phenomena. If elements are hidden in the poles that could rewrite Earth's history or suggest the existence of unknown intelligences, it is possible that governments are trying to control the narrative and protect sensitive information.

Some theorists argue that Lake Vostok may contain traces of non-terrestrial technologies, perhaps the wreckage of an ancient spacecraft that crashed millions of years ago or an underground base that is still active. Although there is no concrete evidence to support this hypothesis, the fact that the magnetic and gravitational anomalies in the region remain unexplained reinforces the idea that there is something beneath the lake that is beyond conventional science.

If these assumptions were true, censorship would be a way to avoid panic or to protect a discovery that could change the fate of humanity. The big question remains: when will the world finally know the truth about what was found in Lake Vostok?

Implications for space research and future missions

The study of subglacial lakes in Antarctica, and Lake Vostok in particular, has implications beyond our planet. Indeed, these extreme environments are perfect analogues to those we might find on Europa, the moon of Jupiter, and Enceladus, the moon of Saturn, both considered among the best candidates for hosting extraterrestrial life in our Solar System.

Europa and Enceladus are covered by thick ice caps, beneath which exist subglacial oceans kept liquid by the internal heat of their respective celestial bodies. If life has managed to survive for millions of years under Antarctic ice, it could do the same in these alien environments. Studying how extremophilic bacteria and other life forms have adapted in Lake Vostok may offer crucial clues about what to expect in future space missions.

Techniques developed to drill through Antarctic ice and collect biological samples can be used to explore icy moons. NASA and ESA are already planning missions to send cryogenic probes, or robots that can drill through the ice and send underwater drones to explore the waters beneath the surface. If we can prove that life can survive in extreme environments like Lake Vostok, we will have concrete evidence that the oceans of Europa and Enceladus could also harbor life forms, perhaps completely different from those on Earth.

In addition, the study of subglacial lakes may provide essential information for human colonization of other worlds. If we colonize Mars or the moons of Jupiter and Saturn in the future, we will need to learn how to extract water from ice and adapt to extreme conditions. Antarctica represents the best natural laboratory on Earth to develop the technologies needed for survival in space.

But the implications go beyond a simple search for alien life. If biological, structural or even technological anomalies exist in the subglacial lakes of Antarctica, their discovery could radically change our approach to space exploration. If we were to find life forms completely different from those we know, we would have to revise our understanding of biology and consider the possibility that life in the universe is far more common and varied than we think.

If, on the other hand, man-made structures are hidden beneath Lake Vostok, this would suggest that our planet has been visited in the past or that ancient civilizations developed advanced technologies before being swallowed by ice. This could change the way we look at space exploration and theories about the presence of intelligent life elsewhere in the universe.

The next space missions could then depend directly on the discoveries we make at Earth's poles. If we learn how to drill through ice, study isolated environments and search for traces of life in forbidding conditions, we can apply this knowledge to explore the icy moons of the Solar System and, perhaps, finally find proof that we are not alone in the universe.

But for this to be possible, it is essential that research at the poles be made transparent and accessible. If information about what has been discovered in Lake Vostok and other subglacial lakes remains secret, we risk missing a unique opportunity to understand our place in the universe.

Perhaps, the real question is not whether we will find life on Europa or Enceladus, but whether we are ready to discover the truth about what already exists, hidden beneath the ice of our planet.

SCIENTIFIC CENSORSHIP

HIDDEN DISCOVERIES ABOUT THE POLES

Why is some research on the poles being secreted?

In recent decades, discoveries made in the poles have often been surrounded by disturbing scientific censorship, raising questions about what is really being found in these remote regions and why such information is not being shared with the public. Although Antarctica and the Arctic are presented as areas of transparent and cooperative scientific research, many discoveries made in the polar regions seem to have been hidden, minimized, or deliberately covered up.

One of the main reasons for secrecy is the strategic value of polar discoveries. If nations involved in polar research, such as the United States, Russia, China, and Europe, have found evidence of new energy resources, revolutionary materials, or even unknown technologies, they may have chosen to keep this information secret to maintain a global strategic advantage. Antarctica, for example, may contain deposits of rare minerals or revolutionary energy resources that, if revealed, could trigger a race for their exploitation and alter the world's economic balance.

Another motivation behind the censorship is the possibility that anomalous life forms or traces of lost civilizations have been discovered at the poles. If organisms with never-before-seen genetic characteristics were found in subglacial lakes or under the ice, this would challenge current theories of evolution and the origin of life on Earth. If they were then the remains of an advanced civilization, their recognition could destabilize the current historical paradigm, leading to a radical change in the understanding of our own existence.

Magnetic and gravitational anomalies detected in parts of Antarctica suggest that there may be non-natural structures beneath the ice, perhaps remnants of an unknown civilization or even advanced technology. If these hypotheses were confirmed, governments would have every interest in studying these discoveries in secret, preventing such knowledge from entering the public domain before its full potential is understood and exploited.

Another aspect concerns the possible presence of anomalous phenomena at the poles, such as entrances to underground cavities, magnetic portals or unexplained electromagnetic phenomena. Some theories suggest that secret bases in the poles may be study centers on unknown energies or advanced interdimensional communication systems. If such phenomena are real, they could represent a revolutionary discovery for physics and human technology, but also a danger if misused.

Censorship could be linked to secret military projects. If new technologies, climate weapons, or advanced propulsion systems are being tested in the poles, it makes sense that information would be controlled and restricted to only a select few individuals. After all, the technological advantage that would come from controlling these discoveries could ensure military and geopolitical supremacy on a global scale.

All of these possibilities explain why much scientific research on the poles is classified, secreted or downgraded, and why only a fraction of the discoveries made are actually made public. But what happens to those scientists who have tried to reveal what they have found?

Scientists who have tried to speak out and have been silenced

Throughout history, several researchers who have conducted studies in the poles have revealed unexplained anomalies, but many of them have suffered mysterious consequences after making their findings public. Some have disappeared, others have seen their careers ruined, while still others have been silenced through political and academic pressure.

One of the most emblematic cases concerns a team of Russian scientists working at the Vostok base. After reaching the waters of the subglacial lake in 2012, some team members made informal statements about possible earth-shattering discoveries, including never-before-seen life forms and unexplained magnetic anomalies. However, soon after, some of them disappeared from the spotlight, while others avoided speaking publicly on the subject. This fueled speculation that their findings may have been censored by Russian authorities.

Another interesting case involves a group of U.S. scientists working on Antarctic research who reported that they had detected geometric structures under the ice in a restricted area. Shortly after submitting their preliminary data, they were fired or transferred to other projects, and their research was halted. Some claimed that the U.S. government allegedly imposed silence on them, preventing publication of their results and seizing the data they had collected.

Another well-known case is that of British researcher Dr. John R. Priscu, a leading expert on polar microbiology. Although he has conducted fundamental studies on Lake Vostok and other subglacial lakes, his public statements have always been highly scrutinized, and much of his most advanced research has never been made available to the public. This has led some to believe that the information he actually discovered was filtered by authorities before being released.

Some researchers involved in the study of magnetic anomalies at the poles also came under pressure not to disclose their data. One physicist working on studies of Hollow Earth and gravitational anomalies in Antarctica reported receiving threats to stop his research, and after a period of intense academic activity, he disappeared from the radar without making any more public statements.

Then there are testimonies from former members of military missions to the poles who have told of seeing anomalous flying objects, artificial structures buried under the ice, and secret activities conducted by highly specialized government teams. Some of these witnesses have been ridiculed or discredited, while others have simply stopped talking after receiving unofficial warnings.

If these accounts are true, it means that some of the discoveries made at the poles are so extraordinary that they should be kept secret. But then, what might have been found?

Could it be evidence that shows that Earth's climate has been manipulated for much longer than we think? Or man-made structures that suggest the presence of advanced civilizations in the distant past? Or even, of life forms so different from those known that they challenge all official biology?

The reality is that the polar zones remain one of the last unexplored boundaries of our planet, and governments seem to want to maintain strict control over what is discovered there. If the truth were made public, it could upset the way we see the world, and perhaps that is precisely why information is being filtered, hidden, or minimized.

The future may reveal many of these truths, but one thing is certain: as long as control over information remains in the hands of a few, the general public will only know a part of reality. How many other scientists have discovered secrets in the poles and been forced into silence? And how many of them will have the courage to speak out, defying the consequences?

Altered or deleted data: evidence of information manipulation?

One of the most disturbing aspects of research in the poles is the manipulation of scientific data, a practice that seems to have been adopted to avoid uncomfortable implications or to control the narrative about the most sensitive findings. Over the years, several independent scientists and analysts have reported anomalies in official data, indicating that some information has been deliberately deleted, altered, or hidden.

One of the best-known examples involves magnetic and gravitational anomalies detected in Antarctica, particularly in the Wilkes Land region. Early satellite data from NASA and ESA showed a strong gravitational anomaly in a large area of the continent, suggesting the presence of a mass buried under the ice, too dense to be a simple natural formation.

However, after some scientists began to speculate that it might be a buried structure or ancient impact crater with unusual features, the data began to disappear from public databases, and subsequent analyses published by space agencies seemed to downplay the issue, reducing the anomaly to simple natural geological effects.

Another emblematic case is related to satellite images of Antarctica, which often show blurred or completely obscured areas, especially in areas where geological anomalies are suspected. Several independent researchers have compared satellite images released at different times, noting that some previously visible regions have subsequently been covered by digital filters or graphic manipulations, preventing accurate analysis of what lies beneath the ice.

Another example involves studies conducted on subglacial lakes, particularly Lake Vostok. When Russia completed the drilling of the lake in 2012, some initial data indicated the presence of unknown microorganisms, with genetic traces that did not correspond to any known life form. However, soon after, official scientific reports were revised, and the results were downplayed, presenting the microorganisms as variants of already existing species. Some Russian scientists who had previously spoken of unique life forms suddenly stopped making statements, and information on the detailed analysis of the samples taken was secreted.

Another controversial incident involves the Amundsen-Scott base, located at the South Pole. In 2016, some researchers reported strange electromagnetic disturbances recorded in the vicinity of the base, suggesting that they might be the result of testing advanced technologies or interactions with local geophysical anomalies. However, shortly after the first data were published, the documents were withdrawn from official databases, and publicly accessible information made no further mention of the anomalies found.

The erasure or modification of data not only affects the most recent discoveries, but also extends to historical maps and geological records. Some ancient maps, such as the Piri Reis map, show Antarctica devoid of ice, suggesting that someone in a remote era may have had advanced geographic knowledge of the continent before its glaciation. However, any attempt to seriously analyze these documents in academia is quickly discredited, and many historians prefer not to delve into the subject to avoid being labeled "pseudoscientists".

If information about the poles is being manipulated or censored, it means that what is there is of enormous strategic, scientific or historical importance. The fact that some data are removed, edited or downplayed suggests that behind the facade of normal scientific research lies something that governments do not want the world to know.

What lies behind the secret about geological anomalies?

Geological anomalies detected at the poles represent one of the most intriguing enigmas in modern science. Although they are officially attributed to natural causes, their characteristics and the reaction of scientific institutions suggest that there is something much more complex at play.

One of the most mysterious aspects concerns the magnetic and gravitational anomalies detected in different parts of Antarctica and the Arctic. In particular, Wilkes Land, a large region in East Antarctica, has shown a huge gravitational anomaly under the ice, which some scientists speculate may be an impact crater formed millions of years ago. However, others believe it could be a buried man-made structure, perhaps belonging to an ancient civilization or an advanced technological installation.

Another intriguing case is that of Queen Maud Land, where regular geometric formations have been detected under the ice. Some researchers suggest that they may be the remains of constructions buried for millennia, perhaps belonging to a preglacial civilization that once inhabited Antarctica. Satellite images showing these structures have often been edited or obscured, fueling suspicions that authorities want to prevent the public from analyzing these anomalies.

Lake Vostok is also at the center of one of the largest geological anomalies on the planet. In addition to its incredible depth and millennia-old isolation, geophysical studies have detected a strong magnetic anomaly in the area below the lake. Some scientists speculate that this may be caused by an underground energy source, such as a magma chamber, while others suggest that it could be an artificial structure with electromagnetic properties.

Other geological anomalies involve underground cavities discovered at the poles. Radar images have revealed huge compartments under the ice, some of which are too large to be explained as simple natural caverns. Some independent researchers believe these cavities could be hidden underground bases, ancient buried cities or entrances to unknown tunnel networks, possibly linked to the controversial Hollow Earth theory.

Antarctica is home to mysterious craters whose origin is still debated. One of the most debated is the Wilkes Land crater, which has a diameter of nearly 500 km and is considered one of the largest impact structures on the planet. However, the absence of obvious signs of impact and the presence of electromagnetic anomalies raise suspicions that it may be something other than a simple meteor crater.

If these anomalies were the result of interactions with unknown technologies, remnants of ancient civilizations, or even geological phenomena never before observed, their discovery could radically change our view of history and geophysics.

The fact that scientific institutions do not delve into these mysteries or, even worse, censor the data, suggests that what lies beneath the polar ice should not be revealed to the world. If one day this information is released, we may be facing one of the greatest revelations in human history. The question is, who is in control of this information and why is it being hidden?

Who controls access to research in the poles?

Access to the polar regions, officially intended for scientific research and international cooperation, is actually tightly controlled by a small group of governments, scientific institutions and military bodies. Although the Antarctic Treaty states that the continent should remain an area dedicated to science and peace, in practice there are numerous restrictions that prevent independent expeditions from freely exploring the area.

The United States, Russia, China, the United Kingdom and other major powers have control over major research bases and determine who can access the most sensitive areas. Many of these bases, such as Amundsen-Scott, Vostok or Neumayer III, are located at strategic points, often near areas where unexplained geological and magnetic anomalies have been detected. Access to these areas is restricted to authorized personnel only, and independent expeditions must undergo strict security and approval protocols, which effectively makes it almost impossible to explore the continent without permission from the authorities.

NASA and ESA, which officially study the poles to better understand Earth's climatic conditions and develop technologies for future space exploration, work with governments to monitor activities in Antarctica and the Arctic. Satellites used for land mapping have often shown censored areas or altered images, suggesting that some areas are being deliberately kept secret. If the poles were not hiding anything important, why should there be areas inaccessible even to independent scientists?

National security agencies, such as the CIA, the Russian FSB and the Chinese Ministry of Security, also closely monitor activities in the poles. Controlling access to certain information could be motivated by fear of revolutionary discoveries being released to the public, or by a desire to exploit exclusive knowledge for the benefit of a single nation or a narrow elite. In some cases, explorers and scientists who have attempted to conduct independent research in the poles have received threats, warnings, or have been blocked by insurmountable bureaucratic obstacles.

Multinational corporations could also play a role in this system of control. If strategic natural resources such as rare earths, fossil fuels, or materials with unique properties exist in the poles, large corporations could be involved in secret agreements with governments to prevent access to these resources until they can be exploited without public opposition.

If control over access to the poles is so tight, it means that what is found there is critically important. The question is: Is this control justified to protect nature and global security, or does it serve to keep secrets that could shock the whole world?

The research that could rewrite our history

If the poles are so closely guarded, it is because discoveries made there could radically change our understanding of Earth and human history. There are clues that suggest that the ice of Antarctica and the Arctic may conceal unimaginable truths capable of rewriting everything we know about the origins of civilization and the geological processes that shaped the planet.

If radar images and magnetic anomalies detected in Antarctica indicate the presence of buried man-made structures, it means that the continent may have hosted an advanced civilization in the distant past, before it was covered by ice. This possibility is supported by ancient maps, such as the Piri Reis map, which show Antarctica without ice in incredibly accurate geographic detail. If these maps are based on pre-existing knowledge, it means that someone thousands of years ago had already explored the continent and knew its topography.

Discoveries in subglacial lakes, such as Lake Vostok, suggest that ecosystems completely separate from the rest of the world may exist under the ice, perhaps containing life forms never seen before, with DNA unlike any other known species. If it were proven that life can survive under such extreme conditions, it would open up the possibility that other icy worlds in the Solar System could also harbor living things, changing our conception of the universe forever.

But there are also even more controversial hypotheses. If materials with extraordinary properties, such as metal alloys with unknown capabilities or structures showing signs of artificial workmanship, have been found at the poles, it could mean that ancient civilizations or even non-terrestrial intelligences played a role in the development of the planet's history. This would explain why some discoveries are immediately classified and why information is filtered before being made public.

Another revolutionary aspect concerns the gravitational and magnetic anomalies recorded in parts of Antarctica. If these anomalies indicate the presence of unknown energy sources or underground structures, it means that the poles could be the location of advanced technology buried under the ice. If these technologies were recovered and studied, they could lead to an evolutionary leap in science and technology, but they could also be used for military purposes or global control, thus justifying the secrecy surrounding them.

If all these assumptions are true, it means that human history is much more complex than we have been taught. We may discover that advanced civilizations lived on Earth long before known civilizations, or that our own species has different origins than we think. We may also be confronted with evidence of contact with alien entities or knowledge that modern science cannot yet explain.

Control over information about the poles is a clear signal that something extraordinary has been found, and that governments and institutions do not want these truths to emerge too quickly. Perhaps because they fear that such a radical change in the way we see the world could destabilize society, or perhaps because they want to maintain a monopoly on discoveries that could give unimaginable power to those who control them.

If one day these discoveries are made public, humanity may be forced to completely revise its history and its role in the universe. The big question is: How long will it be before the truth is revealed? And who will decide when the world is ready to know it?

THE HIDDEN AGENDA OF SPACE AND MILITARY AGENCIES

NASA and polar missions: a suspect interest?

In recent decades, NASA has shown increasing interest in the polar regions, conducting numerous monitoring and research missions to Antarctica and the Arctic. Officially, these operations are aimed at studying climate, atmospheric variations, and extreme geophysical conditions. However, several elements suggest that this interest may conceal much deeper and more secretive purposes.

One of the main reasons for NASA's presence at the poles concerns the parallels between the extreme conditions of Antarctica and extraterrestrial environments. The icy moons of Jupiter and Saturn, such as Europa and Enceladus, are covered by thick ice caps under which are liquid oceans, very similar to the subglacial lakes discovered under Antarctic ice, such as Lake Vostok. Studying these terrestrial environments allows NASA to simulate future missions, but it could also reveal unique and unknown life forms, potentially similar to those that might exist in space.

One curious element is NASA's involvement in polar ice radar exploration missions, some of them classified or conducted in collaboration with national security agencies. If their purpose was simply scientific, why are these projects often shrouded in strict secrecy? Could it be that NASA has discovered something extraordinary at the poles, and the data are carefully filtered before being made public?

Satellite images provided by NASA often show inexplicably blurred or hidden areas, particularly in parts of Antarctica where magnetic and gravitational anomalies have been detected. Some independent researchers have pointed out that the most detailed images of the poles are published only partially or with strange alterations, suggesting that something is being deliberately concealed from the public.

But the link between NASA and the poles may go beyond just terrestrial exploration. Some theories suggest that the poles may contain advanced technologies, perhaps of non-terrestrial origin, and that NASA, along with other space agencies, is secretly studying these discoveries to develop new technologies applicable to space exploration. If fragments of materials with anomalous properties or remnants of unknown structures have been found in the poles, these could represent an invaluable technological and scientific treasure trove, and would explain the reason for strict control over such areas.

Some leaked information suggests that NASA's polar missions may have links to secret projects on advanced propulsion and the study of gravitational anomalies, which opens the possibility that the agency is testing experimental concepts of space travel or manipulation of traditional physics. If this research is taking place at the poles, it is likely that access to data will be tightly controlled to prevent other nations or the public from discovering the true extent of discoveries made in these remote regions.

NASA's interest in the poles, then, may not just be a matter of environmental research, but a piece of a much larger project that could involve the study of unknown life forms, advanced technologies, and physical anomalies that challenge our understanding of modern science.

The Pentagon and the constant monitoring of the polar regions

If NASA is in charge of scientific research at the poles, the Pentagon maintains strict and constant control over these regions, investing significant resources in monitoring and military operations. Officially, the U.S. military's interest in Antarctica and the Arctic is tied to defense strategies, national security, and global surveillance operations, but some evidence suggests that military involvement in the poles is far more complex than is stated.

One of the main reasons for this control is the strategic position of the poles in global security. The Arctic, in particular, has become a contested area among major world powers, with Russia, the United States and China strengthening their presence in this region. However, Antarctica, while officially a demilitarized zone under the Antarctic Treaty, is guarded by sophisticated military systems that regulate access. If there are no obvious threats, why does the Pentagon maintain such tight control over who can access certain areas?

Another reason for military monitoring could be the presence of anomalous phenomena at the poles. Several classified documents indicate that unidentified flying objects have been sighted in these regions, often described as capable of maneuvers impossible for conventional technologies. Some independent researchers speculate that the poles may host secret bases for advanced vehicle experimentation, perhaps related to reverse engineering projects of non-terrestrial technologies.

Antarctica is also where powerful electromagnetic emissions have been detected, some of which interfere with satellites and global communications. The Pentagon, aware of these anomalies, has initiated research projects to understand and possibly exploit these emissions, which could have applications in the military, such as electromagnetic weapons, advanced communication systems or space-time distortion technologies.

Military bases in polar regions, while officially dedicated to scientific research, are often equipped with infrastructure and surveillance systems typical of highly classified military installations. The presence of advanced radar, infrared detection systems, and experimental technologies suggests that the Pentagon is using the poles not only for defensive purposes, but to test cutting-edge technologies that may be too risky or too advanced to be tested in other parts of the world.

Another suspicious element is the fact that information about military activities in the poles is heavily censored, and any attempt at independent investigation is hampered by bureaucratic barriers and restrictions imposed by governments. If there is nothing to hide, why is access to certain areas of Antarctica and the Arctic restricted only to specifically authorized personnel?

Some theorize that the Pentagon is monitoring the poles for even more extraordinary reasons, such as the possible presence of unknown technologies buried under the ice, perhaps inherited from a prehistoric era or left behind by entities outside the Earth. If there are underground installations of unknown origin, the Pentagon would have every interest in studying and protecting these discoveries, preventing them from falling into the hands of other nations or being released to the public.

Intense military and scientific activity at the poles suggests that these regions are much more than just icy expanses. If NASA and the Pentagon are investing so many resources to monitor and control these areas, it means that something incredibly important lies at the poles, something the world is not yet ready to know. Perhaps the real purpose of these operations is not just to explore and monitor, but to prepare for a revelation that could forever change the way we view history and the future of humanity.

The role of ESA and other international space agencies

The interest of international space agencies in the Earth's poles is a phenomenon that has intensified in recent decades, with increasing investments by ESA (European Space Agency), NASA, Roscosmos, CNSA (China) and JAXA (Japan). Officially, these entities claim to study the polar regions to understand climate change, develop exploration technologies and simulate conditions in extraterrestrial environments. However, some of the operations conducted in Antarctica and the Arctic suggest that the space agencies interest may be hiding far more complex and secretive goals.

ESA, for example, is involved in a number of satellite monitoring projects at the poles, using advanced instruments such as the Copernicus program's Sentinel satellites and the CryoSat-2 satellite, whose job is to map ice changes and detect anomalies in the subsurface. Although the stated focus is climate change, some radar images have revealed unexplained geometric structures under the Antarctic ice, leading some independent researchers to speculate that ESA may have discovered something unnatural hidden under the polar ice cap.

Roscosmos, the Russian space agency, has also invested in polar missions, often working closely with Russian military bases located in Antarctica. Vostok Station, located above the mysterious Lake Vostok, is one of the areas most studied by Roscosmos, which has used advanced sensors to detect anomalous magnetic variations and possible energy emissions from underground. Russian interest in this area suggests that the space agency may be aware of extraordinary phenomena, perhaps related to a technological discovery hidden beneath the ice.

CNSA, China's space agency, has recently stepped up its operations in the poles, investing in research bases, advanced drilling technologies and radar mapping missions. China seems particularly interested in the possibility that Antarctica may contain valuable resources or strategic information to be exploited for its own space program. If the Chinese government is investing heavily in polar research, it is likely that it has discovered something to justify such investments.

JAXA (Japan Space Agency) has also shown unusual interest in the poles, with missions such as the GCOM-W satellite to monitor atmospheric and magnetic anomalies at the poles, and the Hayabusa project, which studies the properties of Antarctic ice to compare with materials found on asteroids. Japan's focus on the unique properties of polar ice could indicate that Antarctica contains rare elements or unknown compounds that could have applications in space.

All of these agencies work closely with governments and military forces, which raises questions about the true purpose of their missions. If research in the poles were really limited to climatology, why is there a strong component of secrecy around certain studies and results? Could it be that space agencies have found something much more important, something that could radically change our understanding of science, geology and even the history of our planet?

Could space missions be linked to what lurks in the poles?

One of the most intriguing aspects of the study of the polar regions concerns the possible connection between space exploration and anomalies detected at the poles. Several clues suggest that space agencies may be interested in the poles not only for scientific reasons, but because these regions contain secrets that could be directly related to the universe and advanced technology.

One of the key elements of this connection is the similarity between the conditions of Earth's poles and those of other celestial bodies. Antarctica is considered the closest environment to that of the Solar System's icy moons, such as Europa (Jupiter's moon) and Enceladus (Saturn's moon), both of which are covered by thick ice caps under which liquid oceans are found. If unique and unknown life forms are found in the subglacial lakes of Antarctica, this would increase the likelihood of finding living organisms on these celestial bodies, which would justify the enormous investment of space agencies in polar research.

But the connection between the poles and space may go beyond simple biology. Some magnetic and gravitational anomalies detected at the poles have been compared with similar phenomena observed on Mars and the Moon, suggesting that there are as yet unknown geophysical processes linking our planet to other celestial bodies. If the poles contain anomalous structures or unknown energy sources, it is possible that space agencies are trying to understand how they work in order to apply them to future space missions.

Another theory suggests that the poles could conceal advanced technologies, perhaps of non-Earth origin, and that space agencies are involved in studying these technologies to develop new propulsion systems, alternative energy sources or interstellar communication methods. If artificial structures are found beneath the ice, their analysis could provide clues to advanced civilizations that may have had contact with Earth in ancient times.

Some theorists speculate that Antarctica might even host a space-time portal or a zone of gravitational instability, which would explain the interest of space agencies in constantly monitoring the region. If phenomena that affect time and space exist at the poles, they could be a key to understanding interstellar travel and gravitational distortions, concepts that are still only theoretical today but may have already been observed in practice.

The Arctic also has unexplained anomalies, with unexplained radio signals and magnetic disturbances that have led some theories to suggest that there may be hidden structures under the ice or secret experimental activities going on. If these anomalies are related to electromagnetic wave experiments or testing of advanced technologies, it is possible that space agencies are trying to replicate these phenomena for future applications in space.

If there really are secret underground bases at the poles that house unknown technologies or materials of non-terrestrial origin, then the link between space exploration and polar research becomes even more apparent. Space agencies may be searching for answers that could radically change our understanding of the universe and our place in it.

If all this is true, then space missions may not simply be intended to search for life on other planets, but may be related to the recovery and study of knowledge that has already been found here on Earth, buried under the millennia-old ice at the poles. The question to ask is how long will it be before this information is made public? Or will they remain forever a secret in the hands of a few scientific and governmental elites?

What are satellites really looking for at the poles?

The Earth's polar ice caps are constantly monitored by a network of advanced satellites, officially to study climate change, ice change and weather extremes. However, the intensive use of sophisticated instruments such as ground-penetrating radar, advanced spectrometers, and electromagnetic anomaly detectors suggests that these satellites may be looking for more than just environmental data.

One of the most suspicious elements concerns the way some areas of Antarctica are censored in satellite images. Some independent researchers have noted that specific areas of the polar cap, particularly those where magnetic or gravitational anomalies have been detected, are often obscured or shown at much lower resolution than other areas of the planet. If the polar regions were free of secrets, why would there be a need to hide certain images or alter publicly visible data?

A key aspect concerns the monitoring of subglacial lakes, such as Lake Vostok, the study of which has been intensified in recent years through satellites equipped with instruments capable of measuring thermal variations and geophysical anomalies. Some data collected have shown mysterious heat emissions from beneath the ice, suggesting the possible presence of unknown energy sources or phenomena not yet explained by official science. If there are indeed thermal and magnetic anomalies in the Antarctic subsurface, it could mean that something artificial or extraordinary is hiding under the ice.

In addition, some satellites have been equipped with electromagnetic emission detectors, instruments used to intercept anomalous radio waves or signals of unidentified origin. This has led some scholars to speculate that satellites may be used to detect communications or signals from underground facilities, perhaps secret bases or even non-terrestrial technologies operating under the ice. If the government and space agencies are looking for intelligent signals at the poles, it means they may have already detected something unexpected and are trying to analyze it with increasingly advanced instruments.

Another area of interest is the monitoring of gravitational anomalies at the poles, with missions such as GRACE (Gravity Recovery and Climate Experiment) detecting unexplained variations in Earth's gravitational field in some polar regions. Some theorists suggest that these anomalies could be related to the presence of giant underground cavities or man-made structures buried under the ice, and satellites would be trying to map and understand these phenomena.

The growing interest of satellites in ice movements and structural changes in the polar ice sheet could be linked to a strategy to predict the emergence of buried structures as the ice melts. If climate change is slowly revealing what is hidden beneath Antarctica, governments and space agencies may already be aware of extraordinary secrets and are closely monitoring when and how they might come to light.

If these satellites are looking for more than just climate change, it means that the polar regions could contain crucial information that could rewrite our understanding of the Earth and its history. But the real question is, will this information ever be made public, or will it remain under strict government and military control?

The future of research in the poles: new discoveries or more censorship?

The future of research in the poles seems to be torn between two possible opposing scenarios: on the one hand, technological advancement could lead to breakthrough discoveries that could finally be shared with the world, but on the other, increasing secrecy and government control over information could make access to the truth increasingly difficult.

As ice continues to melt, it is inevitable that new areas of Antarctica and the Arctic will be exposed for the first time in thousands of years. If remains of ancient civilizations, man-made structures, or unexplained geological anomalies are found under the ice, these secrets may emerge naturally over the next century, forcing governments to decide how to handle the information. Will they be revealed in a gradual way to accustom the public to a new reality, or will attempts be made to cover it up to maintain control over the discoveries?

On the other hand, research at the poles is increasingly under the control of government agencies, the military and private corporations, raising fears that the level of censorship may increase even more in the coming years. If pole research reveals information that is too shocking-such as confirmation of buried advanced technologies, evidence of contact with non-terrestrial intelligences, or data that could change our view of history-it is likely that governments will intensify secrecy and restrict access to information even more.

A recent example of this strategy is the gradual increase in restrictions on independent missions to Antarctica, with stricter laws preventing private individuals and small research groups from freely exploring certain areas. If the only access to the poles is controlled by major powers and multinational corporations, it means that any discovery will be filtered and made public only if it is deemed acceptable for information control.

The role of space agencies in polar research could also become even more ambiguous, with increasingly sophisticated projects studying the polar regions without ever fully disclosing the data they collect. If NASA, ESA and other agencies are monitoring the poles for phenomena that might have implications for our understanding of the universe, it is possible that something extraordinary has already been discovered but not yet revealed.

The more troubling question is whether this information will ever be made public. If the discoveries in the poles are so extraordinary that they change our perception of history and science, governments may choose to release the information only in a controlled manner, gradually preparing the public for a new reality. However, if the discoveries in the poles are about advanced technologies, lost civilizations, or past catastrophic events that could be repeated, then censorship is likely to become even more stringent.

In the end, the future of research at the poles will depend on which faction is in control of the information: will scientific transparency be chosen, allowing humanity to know the truth, or will the politics of secrecy prevail, keeping the world in ignorance about what lies beneath the ice?

If history has taught us anything, it is that the most extraordinary information has always been protected by those in power. But as exploration technologies advance and the number of independent researchers questioning these anomalies increases, the truth may slip through the cracks sooner than governments expect.

When that happens, the world may be faced with one of the most incredible revelations in human history. The question is, will we be ready to accept it?

COULD WE SURVIVE SUCH A DISCOVERY?

The burden of truth: how would humanity respond?

If it were to be officially announced tomorrow that a cryptoterrestrial civilization has been discovered under the ice of Antarctica, or that evidence of an unknown presence exists at the poles, humanity would be faced with one of the greatest revelations in history. But how would we react to such a shocking truth?

At the individual level, the reaction would vary according to personality, upbringing and ability to adapt to new realities. For some, the discovery would be an extraordinary opening of the mind, a confirmation that human history is far more complex than we have been taught. These people would embrace the new knowledge with enthusiasm, wanting to know more and radically rethinking their worldview. However, for others, the revelation would be traumatic and destabilizing. The idea that an intelligent life form might exist alongside us, invisible for centuries, or that official history has deliberately hidden certain truths, could generate anxiety, fear and resistance to change.

The phenomenon of cognitive dissonance plays a key role in this dynamic. When information deeply contradicts what one has always believed, the human brain tends to reject it or reinterpret it in a more reassuring way. Many would prefer to deny the finding, believing it to be manipulation, conspiracy, or hoax. This reaction would not only be limited to the most skeptical people, but could also occur among scientists and scholars who are used to a worldview that such a discovery could destroy.

At the collective level, society's reaction would depend on how the discovery would be publicized. If the announcement were handled gradually, preparing the public through studies, documentaries and debates, the transition to a new understanding of reality could be smoother and less traumatic. However, if the revelation were sudden, without adequate preparation, it could trigger panic, confusion and distrust of authorities.

Reactions could also vary according to cultures and religious beliefs. Some traditions might see the discovery as confirmation of ancient legends, while others might interpret it as a threat to the foundations of their faith. It is possible that some groups see this revelation as an eschatological signal or evidence of the intervention of higher forces.

The economic and geopolitical spheres would also be significantly shaken. If unknown technologies were found in the poles, control of these discoveries could redefine the global balance, with a new race among world powers to exploit these resources. If the discovery challenged current scientific theories, a huge ideological battle would open between those who want to accept the new reality and those who want to maintain the status quo.

In the end, acceptance of the truth would depend on time and society's ability to adapt. History has shown that great discoveries-from heliocentrism to evolution-have always met strong initial resistance, but over time have become integrated into common thinking. The difference is that this discovery could completely redefine what it means to be human and our role in the universe.

The reaction of institutions: acceptance or cover-up?

If a discovery in the poles revealed the existence of a cryptoterrestrial civilization or phenomena that cannot be explained by current science, governments, academic institutions and religions would be faced with a crucial choice: accept the truth or cover it up to protect control over the masses?

History teaches us that major institutions tend to react with distrust when faced with discoveries that challenge their power and authority. If it were proven that Earth hosted advanced civilizations in the distant past, many aspects of official history would have to be rewritten, with devastating consequences for academics and governments that for centuries have defended an accurate narrative of our origin and evolution.

Governments, in particular, could adopt several strategies to handle a disclosure of this magnitude. The first option would be to control the information, releasing only part of the truth and filtering out the most sensitive details. They could disclose the discovery gradually, masking it as a simple scientific advance without deeper implications. This would allow them to prepare public opinion without generating panic or social uprisings.

Another possibility is for governments to completely cover up the discovery, using tools such as disinformation, ridicule and censorship to maintain control of the narrative. They could discredit independent sources, label the discovery a conspiracy theory, and even create false versions of the truth to confuse the public. If the discovery had significant technological implications, world powers would have every interest in secretly studying what was found at the poles without revealing it to the rest of the world.

Religious institutions would play a crucial role in managing revelation. Some might reinterpret the discovery in light of their doctrines, seeking to incorporate it into a new religious narrative. However, others might see it as a threat, especially if the discovery challenged the basis of the beliefs on which they were founded. Internal divisions might emerge, with some leaders welcoming the new knowledge and others categorically rejecting it.

Academia would also find itself in a difficult position. If the discovery at the poles disproved established theories about human history and Earth geology, many experts and scholars would risk losing credibility. Academia might initially resist the new knowledge, trying to maintain its authority and control over the information, but over time, if the evidence were irrefutable, it would be forced to revise its positions.

On a geopolitical level, the most powerful nations could compete for control of discoveries made at the poles. If the discovery involved an advanced technology, an unknown energy, or a new form of communication, a covert war between the superpowers could be triggered to grab the strategic advantage. This could lead to new alliances, covert conflicts and unprecedented scientific espionage.

The reaction of institutions would depend on how much the discovery would affect their power and control over society. If it was considered too destabilizing, there would be a massive attempt at a cover-up or manipulation of the narrative. If, on the other hand, the revelation were handled intelligently and strategically, it could mark the beginning of a new era for humanity, prompting us to redefine our identity and our role in the cosmos.

But the real question is: Is there a limit to the control of information? Or will the day come when the truth is so obvious that it can no longer be hidden?

Collapse of certainty and impact on religious beliefs

If the discovery of a cryptoterrestrial civilization at the poles is confirmed, the implications for the world's major religions would be immense. For millennia, humanity has built its spiritual beliefs around the idea of being the dominant and sole species in the divine plane. However, if evidence emerged that there are or have been intelligent beings coexisting with us, religions would be forced to reevaluate their fundamental dogmas.

Some religious traditions might see the discovery as a confirmation of their own scriptures. Stories of beings coming from the sky, deities inhabiting the underground, or entities communicating with humanity could be reinterpreted in light of the new evidence. For example, in Christianity and Judaism there are references to mysterious beings such as the Nephilim, while in Islam there is talk of the Jinn, creatures that would live in another dimension parallel to our own. If cryptoterrestrials were real, they could be likened to these spiritual figures, allowing religions to maintain their role without a total collapse of belief.

However, other religious currents might perceive this discovery as a direct threat. If cryptoterrestrial beings possessed a history older than ours, superior technology or an understanding of reality different from ours, the very concept of humanity as the center of the cosmos would be challenged. This could lead to crises of faith, internal reforms or even outright rejection of the discovery, labeling it a mystification or deception orchestrated by dark forces.

Another critical issue concerns the human creation narrative. Whether cryptoterrestrials are a parallel species, a different evolutionary branch or beings pre-existing humanity, many religions should reconsider the concept of Adam and Eve, divine creation and man's place in the universe. Religions that preach that mankind was created in God's image may be faced with the question: were these beings also created by God? Or is there another plan of creation that has always been hidden?

The concept of cosmic history and interconnectedness among civilizations could change dramatically. If the discovery reveals that cryptoterrestrial beings have had contact with humans in ages past, it could mean that many of our religious traditions have been influenced by these interactions, creating a new interpretation of sacred texts based on the encounter between civilizations rather than human experience alone.

If this revelation were accepted, religions could adapt and reinterpret their view of the universe, or they could face a profound crisis that would lead to a fragmentation of faith. Either way, the impact would be so profound as to mark the beginning of a new era in human spirituality.

Psychological effects on a global scale: between panic and wonder

A revelation of this magnitude would not only affect religious institutions and beliefs, but would also have a devastating emotional and psychological impact on the entire world population. Human reaction to a shocking discovery can range from wonder to disbelief to panic and outright rejection of reality.

One of the first effects that would occur would be collective panic. When certainties are suddenly challenged, the human mind tends to react with fear and confusion. The most psychologically vulnerable people might experience anxiety, paranoia, and post-traumatic disorders, especially if the discovery were presented as a threat or risk to human survival.

Distrust of authorities would also reach extreme levels. If governments and institutions have hidden information about a possible cryptoterrestrial civilization for decades, trust in institutions could suddenly collapse, leading to social uprisings, protests, and a political destabilization. Some groups might interpret the discovery as a deception orchestrated by governments to manipulate the population, while others might embrace more extreme conspiracy theories, believing that cryptoterrestrial beings have already influenced our development and continue to do so in the shadows.

Another significant psychological effect would be the redefinition of reality itself. If it were shown that the story we know is incomplete or manipulated, people might feel disoriented, without reference points. Many might react with a sense of existential bewilderment, wondering who we really are and what our role is in the universe.

However, alongside the fear and panic, there would also be a wave of wonder and excitement. For many people, the discovery of cryptoterrestrial beings would be confirmation that the universe is much larger and more complex than we have always believed. Artists, philosophers and scientists could embrace the new reality with enthusiasm, trying to interpret the implications of the discovery through art, philosophy and technology. Humanity could be pushed to overcome its limitations and seek a deeper connection with the universe.

Scientific research would also undergo an unprecedented acceleration. If a civilization hidden in the poles were revealed, scientists around the world would mobilize to study its biology, technology, and culture, trying to understand how these beings evolved, what knowledge they developed, and whether they could offer us a new way of seeing reality.

Psychological reactions would then be highly polarized. Some would embrace discovery with curiosity and a desire to learn, seeing it as an opportunity to expand the boundaries of knowledge. Others, however, would fall into a state of culture and cognitive shock, unable to accept a reality that contradicts everything they have always believed.

The impact on children and the younger generation would be particularly interesting. Growing up with the knowledge that we were never alone, they could develop a more open mind and a broader understanding of reality.

New forms of thought, art and expression could emerge, based on a more cosmic and interconnected view of the world.

In the end, the overall reaction would depend on how the discovery would be communicated. If it were handled with transparency, education and psychological preparation, humanity could accept this new reality with maturity and open-mindedness. If, on the other hand, the revelation were chaotic and sudden, the risks of panic, social unrest and mass existential crisis would be enormous.

The big question is: Will we be ready to face a discovery that would change our perception of reality forever? Or will we cling to our old certainties, refusing to accept the new truth?

Political and geopolitical consequences of the discovery

If the existence of a cryptoterrestrial civilization in the poles were revealed, global geopolitics would change radically and irreversibly. The major world powers - the United States, Russia, China and the European Union - would not leave a discovery of this magnitude to chance. Rather, they would seek to control it, manipulate it and use it to their own advantage.

The first immediate effect would be a race to access and dominate the polar regions. If an advanced civilization existed or still exists under the ice, then the most powerful nations would fight to be the first to study it and exploit its knowledge. Antarctica, currently protected by the Antarctic Treaty, could become a geopolitical battleground with secret missions to recover artifacts, unknown technologies or even contact with intelligent beings.

This discovery could justify new strategies of control and social manipulation. If it became known that the official story was altered or censored to conceal the existence of these beings, people's trust in governments would suddenly collapse. To prevent riots and social instability, world leaders could control information even more tightly, using the media to filter news and steer public opinion. They could even invent false enemies or global threats to unite humanity under one control and prevent chaos.

Some governments might exploit the discovery to justify an expansion of their own power. If a cryptoterrestrial civilization is revealed, powerful nations could proclaim themselves "protectors of the human race", justifying militarizations, new alliances and increased technological control over the population. They could also use the discovery to intensify surveillance, monitoring of citizens and control of communications, under the guise of protecting humanity from a possible destabilizing social impact.

If the cryptoterrestrial civilization possesses advanced technologies, whoever gets them first could become the dominant nation of the future. The discovery of new energy sources, materials with extraordinary properties or unknown communication systems could give a superpower an unprecedented scientific and military advantage. This could lead to new international tensions, with nations accusing each other of hiding secret technologies and knowledge.

Moreover, if the discovery challenged the very foundations of human history and evolution, a global movement to rewrite our collective identity might arise. Some nations might embrace this new truth, while others might resist, deny or attempt to cover up the deeper implications to maintain their status quo.

If the cryptoterrestrial civilization were still active and aware of our presence, world politics would face an unprecedented dilemma: negotiate, hide or fight? The possibility of dialogue, knowledge exchange or conflict could redefine not only Earth's geopolitics, but also our role in the universe.

Discovery would not automatically lead to an era of openness and information sharing. Rather, it would risk being instrumentalized by the great powers, who could use it to strengthen their own dominance, justify new control strategies and manipulate the population under the illusion of protection.

Should we prepare for such a revelation?

If such a shattering revelation were to occur, humanity would have two possible paths ahead: accept and quickly adapt to a new reality or reject and react with panic and resistance. The key to coping with such a discovery is mental and social preparation, to prevent the change from becoming traumatic or chaotic.

One of the first steps is to accept that our knowledge of history and reality is always evolving. If history has taught us anything, it is that great discoveries were always initially rejected, but over time they became cornerstones of human knowledge. If we prepare ourselves to keep an open mind, we will be able to approach discovery with curiosity and a desire to learn, instead of with fear and rejection.

Critical awareness and control of information will also be crucial. If discovery is going to be handled by governments and the media in a manipulated way, it will be essential that independent groups, scientists, and knowledgeable citizens work to spread the truth transparently. Technology has given us global communication tools, and it will be important to use these tools to prevent discovery from being distorted or exploited.

Psychologically, it will be necessary to prepare the population for a possible paradigm shift. If humanity has lived for millennia thinking that it is the only intelligent life form on Earth, discovering that it is not could be an unprecedented culture shock. Educating people about these possibilities, openly discussing alternative theories to the official story, and promoting dialogue between science and spirituality could help make the transition more gradual and less traumatic.

Even at the societal level, it will be necessary to develop an ethic of coexistence with the unknown. If cryptoterrestrial beings still exist, the first step will be to understand who they are, what their intentions are, and whether peaceful dialogue can be established. Humanity will have to overcome its tendency toward aggression and domination by learning to cooperate rather than conflict with new intelligences.

Another important aspect is the role of technology. If discovery leads to new scientific and technological knowledge, it will be crucial to ensure that this knowledge is used for the collective good and not for military or control purposes. We may be facing an unprecedented technological acceleration, and society will have to be prepared to handle it responsibly.

The biggest question will be how to redefine our place in the universe. If we discover that humanity is not the only Earth civilization, nor the oldest, we will have to redefine our concept of history, evolution and identity. This could destroy many of the structures on which our societies are based, but it could also open up new perspectives, new philosophies and a new sense of global unity.

We must therefore prepare ourselves not only mentally, but also culturally and politically, to prevent such a momentous discovery from becoming a weapon of division rather than an opportunity to unite humanity.

The question is not whether this revelation will happen, but when. And when it happens, the real challenge is not to accept the truth, but to decide how we want to build the future after discovering it.

SECRET PASSAGES IN THE ICE

NATURAL OR ARTIFICIAL TUNNEL NETWORKS?

Hidden tunnels in the poles: geological anomalies or man-made constructions?

Earth's polar regions, seemingly deserted and inhospitable, hide enigmatic underground structures under their thick blanket of ice, discovered thanks to the latest geological exploration technologies. But what exactly are these cavities? Are they simple natural phenomena or could they be traces of ancient man-made constructions, perhaps belonging to an unknown pre-historic civilization?

The first anomalies were detected through ground-penetrating radar (GPR), an instrument that allows one to peer underground and obtain three-dimensional images of what lies beneath the ice. These scans revealed immense tunnels and cavities, some with such perfect dimensions and such regular angles as to rule out a purely natural origin. Some of these formations even appear to be connected by smaller passages, suggesting the presence of a true underground network.

Conventional explanations suggest that these tunnels may be burrows excavated by subglacial water flow, a phenomenon that occurs when geothermal heat or friction from moving ice melts the lower layer of the ice sheet. However, many of these cavities do not exhibit the typical characteristics of natural erosion. In some cases, the tunnels appear smooth, symmetrical, and with solid walls, almost as if they were excavated with advanced tools rather than shaped by nature.

Another hypothesis is that these passages are ancient lava conduits, similar to the volcanic tunnels found in Hawaii or Iceland. However, Antarctica does not have sufficient volcanic activity to explain the quantity and vastness of these tunnels, and their regular alignment defies the laws of conventional geology.

Some researchers suggest that these structures could be ancient man-made constructions, dating back to a time when Antarctica and the Arctic were not yet covered by ice. If this hypothesis were true, it would mean that a technologically advanced civilization inhabited the poles in the distant past, leaving behind a network of passageways and structures buried by time.

Satellite images have also identified strange openings in the ice, which appear to be entrances to hidden tunnels. Some of these entrances, observed in Antarctica, have been inexplicably censored or changed on public maps, fueling theories that governments may be aware of these secret passages and are trying to keep them hidden.

If artificial tunnels do indeed exist under the ice, they may have an as yet unknown purpose. They could be remnants of ancient underground cities, shelters built to protect a civilization from climate catastrophes or global wars, or even passageways used by a nonhuman species that lived on Earth parallel to our own.

The question remains: are we facing a unique natural phenomenon or irrefutable evidence that human history is far more complex than we have been taught?

Military and scientific exploration in polar tunnels

If these tunnels under the ice are real and have anomalous features, then it is logical to assume that the great powers have already launched secret missions to explore them. And indeed, there are multiple clues pointing to clandestine operations conducted by armies and scientific institutions, the purpose of which may be more than just geological exploration.

The U.S. military, Russia, and even China have shown increasing interest in the polar regions, with official research missions that may conceal far more covert purposes. The Pentagon, for example, has funded numerous radar mapping projects of the Antarctic subsurface, justifying them with the study of climate change. However, some former officials have hinted that these missions may have an ulterior motive: to detect anomalous structures and study what lies beneath the ice.

Russia, with its historic Vostok base, has been at the center of numerous suspicious incidents. After drilling into Lake Vostok, a body of water sealed under ice for millions of years, some members of the expedition mysteriously disappeared or were repatriated without explanation. Some sources suggest that they may have found something far more extraordinary than just ancient bacteria.

NASA and ESA have also shown unusual interest in polar tunnels, developing robotic exploration technologies for extreme environments, as if they were testing tools for space missions but applying them in Antarctica. If these agencies are studying the cavities under the ice, it is possible that they are trying to understand their purpose and possible connection to Earth's past or possible hidden life forms.

Some independent explorers and researchers who have tried to investigate these tunnels have been warned not to proceed or have found unexplained difficulties. There are also stories of pilots who reported seeing huge openings in the ice, but their reports were censored or downplayed.

If there is indeed a network of tunnels in the poles, then a crucial question must be asked: why is it that no official institution speaks openly about it?

Whether these passages lead to secret bases, ancient civilizations, or non-human structures, their study could provide unprecedented knowledge about Earth's history and possible contact with unknown intelligences. But at the same time, revealing this truth could completely upset the world order, starting a new race to control these mysterious tunnels.

The most extreme, but not impossible, assumption is that these tunnels are not empty. If they are man-made constructions, it is possible that some-one-or something-is still using them. They could be shelters of a hidden civilization, interdimensional passageways, or even secret bases used for operations that the world need not know about.

For now, the public knows only fragments of information, and secret missions to the poles continue away from the eyes of ordinary people. But the ice is slowly melting, and what has been hidden for millennia may soon come to light.

When this happens, will the world be ready for the truth?

Theories on the connection between the tunnels and the Hollow Earth

The discoveries of immense cavities and underground tunnels in the poles have reignited the debate on one of the most controversial theories in the history of geology: the Hollow Earth Theory. According to this hypothesis, our planet may not be completely solid, but vast caves and, in some cases, even entire habitable ecosystems may exist within it. Some proponents of the theory claim that these tunnels would not be simple geological formations, but real passageways leading to an inner world inhabited by unknown life forms or civilizations that evolved separately from surface humanity.

One of the main clues in favor of this theory comes from magnetic and gravitational anomalies detected at the poles, especially in Antarctica. Some military and scientific expeditions have recorded unexplained variations in the gravitational field, suggesting the presence of cavities of enormous size, much larger than mainstream science thought possible. If these cavities were connected, they could form a network of tunnels stretching thousands of kilometers beneath the Earth's crust, an idea reminiscent of ancient legends of underground cities such as Agartha or Shambhala.

According to some historical sources, even the Nazis were interested in the possibility that Earth had hidden entrances to an underground world. During World War II, expeditions were conducted to Antarctica and other remote areas with the goal of finding secret passages leading to an advanced underground civilization, which some conspiracy theorists believe was a superior race or even an alliance with nonhuman entities.

216

But the connection between the polar tunnels and Hollow Earth is not just based on speculation. There are radar and geophysical data showing the existence of huge gaps under the ice, gaps that cannot be explained by normal glacial movement or subglacial water flow alone. Some theorists suggest that these tunnels could be entrances to man-made structures, perhaps built millions of years ago by a lost civilization.

If the tunnels in the poles are indeed connected to an underground world, the implications would be revolutionary. It would mean that not all terrestrial life has developed on the surface, and that there may be intelligent beings who have chosen (or been forced) to live underground to avoid climate catastrophes or global events. Some even argue that these beings may interact with our civilization covertly, influencing global events without ever revealing themselves openly.

But if indeed these tunnels lead to an underground realm, why has no government ever released information about them? It could be because control of these passages would provide an unprecedented strategic advantage. If unknown ecosystems or resources do indeed exist under the ice, anyone who discovers them would have access to knowledge that could alter world geopolitics forever.

The possibility that the polar tunnels are part of an ancient network of interconnected underground passages is not just a science fiction idea, but a question that modern science may finally be able to answer thanks to new underground exploration technologies.

Advanced technologies to explore the frozen underground

Exploring tunnels under polar ice is one of the most complex challenges in modern science. Extreme conditions, perennial frost and geographic isolation make it difficult to access and map underground cavities, but thanks to technological advances in recent decades, scientists are beginning to obtain increasingly detailed data on what lies beneath the ice caps.

One of the most powerful tools used to explore the polar subsurface is ground penetrating radar (GPR). This technology sends electromagnetic pulses into the ice and soil below and analyzes the reflected waves, allowing three-dimensional images of underground structures to be created. Using this technique, large voids have been discovered under the ice, which could be either natural formations or the remains of ancient man-made structures.

Another revolutionary technology is satellite interferometry, which uses high-resolution satellites to detect minute changes in the ice surface, signaling possible cavities or underground movements. Space missions such as those of ESA (European Space Agency) and NASA have provided valuable data on polar anomalies, some of which cannot be explained by conventional science.

Ultra-low temperature drilling, such as that used to reach Lake Vostok, is another crucial technique. These systems allow penetration into the ice sheet without contaminating subglacial environments, an essential factor in studying any hidden ecosystems or locating intact buried structures.

Another advanced method is three-dimensional sonar, used in regions such as the Arctic to map structures under sea ice. This technology could also be applied in terrestrial areas to detect underground passages and tunnels with unprecedented accuracy.

In recent years, autonomous drones and exploratory robots have been developed that are designed to withstand the extreme conditions of the poles. These robots can navigate tunnels and send images in real time, allowing scientists to explore areas inaccessible to humans. Some of these drones, such as NASA's "Icefin", have been designed to explore not only Earth's ice, but also the icy moons of Jupiter and Saturn, showing that technologies used to study Earth could have applications in space exploration as well.

Recent experiments have tested the use of seismic and vibrational waves to "listen" to the inside of ice, a method that can identify hidden caves and tunnels. If this technology were applied on a large scale, we could obtain a complete map of underground cavities in the poles, revealing whether there are connections between them or whether they lead to as yet unknown structures.

With these increasingly sophisticated technologies, the mystery of the tunnels under the poles could be solved in the next few years. If they turn out to be only natural geological formations, we will still have greatly expanded our knowledge of the polar regions. But if evidence of a lost civilization or man-made structures emerges, then the world will face one of the greatest revelations in human history.

The real question is, when we finally find out the truth, will it be made public or will it be a secret guarded by the world's elites?

Testimonies and documents on secret pole entrances

Theories about tunnels hidden under the polar ice are not just the result of speculation and scientific interpretation. Over the years, numerous witnesses-including former military personnel, researchers, and pilots-have made startling statements about alleged secret entrances that would lead to underground structures of unknown origin.

One of the most notorious cases involves the statements of Rear Admiral Richard E. Byrd, one of the most famous explorers of Antarctica and the Arctic. During Operation Highjump (1946-47), Byrd led a massive U.S. military expedition to Antarctica with more than 4,700 men, supported by warships and aircraft. Although officially the mission was intended for scientific research, several documents and reports suggest that the real objective was to investigate strange geographical anomalies and unexplained phenomena under the ice. According to some accounts, Byrd reported seeing huge entrances in the Antarctic mountains so large that aircraft could pass through.

Another disturbing episode is that reported by former military pilot John Kilroy, who allegedly participated in flyover missions in Antarctica for the Pentagon in the 1980s. Kilroy claimed to have seen huge, perfectly circular openings in the ice, resembling giant underground hangars. According to his testimony, he was ordered not to tell anyone about it, and shortly thereafter his access to mission records was completely revoked.

Russia also has a long history of suspicious missions to the poles. During the Cold War years, numerous Soviet researchers were sent to East Antarctica near the Vostok base. Some of them, including former scientist Dr. Anton Belousov, suggested that the Soviet government was aware of large underground structures under Lake Vostok, accessible through natural or man-made tunnels. After divulging some details, Belousov was silenced, and all information about his research was classified by the Russian government.

In recent years, some private contractors and independent scientists have also reported anomalies at the poles. A former NASA engineer, who preferred to remain anonymous, said that satellites repeatedly detected "geometric structures" under the ice, but each time the images were analyzed, access to the data was blocked or changed.

Adding to these accounts are declassified documents suggesting that the United States and other nations conducted covert operations in Antarctica to explore these tunnels, but the results were concealed from public view. Some of these reports speak of military missions to specific regions of the poles, with specialized equipment for underground exploration and detection of energy anomalies.

If these statements were true, it would mean that governments know more than they reveal and that discoveries made in the polar tunnels could rewrite our understanding of Earth and its history.

What might these tunnels conceal and why is no one talking about them?

If there really is a network of tunnels and underground structures under the polar ice, the most logical question is why is no one talking openly about it?

There are several possible explanations for the silence surrounding these anomalies. The first concerns national security and geopolitics. If remnants of ancient man-made structures or unknown technologies were found in the poles, then whoever controls them would have an unprecedented strategic advantage. If they were secret bases built by world powers for undisclosed experiments, then secrecy would serve to protect sensitive information from rival governments.

Another hypothesis is that these tunnels might contain evidence of an advanced prehistoric civilization, much older than official history acknowledges. If it were proven that a technologically advanced people existed tens of thousands of years ago, entire academic disciplines-from archaeology to geology-would have to be completely rewritten. This would create a huge institutional crisis, undermining the credibility of universities, museums and governments that have supported a different narrative for centuries.

Another reason for secrecy could be fear of social and economic impact. If the public suddenly discovers that nonhuman artificial structures exist beneath the poles, the consequences would be devastating for modern society. Religious institutions could lose credibility, theories of human evolution could be challenged, and entire economic systems based on information and technology management could collapse.

Even the most extreme hypothesis should not be ruled out: what if someone or something was still using these tunnels? If these passages lead to an environment inhabited by an intelligent life form, then governments may have kept the secret to avoid global panic or to establish confidential contact before revealing the discovery to the world.

In addition, the gradual melting of polar ice could make it increasingly difficult to keep the secret. If some of these underground structures were exposed to sunlight, it would be impossible to hide the truth forever. Could this be the reason why governments are intensifying their scrutiny of Antarctic expeditions?

Censoring of polar tunnels could also be related to advanced research projects on unknown energies. Some reports suggest that anomalous electromagnetic fields have been detected in the depths of Antarctica, which could be sources of natural or artificial energy. If these findings are made public, they could revolutionize our understanding of physics and engineering, rendering obsolete many of the technologies on which the world economy is based.

The silence about the tunnels under the poles is not accidental. Something great lurks beneath the ice, something that could rewrite our history and our place in the universe. The question is no longer whether these tunnels exist, but when the world will be ready to know the truth.

The next big discovery may emerge when the ice melts completely, at which point governments will no longer be able to hide what they have known all along. But until then, the mystery of the polar tunnels will remain one of the greatest censures of our time.

THE POSSIBLE THREAT

WHAT DO THE CRYPTOTERRESTRIALS WANT?

Who are the cryptoterrestrials and what are the theories about their origin?

The hypothesis of the existence of cryptoterrestrial beings-nonhuman intelligences that have coexisted with humanity since time immemorial, hidden under the ice or in the depths of the Earth-is one of the most fascinating and disturbing mysteries of our time. But who might these beings really be? And what would be their origin?

There are several theories about their nature, each leading to very different scenarios. One of the most widely accepted theories is that cryptoterrestrials are the descendants of a very ancient Earth civilization, predating humanity as we know it. According to this theory, an advanced people may have inhabited Earth tens or hundreds of thousands of years ago, developing extraordinary technology and perhaps a social organization very different from our own. Catastrophic events, such as climate change, the reversal of the magnetic poles or a global war, may have forced them to retreat to subterranean environments or hide in the poles as humanity started from scratch.

Another possibility is that these beings are not completely terrestrial, but the result of hybridization between ancient human races and visitors from other worlds. Numerous legends around the world speak of "gods" or "heavenly messengers" who descended to Earth in ancient times, teaching advanced knowledge and altering the fate of civilizations. It could be that these beings never really left, but simply decided to observe the evolution of humanity from a hidden position, intervening only at key moments in our history.

Another theory, even more shocking, is that cryptoterrestrials are not biological beings in the conventional sense, but interdimensional creatures. This would mean that our reality is not the only one in existence, but there are multiple levels of existence coexisting in the same space. In this scenario, these beings could travel between dimensions or inhabit a reality parallel to ours, with the ability to make contact with our world through passages or physical anomalies located in the poles and other areas of the Earth.

Some scholars and theorists suggest that their nature might be energetic rather than material, which would explain why physical evidence of their existence is so difficult to obtain. If these beings had a form of existence based on frequencies, electromagnetic waves or other unknown forms of energy, they could make themselves visible only under certain conditions or interact with our reality without leaving obvious physical traces.

If indeed cryptoterrestrials have been present on Earth since time immemorial, the big question is why have they remained hidden? Are they simply waiting for the right time to reveal themselves, or is there a darker reason behind their behavior?

Interactions with humanity: contacts, secrets and manipulations?

If cryptoterrestrials are real, it means that they may have had contact with humanity throughout history, and perhaps influenced some key events in the development of our civilization. But what is the evidence for these interactions?

There are numerous ancient myths and legends about mysterious beings that came from underground or from the depths of the ice. Indigenous peoples of the Arctic, such as the Inuit, tell stories about intelligent creatures living below the surface and occasionally interacting with humans. Similarly, some ancient European and Asian cultures mention entities called "Guardians of the Earth", who are said to be hidden beings, keepers of secret knowledge and able to predict the future.

If we analyze historical events, unexplained episodes emerge that may have been influenced by nonhuman entities. Some ancient texts speak of mysterious encounters with beings who possessed advanced knowledge, much more advanced than that of the time. Some of these accounts have been attributed to deities, others to wise masters, but what if they were instead interactions with crypto-terrestrial beings?

In the modern world, there are accounts from military personnel, pilots and researchers who claim to have witnessed unexplained phenomena at the poles. Some USAF pilots have reported seeing unidentified vehicles emerge from remote areas of Antarctica or the Arctic, with movements and speeds that do not match any known human technology.

There are also cases of researchers sent to the polar regions for geological or scientific exploration who have been warned not to go too far into certain areas, as if there are secrets to be protected at all costs. Some tell of sensing strange electromagnetic interference, as if an unseen force was preventing equipment from working properly.

But why would these beings interact with humanity so selectively? There could be different factions among cryptoterrestrials, some benevolent, some hostile, with different goals. Some might seek to preserve our development without interference, while others might have specific interests in influencing our political, economic and technological choices.

One of the most controversial hypotheses is that these beings may have been manipulating humanity since the beginning of civilization, steering us in certain directions through the control of elites, religions and political institutions. If so, who really governs the world? Human beings, or a hidden entity pulling the strings from the shadows?

There is also the possibility that these beings are afraid to reveal themselves openly. If they have existed for millennia, they may know something that we ignore, such as an external threat that could strike Earth in the future. They may be trying to protect us, or they may simply be trying to protect themselves from a larger force.

A final hypothesis is that cryptoterrestrials may never have been our allies, but merely observers. In this case, their agenda might be completely indifferent to the fate of humanity. They might consider us an evolving race, useful to study but not worthy of direct contact.

If there is indeed a secret agenda behind the interactions between humans and cryptoterrestrials, the big question is when will it be revealed? If these beings are waiting for the right time to reveal themselves, then perhaps that time is closer than we imagine.

But will we be ready to face the truth, whatever it may be?

Are they a threat or a civilization that wants to maintain anonymity?

If cryptoterrestrials exist, their intentionality remains the greatest enigma. Are they mere observers, beings who prefer to remain in the shadows so as not to interfere with humanity's development, or do they have a more complex strategy and a precise agenda?

One of the most popular theories is that these beings are peaceful but highly secretive, for reasons related to their own survival. If they have existed for thousands or perhaps millions of years, it is possible that they have developed a culture based on secrecy, knowing that a sudden revelation could wreak havoc among humans. They may have witnessed catastrophic events in Earth's history, such as wars or extinctions, and may have chosen to isolate themselves to avoid conflict with humanity.

This theory is supported by the idea that polar regions are perfect environments to remain hidden, difficult to explore and devoid of permanent human settlements. If cryptoterrestrials have bases or underground cities in the poles, they might simply wish to live undisturbed, without outside interference. In this scenario, they might monitor humanity to make sure it does not discover them, but without any hostile intent.

However, there is also a more disturbing hypothesis: what if these beings are not mere observers, but active players in the fate of the planet? Some independent researchers suggest that cryptoterrestrials may have a definite plan, and that their isolation is not accidental, but part of a larger strategy.

One possibility is that they are waiting for the right time to reveal themselves, perhaps when humanity reaches a certain level of technological development or adequate social maturity. They may fear that premature contact would trigger conflicts, wars or a collapse of human institutions. After all, history has taught us that more advanced civilizations have often destroyed or subjugated less developed ones. If cryptoterrestrials have experienced similar events before, they may want to avoid a similar fate for themselves or for us.

But there is also the possibility that they are not neutral at all. If their presence has lasted for millennia, they may have secretly influenced human civilization, guiding our development in a specific direction. Some theorists speculate that they selected the world's elites or influenced the birth of the great religions and political ideologies, always maintaining a covert control over our progress.

The real problem is that we do not know for sure what their agenda is. If they were completely hostile, they would have had thousands of years to subdue or eliminate humanity. If, on the other hand, they were peaceful, why have they never sought direct and open dialogue?

Another possibility is that they do not see humanity as an immediate threat, but neither as a trustworthy partner. If our technological development has begun to endanger their hidden habitat, they may have begun to act more directly, influencing world events to slow human progress or divert attention from certain geographical areas.

If their existence were one day confirmed, humanity would face a momentous dilemma: try to establish peaceful contact or consider them a possible threat to be closely monitored?

Occult influence in political and scientific decisions?

One of the most uncomfortable questions about the possible existence of cryptoterrestrials is: are governments and scientific institutions already aware of their presence? And if so, why are they keeping it a secret?

If a hidden civilization has existed for centuries, it is hard to believe that the world's superpowers have never heard of it. There are numerous declassified documents showing that the great powers have a special interest in the polar regions, with scientific expeditions, military bases and secret exploration projects. But if their only goal was climate research or exploitation of natural resources, why maintain such a high level of secrecy?

Some independent researchers suggest that there may be a secret agreement between governments and cryptoterrestrials, a non-interference pact that guarantees both sides can coexist without directly clashing. This agreement could explain why some areas of the poles are strictly off limits to the public, and why governments seem more interested in monitoring certain anomalies rather than explaining them.

There are also hypotheses indicating that cryptoterrestrials have directly influenced world politics and science, guiding strategic decisions behind the scenes. Some theorists argue that humans may have been conditioned not to seek certain truths, through control of historical, academic and scientific narratives.

One possible sign of this influence is the international treaty that protects Antarctica, preventing any nation from claiming its territory and severely restricting independent exploration. Why has such a vast, resource-rich and strategically important continent remained outside the global colonization race? Could it be that those in power know that there are secrets in Antarctica that should not be revealed?

The scientific field may also have been manipulated or piloted so as to minimize or discredit certain findings. Many scientists who have studied anomalies in the poles have seen their studies blocked, their research buried, and, in some cases, their careers ruined. If a discovery about cryptoterrestrials suddenly emerged, would the scientific community be ready for it or would it be immediately silenced?

Another hypothesis is that cryptoterrestrials may be responsible for some of the greatest scientific breakthroughs in history, transmitting knowledge to selected elites while the rest of humanity remains unaware. Some pioneering scientists, such as Nikola Tesla, have claimed to have had sudden insights into advanced technologies, almost as if they had been transmitted from a higher source. What if this source was a hidden intelligence, older and more advanced than us?

If the influence of cryptoterrestrials is real, then their strategy seems clear: to maintain control without being discovered. But how long can this balance be sustained? With technological progress and the growing number of independent researchers, the veil of secrecy may soon fall.

If and when this truth is revealed, humanity will have to decide how to deal with the discovery of a hidden civilization that may have been observing and influencing us for centuries. The question is: Will this revelation lead to a new era of knowledge, or a conflict with an entity that has always preferred to remain hidden?

Assumptions about their ultimate purpose: adaptation, domination, or study?

If cryptoterrestrials do exist, the great enigma remains: what is their purpose? Are they simply neutral observers of our evolution, beings trying to adapt to the human world without interfering, or do they have a more complex agenda and a long-term plan to influence or control our civilization?

One of the most acceptable hypotheses is that these beings are simply studying humanity from afar, without any hostile intentions. According to this theory, cryptoterrestrials could be an extremely ancient species, perhaps a technologically advanced civilization that lived on Earth well before homo sapiens. If so, they might consider us an interesting phenomenon to observe, just as humans study animal behavior in nature reserves.

Another possibility is that their purpose is not just observation, but preparation for future coexistence. Perhaps they know that one day they will be forced to reveal themselves, perhaps because of climate change, our technological advancement, or the melting of polar ice that could expose their underground bases. If this is the case, they may have already begun to study our psychology and social reactions, trying to figure out how we might welcome their existence without panic or conflict.

But there is also a more disturbing hypothesis: what if these beings already exert secret control over society? If cryptoterrestrials really are more advanced than we are, they may have found ways to influence world events, political decisions and even our technological development, without ever exposing themselves openly. Some independent researchers speculate that they may be responsible for certain historical turning points, certain revolutionary technologies or the maintenance of certain global balances of power.

But why would they do this? The motivations may be many. If they are a declining species, they may need humanity to ensure their survival, perhaps through some form of genetic hybridization or assimilation of our culture. If, on the other hand, they have advanced knowledge of the future, they may know that humanity is headed for a global crisis, and they may be secretly trying to guide us toward an outcome that avoids the collapse of civilization.

It cannot be ruled out that their ultimate goal is domination, but in a more subtle form than we imagine. They may not want to conquer the planet by force, but rather maintain a constant influence over power structures, making sure that humanity does not become a threat to them or to the balance of the planet. If cryptoterrestrials already control certain aspects of global politics, energy resources or scientific research, we may never notice their presence, even though their influence is constant.

If their purpose is control, then the real question is: to what extent are we free to decide our own destiny?

If they exist, what should we do?

If the existence of a cryptoterrestrial civilization among us were confirmed tomorrow, humanity would have to prepare for one of the greatest revelations in history. But what would be the most appropriate reaction?

First of all, the crucial first step would be the psychological and social processing of the discovery. Humanity has always lived with the belief that we are the dominant species and the only intelligent life form on Earth. If it turned out not to be so, our entire belief system, religions, history and philosophy would have to be revised and reinterpreted. This could generate a collective shock wave, but also new perspectives and possibilities for cultural evolution.

Another key reaction would be to understand the nature and intentions of these beings. If they have been able to remain hidden for so long, it means that they possess advanced technologies and superior knowledge of reality. Instead of fearing them or automatically considering them a threat, we could try to study them, dialogue with them and understand what they can teach us.

On the other hand, we cannot rule out the possibility that these beings may have goals at odds with the well-being of humanity. If their agenda is not peaceful, then the world will have to be ready to defend itself, not necessarily with weapons, but with a conscious strategy to preserve our independence and our right to self-determination.

Scientific and political institutions should create a step-by-step approach to disclosure, avoiding panic but educating the public about what we know and what it means to coexist with another intelligence on this planet. This means transparency in governments, access to information, and a new global ethic based on how to deal with the fact that we were never alone on Earth.

Humanity's response should be unified. If the discovery is mishandled, it could cause divisions, conflicts among nations and unwarranted fears. If, on the other hand, we decide to deal with it intelligently, collaboratively and with an open vision for the future, we could benefit tremendously from this knowledge.

The most important question remains this: do we really want to know the truth? Is humanity ready to discover that the world has never been as we have been told?

Perhaps the answer is not whether or not cryptoterrestrials exist, but when we are ready to accept that our history, our science and our perception of reality may have to be completely rewritten.

POLES AS THE FRONTIER OF THE FUTURE

WHO WILL CONTROL THIS SECRET?

A new race to conquer the poles

The polar regions, once considered inhospitable territories of no strategic interest, are now at the center of an unprecedented geopolitical competition. As ice melts caused by climate change, new sea routes and immense natural resources are becoming accessible, pushing the world's great powers into a no-holds-barred race for control of the Arctic and Antarctica.

In recent years, the United States, Russia, China and the European Union have increased their presence in the polar regions, both through the construction of research bases and scientific stations and through military and intelligence operations. Antarctica, in particular, is protected by the 1959 Antarctic Treaty, which prohibits territorial claims and military operations, but the future of this agreement is increasingly uncertain. Some analysts fear that once it expires or is renegotiated, it could open the door to a new form of colonization and resource exploitation.

Russia is among the most active countries in the polar region. It has expanded its fleet of nuclear icebreakers, strengthened its bases in the Arctic and launched scientific missions to Antarctica, officially for climate research purposes but with obvious strategic implications. Moscow considers the Arctic a national priority, with plans to exploit oil and natural gas deposits and control new trade routes.

China is also emerging as a key player in the race for the poles. Beijing has stated that it wants to develop a "Polar Silk Road", using the gradual melting of ice to open up new shipping routes and access natural resources. With bases in Antarctica and a growing presence in the Arctic, China is seeking to insert itself into the polar competition, challenging the traditional dominance of the United States and Russia.

The United States, for its part, is trying to catch up. The Pentagon has declared the Arctic an area of strategic interest, increasing its military presence in the region with nuclear submarines, warships and surveillance drones. NASA and other government agencies are also investing billions of dollars in studying the poles, officially to monitor climate change, but some experts believe the goal is also to search for geological or energy anomalies hidden under the ice.

But behind this official race for control of routes and resources, there may be another, much more secret goal. If unknown structures, remnants of ancient civilizations, or advanced technologies exist beneath the poles, then the real reason for the competition may not just be economic, but related to the discovery of something extraordinary that has been hidden for centuries.

This increasing militarization of the polar regions raises a fundamental question: are we facing a simple race for resources, or do governments know more than they want to admit about the anomalies and secrets hidden in the poles?

Hidden resources in the ice: a disputed treasure

In addition to their strategic importance, the poles hide an impressive amount of natural resources, making them one of the planet's last great economic frontiers. While extraction of these resources has so far been limited by extreme weather conditions, the gradual melting of ice is changing the game, making it possible to exploit once inaccessible deposits.

One of the most coveted treasures is oil and natural gas. The U.S. Geological Survey estimates that the Arctic could contain up to 13 percent of undiscovered oil reserves and 30 percent of global untapped natural gas reserves. These numbers are enough to explain why Russia, the United States and other nations are seeking to strengthen their presence in the region, with oil companies preparing to drill new areas as soon as technology allows.

In addition to hydrocarbons, the poles hide immense mineral deposits. It is estimated that significant reserves of gold, platinum, uranium, nickel and rare earths, elements critical to the technology industry and the production of advanced electronic devices, lie beneath the ice of Antarctica. Antarctica, in particular, could become one of the richest mining areas on the planet, but it is currently protected by the Antarctic Treaty, which prohibits the exploitation of natural resources. However, if economic pressures increase, it is likely that powerful nations will seek to change its rules or find legal loopholes to access these riches.

Another invaluable resource is frozen fresh water. The ice caps of Antarctica and the Arctic contain about 70 percent of the planet's fresh water. With global warming and the growing water crisis in many regions of the world, some countries are already considering harnessing icebergs and pole water supplies to replenish desert areas or metropolises with limited water resources. Some companies are already developing technologies to transport whole icebergs to the shores of thirsty countries, a prospect that could open a new era of polar resource exploitation.

But the real conundrum is: in addition to known resources, could the poles be hiding something even more extraordinary? Some researchers believe there may be unknown materials or technologies under the ice, perhaps related to lost civilizations or still unexplained phenomena.

There are several geological anomalies at the poles that scientists are struggling to explain. Some radar scans have revealed regular underground structures that do not appear to have a natural origin. In addition, strange heat emissions have been detected in some areas of Antarctica, incompatible with the extreme temperatures in the region. If these phenomena were signs of buried technology, their value could be far greater than any oil or mineral deposits.

The fact that much information about the poles is classified or subject to government restrictions fuels suspicion that something much more important is lurking beneath the ice. If the great powers are investing enormous resources in competing for control of these regions, does that mean they know something that the rest of the world ignores?

This growing race to conquer the poles is not only an economic and geopolitical issue, but could represent one of the largest cover-up operations in modern history. If structures of unknown origin, traces of a lost civilization or technologies beyond our understanding are found in the poles, their control could become the key to global power in the coming decades.

The real question is: When and how will the world discover the truth about what governments are really looking for under the ice?

The interests of multinational corporations: exploitation or conservation?

While the governments of the great powers vie for strategic control of the polar regions, multinational corporations are already planning the future of business in the poles. The world's most powerful companies, from energy giants to mining industries, are investing in research, lobbying and covert operations to secure privileged access to the riches hidden beneath the ice.

The natural resources of the poles-oil, gas, rare earths, precious minerals and fresh water-are an irresistible attraction for large corporations. As the ice melts, new extraction opportunities are emerging, and multinational corporations are ready to defy environmental constraints and political restrictions in order to secure a slice of this natural treasure.

Oil companies, such as ExxonMobil, Gazprom, BP and Shell, have already explored potential deposits in the Arctic and Antarctica. Although the Antarctic Treaty prohibits commercial exploitation of natural resources, pressure to revise this agreement is mounting. Russia and China, in particular, are pushing for future concessions, and some multinational companies have begun funding studies to assess the feasibility of extraction under extreme conditions.

In parallel, the mining sector is focusing on rare earth deposits, which are essential for the production of batteries, advanced electronics and military technologies. Reserves of these materials, increasingly scarce in the rest of the world, could make Antarctica and the Arctic the new technological Eldorado of the 21st century. Companies such as Tesla, Apple, and various Chinese giants are already considering how to secure supplies of critical minerals from the polar regions, while mining companies such as Rio Tinto and BHP Billiton have opened research labs to develop new mining techniques in extreme environments.

However, as some companies prepare to exploit polar resources, others are pushing for their protection. The renewable energy sector and multinational corporations linked to sustainability, such as Tesla, Patagonia and large environmental NGOs, are trying to counter extraction plans by promoting initiatives to turn the poles into permanent conservation zones. Some environmental groups argue that the future of humanity depends on protecting the polar ice caps, as melting ice could accelerate global warming and destabilize the world's climate.

As a result, the debate between exploitation and conservation is intensifying. On the one hand, industrial lobbies are pressing governments for access to resources, while on the other, environmental movements and scientists are trying to block commercial activities in the poles to preserve the fragile balance of the polar ecosystem.

Some experts speculate that, in the near future, we may see a division of polar territory: some areas earmarked for economic exploitation, while others will be protected under international agreements. But the real question is: Will multinational corporations really respect the limits imposed or will they use their economic power to circumvent them?

The role of large corporations in the poles will be crucial in shaping the future of the polar regions. If corporations were to gain total control of resources, the risk of unbridled exploitation and irreparable environmental damage would be extremely high. Conversely, if environmental forces succeed in asserting themselves, the poles could become a global laboratory for new sustainable technologies and a model of conservation for the rest of the planet.

In the end, the fate of the poles will depend on political will and the ability of nations to resist economic pressures. But with such high financial interests at stake, the battle for control of these pristine lands will be anything but simple.

How climate change will redefine the control of the poles

Climate change is accelerating the transformation of the polar regions, and with it the geopolitical and strategic dynamics related to these areas. As the world debates the effects of global warming, major powers are already planning how to exploit the new scenario that will emerge as the ice melts.

One of the most visible effects of global warming is the opening of new shipping routes in the Arctic. The Northeast Passage, which connects Europe to Asia via the Arctic Ocean, is becoming increasingly navigable for extended periods of the year. This could revolutionize global trade, reducing transportation time and costs compared to traditional routes through the Suez Canal. Russia and China are among the first countries to invest in creating infrastructure to take advantage of these new trade routes, while the United States and the European Union seek to maintain control over maritime security.

But the real impact of climate change in the poles concerns the exploitation of natural resources. As ice melts, previously inaccessible areas will become fertile ground for the extraction of oil, gas and minerals. Energy companies are already experimenting with new technologies to drill into permafrost and operate in extreme environments, preparing to exploit the immense reserves that lie beneath the ice.

Antarctica, in particular, could become the planet's next great mining frontier. As the ice sheet melts, lands rich in valuable resources could emerge, ready for exploration and exploitation. However, this could spark new international tensions, with some countries pushing to amend the Antarctic Treaty to allow mining activities, while others will fight to keep the area protected.

Scientific bases at the poles are also undergoing transformations. Whereas until a few years ago Antarctica and the Arctic were used almost exclusively for environmental and climate research, today many research stations have become strategic and technological outposts for monitoring natural resources and rival activities. Some analysts argue that, in the future, they may be converted into full-fledged operational bases for the economic exploitation of polar resources.

Another effect of climate change concerns global geopolitical stability. If global warming continues to intensify, some nations may find themselves in such a water and energy crisis that governments may have to make extreme decisions. In this scenario, the poles could become the last frontier for sustaining global economies, leading to an even more frantic race for their control.

The big question is: Will the world be able to manage this transformation in an equitable and sustainable way, or will we witness a new kind of industrial colonization, driven by the interests of superpowers and multinational corporations?

The only certainty is that the poles will no longer be remote and forgotten places, but will become the focus of a new geopolitical and environmental era, in which control of these regions could determine the future of nations and the entire planet.

The military use of the poles: secret bases and global surveillance

While the poles are increasingly seen as a strategic resource for the future of humanity, their military use is already an established, though rarely publicly admitted, reality. The superpowers the United States, Russia and China have invested substantial resources to set up secret bases, develop advanced technologies and constantly monitor these regions, turning them into veritable laboratories for the warfare of the future.

One of the most disturbing aspects is the presence of underground bases hidden under the ice, facilities that officially do not exist but that some sources say would house experimental weapons, global surveillance systems and research laboratories on phenomena not yet disclosed to the public. Some declassified documents suggest that, during the Cold War, both the United States and the Soviet Union built secret installations in the poles, officially to monitor rival activities, but with much broader and more secret purposes.

One of the best known examples is Camp Century, a secret military base built by the United States under the ice of Greenland in the 1960s. Officially it was a science project, but in reality it hosted tests for the placement of nuclear missiles under the ice. This shows how the poles have always been considered an area for military experimentation, away from prying eyes.

Today, with the advancement of technology, the poles have become centers of global surveillance, thanks to the use of satellites, drones and hypersensitive radar. The United States has deployed advanced satellite surveillance systems in Antarctica and the Arctic under the guise of monitoring climate change, but some experts believe these tools are also being used to monitor rival operations and search for anomalies under the ice.

Russia has also invested heavily in militarizing the poles. In recent years, Moscow has strengthened its presence in the Arctic, building air bases, command centers, and hypersonic missile launch facilities, a clear signal that it considers this region a key strategic area for the future. Some reports suggest that Russia is also testing directed-energy weapons and electronic warfare systems in the poles, taking advantage of geographic isolation to develop technologies that could change the global military landscape.

China, although officially without military bases in the poles, is rapidly expanding its influence in the region through a combination of scientific expeditions and strategic investments. Beijing has already developed satellites dedicated to monitoring the Arctic and Antarctica, while its space program appears interested in studying magnetic and geological anomalies at the poles, a move that could conceal military or intelligence purposes.

But the most sensitive issue concerns the development of new weapons in the poles. The extreme environments of the polar regions provide an ideal laboratory for testing advanced military technologies, from climate weapons to electromagnetic warfare systems. According to some speculation, secret experiments would be conducted to modify atmospheric conditions, with the goal of creating new forms of environmental warfare.

If these theories are confirmed, it would mean that the poles are not only a geopolitical and economic frontier, but also the hidden battlefield of a secret technological war. But as long as these operations remain classified, the public will never have access to the truth about what is really going on under the ice.

What future for the poles: openness to the world or elitist domination?

In the coming decades, decisions made about the polar regions will define the future of all humanity. The key question is: Will the poles become a common good accessible to all, or will they be controlled by a small elite of governments and multinational corporations?

If the current situation continues, the poles are likely to become areas of exclusive control of superpowers and large corporations. The resources hidden beneath the ice, their strategic location, and possible scientific or technological breakthroughs mean that no government will want to relinquish control over these areas.

One possible scenario is that once the ice melts, the most powerful nations will begin to claim polar territories, seeking to divide them into zones of influence. Already Russia has claimed vast tracts of the Arctic, while China is developing a scientific presence in Antarctica for purposes that could go beyond climate research. The United States, on the other hand, is accelerating plans to increase its military and commercial presence in the poles, fearful of losing control over a region that could become the focus of global power in the future.

However, there is also the possibility of more equitable and sustainable management of the poles. Some scientists and activists are pushing to turn these regions into World Heritage Sites, protected areas where natural resources cannot be indiscriminately exploited. The problem is that with economic and strategic interests so high, it will be difficult to prevent the most powerful nations from taking control by force or through covert diplomacy.

Another key factor in the future of the poles is technological development. If new sources of energy or revolutionary materials were discovered at the poles, their control could become even more elitist, with a small circle of governments and companies monopolizing access to these resources. If, on the other hand, the poles remained zones of research open to all nations, they could become a global laboratory for the study of climate change, geology and astronomy.

But the real mystery concerns the discoveries that may emerge as the ice melts. If ancient structures, unknown technologies or evidence of an advanced prehistoric civilization exist beneath the polar ice caps, then information management will become the real battle of the future. Global elites may hide the truth to maintain control, while independent researchers may struggle to reveal to the world what has remained buried for centuries.

In the end, the fate of the poles will depend on the political will and awareness of global society. If humanity allows decisions to be made only by a small power elite, the poles will become an inaccessible fortress, controlled by the few who will profit from them. If, on the other hand, the world's population begins to demand transparency and a more equitable approach, then there may be hope that the poles will remain an asset shared by all humanity.

The final question is: Will the whole truth about the poles ever be revealed to us, or will they continue to be the planet's most protected secret?

WHEN THE ICE MELTS

WILL THE TRUTH COME TO LIGHT?

Poles are melting faster than expected

The polar ice caps, once considered impenetrable barriers of eternal ice, are now disappearing at an unprecedented rate. The latest scientific data show that ice melt in Antarctica and the Arctic is accelerating beyond all predictions, with dramatic consequences not only for the global climate but also for what might emerge from beneath these vast expanses of ice.

According to the National Snow and Ice Data Center (NSIDC), Arctic ice loss has reached record levels in recent decades, with ice cover reduced by more than 40 percent from 20th century averages. Antarctica, which until a few years ago seemed more resilient to climate change, is now undergoing an unprecedented decline: in 2023, scientists recorded the lowest ever documented extent of the Antarctic ice shelf, with ice loss amounting to millions of square kilometers.

But the real alarm is that this phenomenon may be irreversible. As global temperatures rise, the natural mechanisms that have until now kept the polar ice caps stable are collapsing, leading to a ripple effect that could change the geography of the planet forever.

Sea level rise caused by melting ice is already putting hundreds of coastal cities at risk, while altering ocean currents could trigger extreme weather phenomena around the world. But there is another aspect of this transformation that few consider: as the ice retreats, secrets buried for millennia could emerge, revealing stories, life forms, and perhaps even unknown structures that until now have remained sealed under miles of ice.

If the current trend continues, within a few decades large portions of Antarctica and the Arctic could become accessible for the first time in modern history. And when this happens, what will we actually find under the ice?

What has already emerged from melting ice?

Although the true impact of global melting is still ongoing, some extraordinary discoveries have already emerged in recent years, fueling theories and questions about what may still be hidden beneath the ice.

One of the most significant findings is that of ancient microorganisms and viruses frozen for millions of years. Scientists extracted ice samples that contained unknown bacteria and viruses dating back to prehistoric times. Some of these organisms have been reanimated in the laboratory, demonstrating that unknown life forms can survive for ages under the ice, and raising concerns about the possibility that ancient pathogens may re-emerge and pose a new biological threat to humanity.

But the ice has preserved more than just microscopic life forms. In 2016, a scientific expedition to Siberia discovered a perfectly preserved cave lion cub that had been trapped in permafrost for more than 30,000 years. This discovery paved the way for the possibility of recovering DNA from extinct species and, perhaps, bringing them back to life through cloning. If the ice has guarded vanished creatures for millennia, could it also hide human remains of forgotten civilizations?

Another extraordinary case is the fossil forests that have emerged in Antarctica. In several regions of the frozen continent, researchers have found traces of ancient plants and trees, proving that Antarctica was once not covered with ice but was home to lush vegetation. This confirms the hypothesis that the continent had a temperate climate in ancient times, opening the door to the possibility that it was inhabited by humans or other intelligent life forms much earlier than official history recognizes.

242

But perhaps the most enigmatic discoveries involve the anomalous geometric structures detected under the ice. Using ground-penetrating radar technology, huge voids have been detected under the Antarctic ice sheet, some of which appear to have regular contours, as if man-made in origin. One of the most mysterious anomalies was detected in the Wilkes Land area, where radar scans revealed a giant circular depression buried under the ice, hypothesized by some to be the crater of a meteoritic impact, while others link it to possible man-made underground structures.

At the same time, numerous independent explorers and researchers have reported sightings of mysterious entrances in the ice, often visible for brief periods before being hidden by new snowfall or censorship in official satellite images. Some theories suggest that secret tunnels and openings could lead to underground bases or even hidden cities under Antarctica, but to date no official expedition has confirmed or denied these hypotheses.

If these early findings are only a preview of what is emerging, then it is fair to ask: what will we find when the ice melts completely?

Could traces of lost civilizations emerge, structures showing that Antarctica was inhabited in ancient times, or perhaps even technological remains of unknown origins?

Or could the retreat of the ice reveal new life forms, unknown beings that have survived for millennia in isolated environments and that could change our understanding of biology and evolution?

The only certainty is that the process is unstoppable. In the coming years, new discoveries could rewrite our understanding of the history and geology of the planet.

But will the world be ready to accept the truth? Or will the great powers and global elites try to cover up the most shocking discoveries while maintaining control over the information emerging from the poles?

Perhaps the real battle will not be between humanity and climate change, but between those who want to reveal the past hidden under the ice and those who will do anything to keep it secret.

Viruses and bacteria trapped in ice: a danger to humanity?

As the world watches the melting of the polar ice caps with concern, a silent danger may be emerging from the depths of the ice: ancient viruses and bacteria that have been trapped for millennia could come back to life and pose an unprecedented biological threat to humanity.

In recent years, scientists have discovered that Siberian polar ice and permafrost contain numerous prehistoric pathogens, some of which are still active and potentially infectious. In 2016, one case shook the scientific community: in Siberia, a wave of anthrax struck the local population, killing one child and infecting dozens of people. Scientists discovered that the bacterium responsible for the outbreak came from a dead reindeer carcass 75 years earlier that had been buried in permafrost and resurfaced due to global warming.

If a simple bacterium like anthrax can survive for decades and become active again as the ice melts, what might happen with much older viruses, dating back tens of thousands or even millions of years?

In 2014, a team of French scientists revived a 30,000-year-old prehistoric virus extracted from the permafrost of Siberia. This virus, called Pithovirus sibericum, was still capable of infecting modern cells, raising alarms about the potential risk that other unknown viruses could return to the environment, finding vulnerable hosts that never developed immune defenses against them.

Some scientists fear that among the viruses and bacteria trapped in the ice may also be strains of deadly diseases that humanity has never encountered, or even primitive versions of viruses such as influenza, plague or smallpox, which could be far more dangerous than modern variants.

If a prehistoric pathogen were to re-emerge and prove highly contagious, it could trigger a global pandemic for which there would be no immediate cure or vaccine available. Modern sanitation measures may not be sufficient to contain a virus that has had millions of years to evolve under extreme conditions, potentially making it more resistant and difficult to treat.

Scientists are trying to closely monitor at-risk areas by taking ice samples to analyze the presence of unknown pathogens. However, the problem is that the melting process occurs in an uncontrolled manner, making it impossible to predict exactly when and where these microorganisms might emerge.

In addition, some theorists suggest that governments might withhold information about these viruses to avoid panic or to exploit any discoveries for military purposes. If some of these prehistoric microorganisms contained elements useful for biotechnology or biological warfare, they could become the subject of secret research, raising questions about the transparency of scientific and political institutions.

In the end, the real danger is not just melting ice, but our unpreparedness to deal with the consequences of what will be released into the environment. Global warming is not just a climate crisis: it could also be the trigger for an unprecedented biological crisis capable of changing the balance of species on Earth forever.

Global climate impact and implications for the future

The accelerated melting of polar ice is not just a local environmental issue, but a phenomenon that will have global repercussions on an enormous scale. Scientists warn that if the current trend continues, we could see irreversible changes in the climate, ocean ecosystem and geography of the planet.

One of the most immediate and devastating effects will be rising sea levels. The polar ice caps contain enough water to cause the oceans to rise more than 60 meters if they were to melt completely. Even if this extreme scenario is not reached in the next century, it only takes a few meters of rise to submerge entire coastal cities. New York City, London, Venice, Tokyo, Shanghai and Miami are just a few of the metropolises at risk of disappearing partially or totally under water, forcing millions of people to move inland.

But rising sea levels are not the only problem. Melting ice is altering the salinity of the oceans, a phenomenon that could disrupt the ocean currents that regulate global climate. One of the most critical currents is the

Gulf Stream, which carries warm water from the equator to Europe and North America, keeping temperatures stable. If this current weakens or is disrupted, we could see glacial winters in Europe and North America, while other areas of the planet would become excessively warm and arid.

Other climate effects include increasingly frequent extreme weather events, such as more powerful hurricanes, devastating heat waves, prolonged droughts and torrential rainfall. The change in global average temperature could also trigger a chain reaction in ecological systems, leading to the extinction of key species and the collapse of entire ecosystems.

But there is another, less discussed aspect: melting ice could unlock geological and biological secrets that could change our understanding of the Earth. If the polar ice caps have sealed evidence of a different past for millions of years, their melting could reveal traces of ancient civilizations, unknown resources or even life forms that have adapted to extreme conditions.

Some scientists speculate that melting ice could reveal new sources of energy, such as hitherto inaccessible gas and oil deposits, or new forms of bacteria and extremophilic organisms, capable of surviving in extreme environments and inspiring technological and pharmaceutical innovations.

The main problem is that if these discoveries are made, who will have control over them? Will they be accessible to all of humanity or will they become secrets guarded by a few elites and corporations?

Melting ice is not only a climate crisis, but also a geopolitical, scientific, and cultural challenge that could change the future of humanity forever. The ultimate question is not whether the ice will melt, but what will come to light when it does.

And most importantly, will we be ready for it?

Could global warming reveal lost cities?

While the world focuses on the immediate consequences of melting ice, an even more mysterious aspect may emerge in the coming decades: global warming may reveal the ruins of ancient, forgotten civilizations buried for millennia under the polar ice caps.

The idea that Antarctica may have hosted an advanced civilization in the past is not pure fantasy, but finds support in several geological, cartographic and archaeological anomalies. We know that in ancient times the Antarctic continent was not covered with ice, but was a temperate environment with forests, rivers and lush fauna. Evidence for this has been uncovered in recent decades, with the discovery of tropical plant fossils, forest remains and even pollen, suggesting that millions of years ago Antarctica was a livable continent.

But if the climate was so different, could it have been inhabited by humans or an advanced prehistoric civilization?

Some of the most intriguing evidence comes from ancient maps showing ice-free Antarctica, including the famous Piri Reis Map, dated 1513. This map, based on much older nautical charts, depicts the coast of Antarctica with amazing accuracy, compatible with modern satellite surveys. But how could a 16th-century cartographer know the morphology of a continent that, officially, had not yet been discovered?

Scientists, using technologies such as ground-penetrating radar (GPR), have detected anomalous geometric structures under Antarctic ice. Some of these data show large underground cavities and formations that appear to have regular contours, suggesting man-made constructions buried under layers of ancient ice.

The idea that a civilization may have existed in Antarctica clashes with official history, which states that mankind could not have colonized the continent before its glaciation some 12 million years ago. However, some independent researchers argue that there may have been an advanced civilization long before ours, capable of adapting to different climatic conditions or using unknown technologies.

If global warming continues to melt the polar ice caps, what lies beneath the ice may finally come to light. Some scenarios include the possible discovery of ruins of lost cities, ancient temples or even advanced technological artifacts that could rewrite human history.

If this happens, will the great powers allow the truth to be revealed, or will they try to cover up the discoveries to exploit them for their own benefit? If lost knowledge, advanced technology or evidence of extraterrestrial contact in the past is hidden under the ice, then control of these discoveries will become one of the most important issues in the near future.

Is climate change only natural or is there a hidden agenda?

While science acknowledges that climate change is a complex phenomenon influenced by multiple factors, some argue that there may be more behind global warming than what is officially being said. The debate is divided between those who believe that climate change is solely caused by human activities and those who suggest that there may be geopolitical and scientific forces that are accelerating it for covert purposes.

One of the most discussed theories concerns the possibility that some governments and power groups are exploiting global warming to gain access to resources and secrets buried under the ice. If the polar ice caps hold ancient ruins, exotic materials, or even unknown sources of energy, then the retreat of the ice could be seen not just as a crisis, but as a strategic opportunity.

There are historical precedents that show how climate change has been used as a pretext to alter political and economic balances. For example, the race for the Arctic has intensified in recent years, with Russia, the United States and China investing heavily in bases, infrastructure and extraction projects. The official pretext is environmental monitoring and scientific research, but many suspect that the real reason is to control the new resources that are becoming accessible as the ice melts.

Another suspicious element involves geoengineering, a discipline that studies methods to intentionally alter the climate. Some experts have speculated that secret experiments may be underway to accelerate global warming in certain regions, with the aim of gaining faster access to hidden resources at the poles. This raises questions about the possibility that some extreme weather events may not be entirely natural, but the result of scientific and military manipulation.

If this theory were true, it would mean that some governments and power groups may have a secret agenda related to climate change, using it as a cover to accelerate secret research and covert operations in the poles.

Another even more controversial hypothesis suggests that global warming might be part of a much larger natural cycle already known to certain elites, who would have decided not to share this knowledge with the public in order to maintain control over resources and the scientific narrative. If so, it would mean that past civilizations may have already experienced similar events, and that some crucial information may have been deliberately concealed so as not to reveal that human history is cyclical and far older than we know.

In any case, the reality is that the world is changing rapidly, and information about climate, research at the poles, and discoveries made under the ice are not always transparently disclosed. If global warming really does unearth lost cities, ancient technologies or secrets buried for millennia, then the real question will be: who will control these discoveries?

Is humanity ready for a truth that could rewrite its history? Or will the world continue to be manipulated by those in power, exploiting climate change for ends the public need not know?

Perhaps the answer will come only when the last layer of ice has melted, and with it the secrets that have been buried beneath the surface for millennia.

CONCLUSIONS

Do we have enough evidence to rewrite history?

After a long journey through the anomalies, discoveries and theories related to the poles, the biggest question remains: is there enough evidence to rewrite the history of humanity and our planet?

When considering all the information analyzed, a picture emerges that challenges the traditional narrative. On the one hand, official science claims that the poles are simply extreme environments with a complex geological history, but lacking revolutionary elements. However, the anomalies found-from ancient maps showing ice-free Antarctica, to geometric structures detected under the permafrost, to mysterious light and magnetic phenomena-indicate that there is still much to be discovered and that some truths may have been hidden or intentionally ignored.

Evidence already available shows that Antarctica was not always a wasteland, but was once home to forests, rivers and conditions suitable for life. This raises a crucial question: if the continent was habitable, who or what might have lived there before glaciation?

Modern technologies, such as ground-penetrating radar and advanced satellite imagery, have detected unexplained cavities and geometric structures buried under the ice. Some scientists speculate that they could be natural formations, but others argue that their arrangement and symmetry suggest an artificial origin. If so, it would mean that an advanced civilization existed far earlier than official history acknowledges.

Accounts from explorers, military personnel and researchers have often reported sightings of unexplained phenomena at the poles, such as unidentified flying objects, anomalous lights and mysterious ice entrances. If these events are real, it could mean that the poles conceal secret bases, extraterrestrial activity or even dimensional gateways.

In addition, global warming is gradually revealing what has been buried for millennia. Fossil remains, ancient microorganisms, and even unknown life forms are emerging from melting ice, and some experts believe we may uncover even more surprising evidence in the coming decades.

If we put all these elements together, it becomes clear that there is a much more complex historical and scientific picture than we have been taught. The real question is not whether we have enough evidence, but whether we are ready to accept it and rewrite what we know about our history and our place in the universe.

Why do many of these topics remain shrouded in mystery?

If indeed the evidence suggests that the poles harbor shocking secrets, why is this information not accessible to the public? Why do so many findings seem to be censored, downplayed, or ignored?

One of the main reasons is geopolitical and strategic in nature. The poles represent an area of critical interest to the world's great powers, not only for their natural resources, but also for the scientific and technological potential they might conceal. If the most powerful nations discovered remains of ancient civilizations, advanced technologies or extraordinary geological anomalies, they would have every interest in keeping this information secret in order to exploit it to their own advantage.

Moreover, the information could be hidden to avoid global panic. If it were confirmed that an advanced civilization inhabited Antarctica long before official history, or that unknown life forms existed beneath the ice, the world could face an unprecedented cultural, scientific and religious crisis. Academic institutions, major religions and governments would have to completely rethink their narratives about the human past, a process that could generate chaos and social instability.

Another key factor is the control of information by scientific and governmental elites. Scientists and space agencies working in the poles often operate under strict confidentiality protocols, and much of their research is never fully disclosed. If discoveries of historical or biological significance are made, they could be classified and used for military or technological purposes rather than being made public.

Some theories suggest that the poles could be used as a secret laboratory for advanced experiments, including genetic testing, research into new forms of energy, and even climate manipulation. If so, governments would have every interest in keeping the public from focusing too much on what is happening in these isolated regions.

Then there is the question of the role of multinational corporations and economic interests. Large corporations see the poles as a source of huge profits, both from resource extraction and research into new materials and technologies. If crucial information about polar anomalies were revealed, it could change the global economic balance, threatening established business models and entrenched power systems.

The possibility exists that the truth is so shocking that it is simply incompatible with our current understanding of reality. If evidence of an extraterrestrial civilization, of a nonhuman form of intelligence, or of phenomena that defy the laws of known physics were hidden in the poles, society might not be prepared to handle this revelation.

History has taught us that knowledge is power, and those who hold the most important information have control over the masses. If the poles hold the key to understanding humanity's true past, the origin of civilization or our role in the cosmos, then it is understandable that there are forces that want to prevent these truths from emerging.

The real question is, how long can they hide the reality?

As technologies advance, as independent satellite imagery becomes increasingly accessible, and as more explorers and researchers go off the grid, the time may come when the evidence becomes so numerous and irrefutable that any cover-up will be impossible.

Perhaps, in the next few years or decades, the truth about the poles will finally be revealed, and the world will discover that the history of humanity is far more complex, fascinating and mysterious than we ever imagined.

The final decision is up to us: to follow the evidence and continue to search for answers, or to accept the unknown and let the mystery remain forever sealed under the ice?

What might the future of polar exploration reveal?

New and emerging technologies are transforming the way we explore the planet, and the polar regions are no exception. As ice melt accelerates, opportunities for exploration are increasing, paving the way for discoveries that could fundamentally change our understanding of Earth's past and present.

One of the most promising tools for future polar exploration is ground-penetrating radar (GPR), which makes it possible to map ice depths without direct excavation. This type of technology has already made it possible to detect anomalous cavities under the Antarctic ice, and with its continued improvement we may soon get clearer details about what lies beneath the polar ice caps. If man-made structures, underwater cities or even signs of ancient civilizations exist, advanced GPR could finally confirm their existence.

Another key technology will be neutrino tomography, an innovative method that could allow people to "see" through layers of ice and rock, revealing the presence of structural anomalies and buried objects. This technique could be key to identifying areas of archaeological or geological interest without the need for invasive drilling.

The use of autonomous drones and underwater robots is also proving essential. With these devices, subglacial lakes, such as Lake Vostok, which has been sealed for millions of years, will be explored in detail. If these lakes harbor unknown life forms or remnants of prehistoric ecosystems, we could make discoveries that challenge our understanding of biological evolution.

Space missions could also provide advanced technologies for polar exploration. NASA and other space agencies are developing instruments to search for life on icy worlds, such as Europa and Enceladus, the moons of Jupiter and Saturn. These technologies could be adapted to study the deep layers of Antarctica, providing crucial data on possible biological or geological anomalies.

Another revolutionary development could be laser drilling and thermal fusion, which would allow depths never before explored to be reached without the risk of contaminating the environment with mechanical equipment. If underground caverns or passageways exist that lead to unknown geological systems, these technologies could pave the way for their exploration.

But perhaps the biggest breakthrough will come with the democratization of access to satellite data. Today, images of the poles are controlled by governments and scientific institutions, and many are obscured or edited before being made public. With the advent of high-resolution commercial satellites and artificial intelligence for image analysis, it will become increasingly difficult to hide any anomalies.

If unexplained structures, gravitational anomalies, or signs of ancient civilizations are found in the coming years, questions will become inevitable: who knew? Why was this information hidden? And what does it mean for human history?

The future of polar exploration may reveal truths that humanity is not yet ready to face. But if there is a secret under the ice, technological progress will make it increasingly difficult to keep it hidden.

How should humanity react to these findings?

If irrefutable evidence of anomalies in the poles emerged in the coming decades-whether in the form of man-made structures, ancient civilizations, unknown life forms or advanced technologies-humanity would face a momentous challenge. The collective reaction could range from enthusiasm to fear, from curiosity to rejection.

From a scientific point of view, a discovery of this magnitude would require a complete overhaul of historical, biological and geological knowledge. If Antarctica had been inhabited in ancient times, what implications would it have on our understanding of human history? We might have to rewrite entire chapters of evolution and reconsider the origin of ancient civilizations.

Politically and geopolitically, the discovery of unique resources or unknown technologies could lead to new international tensions. Governments would seek to monopolize information and maintain control over what is revealed to the public. They could classify discoveries as state secrets and justify increased militarization of poles to protect what was found.

The reaction of civil society would be equally complex. Some people would welcome the discoveries with enthusiasm, seeing them as a step toward a greater understanding of our existence. Others might reject these revelations, unable to accept that the history taught for centuries may have been manipulated or incomplete.

If the findings revealed evidence of a technologically advanced, extraterrestrial or cryptoterrestrial civilization, the consequences would be even more profound. Traditional religions might be forced to reconsider their doctrines, while governments and scientific institutions would have to explain why this information has been ignored or hidden for so long.

The socio-psychological impact would not be underestimated. Our civilization has always lived with the idea that we are the only form of intelligence on Earth. Discovering that we are not alone, or that there has been an advanced technological past buried under the ice, could create a wave of collective identity crisis. Some might react with fear and paranoia, others with excitement and a desire to explore.

One critical aspect would be the management of disclosure. If governments decided to release only part of the information, the risk of speculation and conspiracy theories would increase exponentially. If, on the other hand, full transparency were adopted, the world might face questions for which it is not yet ready.

But the crucial point remains this: if the truth came out, would humanity be able to handle it rationally and constructively?

Perhaps the greatest lesson we can learn from the mysteries of the poles is that we can no longer afford to ignore the unknown. Humanity is a species born to explore, to seek answers, to confront the incredible and the mysterious.

If the poles truly hold millennia-old secrets, then it is our duty to discover, understand and integrate them into our knowledge.

And perhaps, when the ice melts completely, we will be faced with the greatest revelation in human history.

Should we accept the mystery or look for answers?

Humanity has always been faced with a fundamental choice: accept the unknown as part of our existence or challenge the limits of knowledge to find answers? History shows that every great discovery, from the depths of the ocean to interstellar space, has been achieved because someone refused to accept mystery as a definitive barrier.

The Earth's poles represent one of the last great enigmas of our planet, a boundary between the known and the unexplored, between the visible and what still lies beneath the ice. For centuries, humanity has looked at these regions with awe and respect, telling myths about lost lands, vanished civilizations and unexplained phenomena. But now, as technology advances and climate change advances, we are nearing a turning point: the mystery can no longer remain hidden.

Accepting mystery as definitive would mean giving up our nature as explorers, letting others-governments, scientific institutions, economic elites-decide what we can know and what must remain in the shadows. But seeking answers means challenging official narratives, expanding the boundaries of science and, most importantly, being ready to question everything we believed to be true.

If there are indeed ancient structures under the ice, if there are unexplained magnetic phenomena, if Earth's past is much more complex than we have been taught, then we cannot just accept the mystery. We must investigate, investigate further, demand transparency and not be satisfied with conventional answers.

However, this requires courage and open-mindedness. Not all answers will be comfortable. Some may completely overturn the way we view history and reality. But the real progress of humankind has always been built on the most difficult questions, those that initially seemed absurd or uncomfortable, and then turned out to be fundamental to our evolution.

The poles are not only huge expanses of ice, but treasure chests of secrets, of buried knowledge that could illuminate our past or point us to an unexpected future. If we stop looking for answers, we let these secrets remain the property of a few, perhaps forever.

The questions that remain open and the role of the investigator

Even after all the research, scientific studies and evidence collected, many questions remain unanswered. Satellites and radar scans have revealed anomalies under the ice, but still no one has directly explored these cavities to verify their nature. If the geometric structures identified were man-made in origin, who built them? When? And why?

Are the mysterious light and magnetic phenomena occurring in the polar skies simply natural anomalies or signs of something that eludes our scientific understanding? If dimensional gaps or space-time distortions exist at the poles, as some theorists claim, what would that mean for our view of reality?

And then there is the issue of government restrictions and secrecy. Why do some areas of Antarctica remain inaccessible, despite the fact that the Antarctic Treaty declares that the continent should be open to international scientific research? Why do space and military missions constantly monitor these regions, without releasing detailed public explanations?

These questions are not only for scientists and researchers, but for anyone who wants to understand what is really happening at the poles. The public plays an essential role in the search for truth. Access to satellite images, analysis of declassified documents, and gathering independent testimony are powerful tools that can help bring hidden information to light.

Scientific outreach and independent investigation are now more accessible than ever before. The Internet, data sharing, and new technologies allow anyone to be part of the discovery process. If more and more people start asking questions, investigating, and disseminating information, it will be increasingly difficult for those in control of knowledge to keep secrets buried under the ice.

Perhaps we will never discover the whole truth about the poles. Perhaps some answers will remain forever shrouded in the unknown. But the search for truth is an ongoing process, one that does not stop in the face of obstacles, censure or convention.

Past civilizations have left traces of knowledge that we struggle to understand today. Our task is to decipher them, explore them and, if necessary, rewrite history. For mystery is not meant to be passively accepted, but to be faced with courage and a thirst for knowledge.

The ice is melting. The question is not whether answers will emerge, but whether we will be ready to recognize them when they come.

AFTERWORD

We went through a journey through the most unfathomable mysteries of the poles, from secret bases to lost civilizations, from unexplained magnetic phenomena to anomalies revealed by the most advanced technologies. Each chapter raised questions that challenge the official versions of history and science, leading us to ponder how much is still hidden from us and what the future might reveal.

Now that we have come to the end of this investigation, one question remains suspended: are we really ready to know the truth?

The world has changed rapidly in recent decades. Technology has enabled us to observe the Earth with unprecedented precision, to explore the depths of the ice with advanced instruments, and to discover anomalies that, until recently, would have been considered pure science fiction. However, much information remains confined within inner circles, among scientific institutions, governments and industry sectors that see the poles not only as a final frontier, but also as a huge opportunity for power and control.

Global warming is slowly unearthing secrets that have been frozen for millennia. If there are remains of lost civilizations, ancient technologies, man-made structures buried under the ice, it will be impossible to hide them forever. But history has taught us that knowledge is power, and those who control information decide the fate of an entire civilization.

What will happen when the evidence becomes irrefutable? Will governments and academic institutions admit that they have always known more than we have been told? Will the great powers divide up the secrets of the poles as they did with natural resources? Or will the whole world gain access to these discoveries, ushering in a new era of awareness about our history and the as yet untapped potential of our species?

The truth cannot be kept hidden forever. As exploration technologies advance, as independent research tools proliferate, and as interest in the mysteries of our planet grows, answers will emerge sooner or later.

But the most important question is not only what will be revealed, but how humanity will react.

If the history of the poles is different from what we have been told, if there are traces of intelligent beings that lived before us or next to us, if technologies or anomalies that could change our future are hidden under the ice, we will face a radical revision of our conception of reality.

The implications are not only scientific or historical, but also philosophical, social and even spiritual. We will have to rethink our place in the world, our origins, the potential of human beings, and the limits of knowledge that we have always taken for certain.

That is why, at the end of this journey, the choice remains in the hands of the reader. Accept the mystery and let the decisions be made by a few, or continue to search, to investigate, to challenge the official narrative, unafraid of discovering something bigger than ourselves.

The poles are watching us, silent, as they have for millennia. Perhaps they are just waiting for humanity to be ready to look beyond the ice and finally see what has always been there, hidden from view but not from truth.

Thank you for embarking on this journey through the mysteries of the poles, and for choosing to engage with uncomfortable, but necessary, questions.

Each chapter was written with the intent to offer a clear-eyed, well-documented, and provocative look at truths that are often ignored, downplayed, or hidden.

If this reading has sparked your curiosity, challenged your thinking, or led you to see the world through new eyes, then it has fulfilled its purpose.

Your support-through a review on Amazon-can make a real difference.

Your words not only help other readers discover independent, unconventional content, but also help keep inquiry, dialogue, and the pursuit of truth alive.

Thank you, sincerely, for walking this frontier with me.

The mystery continues.

AUTHOR'S NOTE

This book was born from a deep need: to go beyond the surface, beyond official versions, and explore what is often pushed to the margins of science and history.

The poles-seemingly immutable and remote-hide secrets that defy all conventional logic. The evidence gathered in the previous chapters (testimonies, geological studies, anomalies detected by radar and satellites, historical discrepancies) forms a mosaic that, when viewed as a whole, calls into question the very foundations of what we think we know about the world.

My aim is not to provide definitive answers, but to ask the right questions.

To give voice to what has for too long been ignored, silenced, or dismissed as "fantasy".

The sources I consulted-listed in the bibliography-are both official and independent, because I firmly believe that truth can only emerge through the confrontation of different perspectives, not through dogma.

To the reader, my invitation is simple: never stop searching.

Never stop questioning, digging, challenging.

If even one of the hypotheses explored in these pages proves to be true, then our world, our history, our identity would need to be rewritten. And that is not a risk to fear-but an opportunity to embrace with an open mind and critical spirit.

The ice is melting. The veils are lifting.

Truth won't stay hidden much longer.

BIBLIOGRAPHY

Polar Geography, Climatology, and Environmental Change

Bell, Robin E. "The Role of Subglacial Water in Ice-Sheet Mass Balance." Nature Geoscience 1, no. 5 (2008): 297-304.

Christner, Brent C., Jill A. Mikucki, Christine M. Foreman, John Denson, and John C. Priscu. "A Microbial Ecosystem Beneath the West Antarctic Ice Sheet." Nature 512, no. 7514 (2014): 310-313.

Hansen, James, Makiko Sato, Paul Hearty, et al. "Ice Melt, Sea Level Rise and Superstorms: Evidence from Paleoclimate Data, Climate Modeling, and Modern Observations." Atmospheric Chemistry and Physics 16, no. 6 (2016): 3761-3812.

NASA Earth Observatory. "Antarctica Melts Under Its Hottest Days on Record." February 21, 2020.

Rahmstorf, Stefan. "Ocean Circulation and Climate During the Past 120,000 Years." Nature 419, no. 6903 (2002): 207-214.

Rignot, Eric, Jérémie Mouginot, and Bernd Scheuchl. "Ice Flow of the Antarctic Ice Sheet." Science 333, no. 6048 (2011): 1427-1430.

Scambos, Theodore, Christina Hulbe, Mark Fahnestock, and Jennifer Bohlander. "The Link Between Climate Warming and Break-up of Ice Shelves in the Antarctic Peninsula." Journal of Glaciology 46, no. 154 (2000): 516-530.

Shepherd, Andrew, Erik Ivins, Angelique Barletta, et al. "Mass Balance of the Antarctic Ice Sheet from 1992 to 2017." Nature 558, no. 7709 (2018): 219-222.

Steffen, Will, Johan Rockström, Katherine Richardson, et al. "Trajectories of the Earth System in the Anthropocene." Proceedings of the National Academy of Sciences 115, no. 33 (2018): 8252-8259.

History, Exploration, and Eyewitness Accounts

Byrd, Richard E. Alone. New York: G. P. Putnam's Sons, 1938.

Fogg, Gordon E. A History of Antarctic Science. Cambridge: Cambridge University Press, 1992.

Siple, Paul A., ed. Scientific Results of the Second Byrd Antarctic Expedition 1933-1935. New York: American Geographical Society, 1947.

United States War Department. Army Observers' Report of Operation Highjump. Washington, DC: U.S. Government, 1947.

Wilkins, Hubert. Under the North Pole. New York: Brewer and Warren, 1931.

Ancient Maps and Anomalous Cartography

Buache, Philippe. Carte des Terres Australes. Paris: Imprimerie Royale, 1739.

Fine, Oronce. Nova et integra universi orbis descriptio. Paris: Jacob Kerver, 1531.

Hapgood, Charles H. Maps of the Ancient Sea Kings: Evidence of Advanced Civilization in the Ice Age. Philadelphia: Chilton Books, 1966.

McIntosh, Gregory C. The Piri Reis Map of 1513. Athens: University of Georgia Press, 2000.

Topkapi Palace Museum Library. Piri Reis Map. Codex TSMA A.6. Istanbul.

Geophysics, Magnetic Anomalies, and Radar Surveys

Barletta, Valentina R., Louise S. Sørensen, and René Forsberg. "Scatter of GPS Residuals and GRACE Gravimetry: A Comparison for Greenland." Geophysical Research Letters 40, no. 16 (2013): 4214-4219.

Cammarano, Fabio, Barbara Romanowicz, and Yu-shen Gung. "Anomalous Low-Temperature Upper Mantle Beneath the North Pole." Geophysical Research Letters 30, no. 11 (2003): 1545.

Jordan, Tom A., Fausto Ferraccioli, Hugh F. J. Corr, and Philip T. Leat. "Inland Extent of the Weddell Sea Rift Imaged by New Aerogeophysical Data." Tectonophysics 585 (2013): 137-160.

Polar Microbiology and Ancient Ecosystems

Claverie, Jean-Michel, and Chantal Abergel. "Mimivirus and Its Virophage." Annual Review of Genetics 50 (2016): 493-512.

Legendre, Matthieu, Julien Bartoli, Lyubov Shmakova, et al. "Thirty-Thousand-Year-Old Distant Relative of Giant Icosahedral DNA Viruses." Proceedings of the National Academy of Sciences 111, no. 11 (2014): 4274-4279.

Willerslev, Eske, and Alan Cooper. "Ancient DNA." Proceedings of the Royal Society B 272, no. 1558 (2005): 3-16.

Archaeology, Myth, and Alternative Theories

Bauval, Robert, and Adrian Gilbert. The Orion Mystery. New York: Crown Publishers, 1994.

de Santillana, Giorgio, and Hertha von Dechend. Hamlet's Mill. Boston: David R. Godine, 1969.

Fort, Charles. The Book of the Damned. New York: Dover Publications, 1941.

Hancock, Graham. Fingerprints of the Gods. New York: Crown Publishers, 1995.

von Däniken, Erich. Chariots of the Gods?. New York: Putnam, 1968.

Official Reports and Declassified Documents

Central Intelligence Agency. Antarctic Anomalies and Reports. CIA FOIA Reading Room, 2007.

European Space Agency. CryoSat-2 Mission Data Summary. ESA Publications, 2015.

Joint Publications Research Service. The Antarctic: Main Results of 20 Years of Research in the Antarctic. JPRS L/8246, 1978.

National Geospatial-Intelligence Agency. Arctic Surveillance and Imagery Reports, 2001-2020.

U.S. Geological Survey. Polar Imagery Archive, 1975-1990.

Independent Research and Testimonies

Dolan, Richard M. UFOs and the National Security State: Chronology of a Cover-Up, 1941-1973. Rochester, NY: Keyhole Publishing, 2002.

Farrell, Joseph P. The Third Way: The Nazi International, European Union, and Corporate Fascism. Kempton, IL: Adventures Unlimited Press, 2015.

Redfern, Nick. The Secret History of Antarctica: Operation Highjump, UFOs and the Hollow Earth. Detroit: Visible Ink Press, 2017.

Tellinger, Michael. Slave Species of the Gods: The Secret History of the Anunnaki and Their Mission on Earth. Johannesburg: Zulu Planet Publishers, 2006.

Printed in Dunstable, United Kingdom

66641274R00161